MORAL THEOLOGY OF THE CONFESSIONS OF ST. AUGUSTINE

THE CATHOLIC UNIVERSITY OF AMERICA
STUDIES IN SACRED THEOLOGY
(SECOND SERIES)
No. 55

Moral Theology of the *Confessions* of Saint Augustine

A DISSERTATION

SUBMITTED TO THE FACULTY OF THE SCHOOL OF SACRED THEOLOGY OF THE CATHOLIC UNIVERSITY OF AMERICA IN PARTIAL FULFILLMENT OF THE REQUIREMENTS FOR THE DEGREE OF DOCTOR OF SACRED THEOLOGY

BY

JOHN F. HARVEY, O.S.F.S., S.T.L.

Reproduced by permission of
The Catholic University Press of America

Wipf & Stock
PUBLISHERS
Eugene, Oregon

NIHIL OBSTAT:

THOMAS OWEN MARTIN, S.T.D., PH.D., J.C.D.

Censor Deputatus

IMPRIMI POTEST:

WILLIAM D. BUCKLEY, O.S.F.S., M.A.

Superior Provincialis

IMPRIMATUR:

✠ PATRICK J. O'BOYLE, D.D.

Archiepiscopus Washingtoniensis

Washington, D. C.
Die 2 Junii, 1950

Wipf and Stock Publishers
199 W 8th Ave, Suite 3
Eugene, OR 97401

Moral Theology of the Confessions of Saint Augustine
By Harvey, John F.

ISBN 13: 978-1-60608-423-6
Publication date 2/24/2009
Previously published by Catholic University of America Press, 1951

Gratefully Dedicated

TO THE VIRGIN MOTHER OF GOD

FOREWORD

The writer thanks those who made possible the opportunity for this research, particularly his major and local superiors, the Very Reverend William D. Buckley, and the Reverend Doctor Edward J. Carney. He is equally grateful to those who guided him to the completion of the dissertation. To the Reverend Doctor Thomas O. Martin, who, as major professor, suggested the topic of research and followed its progress step by step the writer is deeply indebted; he is likewise appreciative of the help that he received from the two readers, the Reverend Doctors Stanislaus Grabowski and Francis J. Connell, C.SS.R., whose helpful suggestions and corrections were incorporated into the final draft of the thesis. Finally, the writer voices a grateful prayer for many others who aided him in a variety of ways.

TABLE OF CONTENTS

LIST OF ABBREVIATIONS

Augustine's Works:

Conf., *Confessiones.*
Contra acad., *Contra Academicos.*
Contra advers. leg. et proph., *Contra Adversarium Legis et Prophetarum.*
Contra Ad., *Contra Adimantum.*
Contra Faust., *Contra Faustum.*
De civ. Dei, *De Civitate Dei.*
De doct. Christ., *De Doctrina Christiana.*
De dono persev., *De Dono Perseverantiae.*
De lib. arbit., *De Libero Arbitrio.*
De mus., *De Musica.*
De Trin., *De Trinitate.*
De vera rel., *De Vera Religione.*
Epist., *Epistula.*
Enar. in Ps., *Enarratio in Psalmum.*
Quaest. in Hept., *Quaestiones in Heptateuchum.*
Retract., *Retractationum Libri Duo.*
Serm., *Sermo.*

References to the *Confessions* have been taken from the critical text of M. Skutella, who revised the Knöll CSEL text; quotations from other works of the Saint have been drawn from the most critical editions, and, in certain cases, from Migne, whenever a more critical text was lacking. The translation of Sir Tobie Matthew, revised by Dom Roger Hudleston, was utilized for the English rendering of quotations in the text of the thesis, unless it is otherwise noted in the footnotes.

Other Works:

CSEL, *Corpus Scriptorum Ecclesiasticorum Latinorum.*
DTC, *Dictionnaire de Théologie Catholique.*
ML, Migne, J., *Patrologia Latina.*
S.T., *Summa Theologica.*

BIBLIOGRAPHY

I. Texts and Translations of St. Augustine's *Confessions*

Campbell, James M., and McGuire, Martin, *The Confessions of St. Augustine,* Books 1-9 (Selections), With Introduction and Notes, New York: Prentice Hall, 1936.

Capello, Joseph, *Confessionum libri tredecim,* Rome: Marietti, 1948.

Knöll, Pius, *Confessionum libri tredecim,* Leipzig: Teubner, 1898.

Labriolle, Pierre de, *Saint Augustin, Confessions,* 2 vols., a revision of CSEL text, and translated into French by the same; Paris: Societé D'Édition "Les Belles Lettres," 1925-1926.

Matthew, Sir Tobie, *The Confessions of St. Augustine,* English translation revised and emended by Dom Roger Hudleston, London: Burns, Oates and Washbourne, 1923.

Pusey, Edward, *The Confessions of St. Augustine,* English translation, Oxford: 1838. Reprinted by "Everyman's Library"; New York: Dutton, 1936.

Sheed, Frank J., *The Confessions of St. Augustine,* English translation, London: Sheed and Ward, 1949.

Skutella, Martin, *Confessionum libri tredecim,* revision of CSEL text, Leipzig: Teubner, 1934.

Vega, Angel, *Obras de San Agustin,* "Bibliotheca de autores cristianos"; Madrid: La Editorial Católica, S.A., 1946.

Wangnereck, Heinricus, *Notae in Confessiones Sancti Augustini,* Dillingen, 1631. Reprinted by Marietti: Rome, 1938.

II. Literature

A Monument to St. Augustine (Symposium), London: Sheed and Ward, 1930.

Aquinas, Thomas, *Summa Theologica,* with notes by De Rubeis, Billuart, and others, Rome: Marietti, 1938.

Adler, Mortimer, *What Man Has Made of Man,* New York: Longmans, Green and Co., 1937.

Alfaric, Prosper, *L'évolution intellectuelle de saint Augustin,* Paris: Nourry, 1918.

Allers, Rudolph, *Self Improvement,* New York: Benziger, 1939.

Aristotle, *Nichomachean Ethics,* translation by Browne, London: Henry G. Bohn, 1914.

Augustinus, Sanctus Aurelius, *Contra Adversarium Legis et Prophetarum*, ML 42.603-666.

———, *Contra Academicos*, CSEL, ed. by P. Knöll, 1922, 63.3-81.

———, *Contra Adimantum Manichaeum*, CSEL, ed. by J. Zycha, 1891, 25.115-190.

———, *Contra Faustum Manichaeum libri tres et triginta*, CSEL, ed. by J. Zycha, 1891, 25.251-787.

———, *De Civitate Dei libri viginti et duo*, 2 vols., ed. by B. Dombart-Kalb, fourth edition; Leipzig: Teubner, 1928-1929.

———, *De Doctrina Christiana libri quattuor*, ML 34.15-122.

———, *De Dono Perseverantiae ad Prosperum*, ML 45.993-1034.

———, *De Libero Arbitrio libri tres*, ML 32.1221-1310.

———, *De Musica libri sex*, ML 32.1081-1194.

———, *De Trinitate libri quindecim*, ML 42.817-1098.

———, *De Vera Religione*, ML 34.121-172.

———, *Epistola* 231, CSEL, ed. by Al. Goldbacher, 1911, 57.504-508.

———, *Enarrationes in Psalmos*, ML 36.57-1028.

———, *Quaestiones in Heptateuchum*, CSEL, ed. by J. Zycha, 1895, 28: 2.3-506.

———, *Retractationes libri duo*, ML 32.583-656.

———, *Sermones*, 1-363, ML 39.1493-1638.

Battifol, Pierre, *Le Catholicisme de saint Augustin*, Paris: Gabalda, 1929.

Bourke, Vincent, *Augustine's Quest of Wisdom*, Milwaukee: Bruce, 1945.

Boyer, Charles, *Christianisme et Néo-Platonisme dans la formation de saint Augustin*, Paris: G. Beauchesne, 1920.

———, "De fundamento moralitatis secundum Sanctum Augustinum," in *Acta Hebdomadae Augustinianae-Thomisticae*, Turin: 1931, 97-109.

———, *Essais sur la doctrine de saint Augustin*, Paris: G. Beauchesne, 1932.

———, *L'idée de vérité dans la philosophie de saint Augustin*, Paris: G. Beauchesne, 1920.

Burkitt, Francis, *The Religion of the Manichees*, Cambridge: University Press, 1925.

Garvey, Sister Mary Patricia, *St. Augustine: Christian or Neo-Platonist?* Milwaukee: Marquette University Press, 1939.

Gilson, Étienne, *Introduction à l'étude de saint Augustin*, Paris: J. Vrin, 1931.

Henry, Paul, *Plotin et L'Occident*, Louvain: 1934.

Hughes, Philip, *A History of the Church*, vol. three, New York: Sheed and Ward, 1947.

Maritain, Jacques, "St. Augustine and St. Thomas," in *A Monument to St. Augustine*, London: Sheed and Ward, 1930, 199-223.

Mausbach, Joseph, *Die Ethik des heiligen Augustinus*, 2 vols., 2 ed., Freiburg in Br., 1929.

Merkelbach, Henry, *Summa Theologiae Moralis*, 2 vols., Paris: Desclée, 1938.

Migne, Jacques, *Patrologiae Cursus Completus,* Series Latina, 221 vols., Paris: 1843-1864.

Moore, Thomas V., *Personal Mental Hygiene,* Grune and Stratton, New York: 1944.

Ottley, Robert L., *Studies in the Confessions of St. Augustine,* London: Scott, 1919.

Platz, Philipp, *Der Römerbrief in der Gnadenlehre Augustins,* "Pontificia Universitas Gregoriana," Würzburg: Rita-Verlag und Druckerei, 1937.

Portalié, Eugene, "Augustin," in *Dictionnaire de Théologie Catholique,* Paris: 1909, 1.2268-2472.

Roland-Gosselin, Bernard, "St. Augustine's System of Morals," in *A Monument to St. Augustine,* London: Sheed and Ward, 1930, 225-248.

———, *La morale de saint Augustin,* Paris: Rivière, 1925.

Sales, St. Francis de, *Oeuvres de saint François de Sales,* vols. 13-14, Annecy: Abry, 1906.

Switalski, Bruno, *Plotinus and the Ethics of St. Augustine,* Chicago: Capitol Press, 1946.

Tertullian, *Liber de praescriptionibus adversus haereticos,* ML 2.9-74.

Van Hoonacker, A., *Les Douze Petits Prophètes,* Paris: J. Gabalda, 1908.

INTRODUCTION

The purpose of this thesis is to explain the *moral* content of the *Confessions* of St. Augustine. Accordingly, other works of the Saint, as well as commentators on the *Confessions* will be used solely to clarify the main moral tenets of this work. Since moral principles, moreover, are found not merely in the expressed ideas of St. Augustine, but are also embodied in his actions, moral principles will be gleaned and illustrated from both sources.

Before undertaking such an analysis, however, it seems well to consider briefly the nature, purpose, validity, and sources of the *Confessions,* as well as other pertinent background information. According to the double meaning of the word, the *Confessions* are both a prayer of praise and thanksgiving for the care that Divine Providence has lavished upon the Saint and a humble acknowledgment of the wanderings and sins of the Saint during the years that preceded his Baptism.[1] A tone of theocentrism dominates throughout all the books of the *Confessions,* so that they are never mere autobiography. Even in reflecting upon his own past life, the Saint stands, as it were, apart from himself, and assumes an impersonal objective tone.[2]

When, moreover, the *Confessions* consider man, they view him

[1] See J. Mausbach, *Die Ethik des heiligen Augustinus* (2. ed., Freiburg i. Br., 1929), 1.8-9: Augustins Konfessionen sind keine Chronik, kein Tagebuch: sie wollen—dem Doppelsinn des lateinischen Wortes entsprechend—die Irrgänge des eigenen Lebens und Strebens bekennen und Gott für seine gnadenvolle Führung danken. See also A. Vega, *Obras de San Agustin* (*Bibliotheca de autores cristianos,* Madrid, La Editorial Católica, S.A., 1946), 301, who says the same.

[2] See J. Campbell and M. R. McGuire, *The Confessions of St. Augustine* (N. Y., Prentice-Hall, 1936), 16-17: But this theocentric consciousness conditions his style throughout and gives even his *Confessions,* despite all their passion, an impersonal objective tone. See also E. Pusey, *The Confessions of St. Augustine* (Oxford, 1838). Reprinted by "Everyman's Library," N. Y., Dutton, 1936), Preface, 15-28, where the author points out that the Saint uses incidents from his own life as occasions to discuss objectively principles of theology and of philosophy.

in the same theocentric fashion, in his relationship to God, and so reaffirm frequently that the happiness of man is inseparably linked with the knowledge and worship of God, the supreme Good, and the cause of all moral good.[3]

In writing his *Confessions* Augustine had several purposes in mind. First of all, he wanted to praise and to thank God for His mercy in drawing him from the abyss of sin to Divine friendship, and at the same time he demonstrated the efficacy of Divine grace in his own life. Again, the Saint hoped by his narrative to raise the minds and hearts of his readers to the contemplation of the God who had been so good to him; and especially did he direct his narrative to those who were in the same state that he had been in as a message of *encouragement* to break the bonds of habitual sin.[4]

Finally, Augustine wanted to correct exaggerated accounts of his past by setting down clearly the *truth* about himself, so that men might understand that whatever goodness he had acquired had come from God alone. He believed that the *truth* would lead men to praise God.[5] Thus, implicit in the very purpose of this work is its *validity*.

Inasmuch as the *validity* of the *Confessions* has been called into question by Alfaric and others who hold that Augustine exaggerated

---

[3] See B. Switalski, *Plotinus and the Ethics of St. Augustine* (Chicago, Capitol Press, 1946), 40: Behold the theocentrism of St. Augustine: God is the cause and end of everything, and consequently in ethics He is the supreme good and cause of all moral good. Switalski affirms also that St. Augustine's interest in man is permeated by the same theocentric viewpoint (*op. cit.*, 57 ff.).

[4] See *Conf.*, 2, 3, 5. See also *ibid.*, 10, 3-4, 4-6. See also A. Vega, *op. cit.*, 298, who sets down three purposes for the writing of the *Confessions*: the glorification of God, the edification of fellow Christians, and the conversion of his former companions in error; V. Bourke, *Augustine's Quest of Wisdom* (Milwaukee, Bruce, 1945), 146-148, who points out that St. Augustine wanted to reveal the efficacy of Divine grace in his own life.

[5] See *Epistula*, 231, 6 (CSEL 57.508-9, ed. Goldbacher, 1911): Ibi non aliis de me crede, sed mihi, ibi me adtende et vide, quid fuerim in me ipso per me ipsum. See also *De dono persev.*, 20, 53 (ML 45.1026): Quid autem meorum opusculorum frequentius et delectabilius innotescere potuit quam libri *Confessionum* mearum? In eis certe dixi Deo nostro, et saepe dixi: 'Da quod jubes, et jube quod vis.'

his sins of his sixteenth year in order to bring out the healing power of grace, Boyer develops at length an argument for their validity. Basically, his argument may be reduced to three points: (1) the exceptional gravity of the witness, who addresses his recital to God, and calls Him to witness that he is relating events exactly as he remembered them; (2) the conscientious precision of details; and (3) the general religious tone of the narrative.[6]

In developing these arguments Boyer points out that the Saint's choice of certain events from his personal history to illustrate the action of Divine grace on his soul does not affect adversely the validity of his work. Thus Augustine chooses incidents that are meaningless from points of view other than his own. The jealousy of the infant and the looting of the pear tree are incidents that cause him to dilate upon the effects of Original Sin and the perversity of the human will.[7] To the objection that the mind of

---

[6] See Pr. Alfaric, *L'évolution intellectuelle de saint Augustin* (Paris, Nourry, 1918, Preface, 3-4 and 380-381, where the author denies the validity of the *Confessions*. In opposition to this view Boyer (*Christianisme et Néo-Platonisme dans la formation de saint Augustin,* Paris, Beauchesne, 1920, 11-13) develops the following points: (a) the exceptional gravity of the witness: On ne saurait trop réfléchir à l'exceptionnelle gravité du témoin. Sa sincérité ne peut être mise en question . . . ; (b) the conscientious precision of details: Ses intentions doctrinales ont dirigé la mise en oeuvre de ses souvenirs. Mais elles ne l'ont certainement jamais amené à défigurer sciemment le moindre fait. . . . Il n'y a pas dans les *Confessions* d'inexactitude volontaire; (c) the general religious tone of the narrative: De plus, c'est devant Dieu, c'est en parlant à Dieu lui-même, et parfois en le prenant à témoin de sa parole, que l'évêque d'Hippone relate ses souvenirs. Une manière si hardie n'est point un procédé littéraire, mais la forme spontanée d'un sentiment religieux profond. . . .

Again, Boyer points out that the Saint's description of his sixteenth year refers to actual sins of impurity (*op. cit.,* 11, 12, 15, 27, 192); finally, in the conclusion of his work he repeats his arguments for the validity of the *Confessions* (192-193).

See also E. Gilson, *Introduction à l'étude de saint Augustin* (Paris, J. Vrin, 1943), 330, where the author evaluates Boyer's study of the formation of St. Augustine in these words: le plus pondéré, et à notre sens, le plus juste que l'on ait consacré à cette delicate question.

[7] See C. Boyer, *op. cit.,* 12: Il insiste sur des incidents qui, à d'autres points de vue que le sien, sont insignifiants. Il s'arrête à méditer sur la jalousie injustifiée d'un bébé à la mamelle, parce qu'il y voit un désordre

the Saint would have forgotten many things during the interval between his conversion and the composition of the *Confessions,* Boyer replies that the period of time was not so long as to cause Augustine to forget *significant* events. (Probably the time interval was no more than twelve years.)[8]

Additional arguments for the validity of the *Confessions* are found in subsequent references to this work in other books of the Saint, and most notably in his *Retractationes,* where he speaks with approval of the widespread circulation of the *Confessions,* and makes a few minor corrections. Previously, moreover, in two other references he writes of his *Confessions* as a *true* picture of himself.[9] In short, the very nature of the work, the veracity of the author, and his subsequent approval of this early work are facts forming a strong cumulative argument for the validity of this work, which is accepted by the vast majority of critics.[10]

Another point of interest for our study is the sources of the *Confessions.* One finds an extremely large number of Scriptural quotations and allusions, which are drawn from over fifty books of both Testaments, and most especially from the Psalms of David and the Epistles of St. Paul, the two favorite readings of the

---

introduit par le péché d'Adam. Dans le larcin qu'il commit un jour de quelques méchantes pommes, il scrute longuement les motifs de la volonté mauvaise.

[8] For the date of the *Confessions,* see A. Vega, *op. cit.,* 302, where he holds that the work was written about A.D. 398. Bourke holds that they were written no later than 401 (*op. cit.,* 147), and in this opinion he follows de Labriolle, *Les Confessions de saint Augustin* (Paris, Societé d'Édition "Les Belles Lettres," 1925, Intro., v-vi. It is safe to say then that approximately twelve years elapsed from the date of the Saint's conversion until the composition of this work.

[9] See *Retractationes,* 2, 6 (ML 32.632): Interim quod ad me attinet, hoc in me egerunt cum scriberentur, et agunt cum leguntur. Quid de illis alii sentiant, ipsi viderint; multis tamen fratribus eos multum placuisse et placere scio. A primo usque ad decimum de me scripti sunt, in tribus caeteris, de Scripturis sanctis. . . . See also *supra,* n. 5; and A. Vega, *op. cit.,* 275 ff., where the author stresses the evident sincerity of the Saint's recital.

[10] See C. Boyer, *op. cit.,* 137-140; 192-193 on this point. See also Campbell and McGuire, *op. cit.,* 55, where the historicity of the *Confessions* is treated.

Saint.[11] In addition to this predominant influence of Holy Scripture, the *Confessions* reflect traces of Neoplatonic thought, which deserve brief discussion.

The influence of Plotinus is most marked in the *Confessions.* In this work the Saint speaks of the "libri Platonicorum" (*Conf.* 7, 9, 13), which Switalski identifies with the *Enneads* of Plotinus. Thus, it was the *Enneads* of Plotinus, and not other Neoplatonic writings, that influenced the thought of the *Confessions.*[12] This influence was studied by Boyer, Switalski and Henry, whose conclusions are stated here.

According to Boyer, this work of Plotinus contributed to the thought of the *Confessions* on the following points:

(1) It gave St. Augustine the concept of a spiritual God, who is Truth Itself, and thus it dispelled his materialistic notion of the Deity.
(2) This Truth is a creative force, through which all things are made.
(3) This same Truth enlightens every human mind and in its possession brings happiness.
(4) This Truth is acquired through purification, i.e., one must strip his mind of worldly images and cares.

In short, the *Enneads* clarified the thought of Augustine from materialistic concepts and stimulated the development of his mind: but they were inefficacious in his moral life.[13]

---

[11] See P. Knöll, *Confessionum* (Teubner, Leipzig, 1898), 334-345 for an index of Scriptural references in the *Confessions.* See also Campbell and McGuire, *op. cit.*, 51-52, where the authors say that the extremely large number of Scriptural allusions in the *Confessions* "enter into the very fabric of the whole work."

[12] See B. Switalski, *op. cit.*, 82: "We may infer that Plotinus is the author, because the context gives synopses of these books, whose contents are the same as the *Enneads* and the *Enneads* only." Again, the author adds (89): "Although Augustine does not use Plotinus' name in his *Confessions,* we already know that the expression 'Libri Platonicorum,' if not always, is at least mostly identical with the *Enneads.*" And, finally, he points out (95): "Only in the *Confessions* . . . does Augustine designate the *Enneads* of Plotinus as 'Libri Platonicorum.'"

[13] See C. Boyer, *op. cit.*, 79-102.

It was the Faith of St. Augustine, Boyer continues, which determined his evaluation of the *Enneads*. Thus in a figure of speech the Saint declared that he had taken from the Egyptians only the gold of truth, which had come to them from God; and that he had condemned the idols which they had fashioned with it. Thus, while rejecting the polytheism of this system, he admits that their doctrine on the *Verbum* approaches that of Christianity.

From his analysis, then, of Plotinus' influence Boyer concludes: (1) However considerable the influence of Neoplatonism was upon the mind of Augustine, it was subordinate to the primary influences of Christianity; and (2) the widespread opinion that Augustine became a Neoplatonist without the previous intervention of Christianity and that Neoplatonism conducted him to the Faith is without solid foundation. Far more efficacious than the *Enneads* were good example, the writings of St. Paul, and the internal operation of Divine grace.[14]

---

[14] See *ibid.*, 131: C'est l'Écriture, c'est la vie des parfaits chrétiens . . . ; c'est la prière; c'est une exhortation providentielle de Saint Paul qui l'ont renouvelé. . . . (137) Conviction de la misère propre, confiance dans le secours de Dieu, tels sont les sentiments fondamentaux qui permettent au phénomène conversion de se développer. See also *ibid.*, 118-119: L'opinion, si répandue, qui veut que saint Augustin soi devenu néo-platonicien, sans aucune intervention du christianisme, et qu'il ait été ensuite conduit à la foi par le néo-platonisme nous parait être une erreur.

In regard to the Neoplatonic doctrine on the *Verbum,* Boyer points out that the Saint took from it whatever was not contrary to the Faith: Augustin reçoit, en ce cas, les développements néo-platoniciens comme un bien qui revient de droit aux catholiques et qui sert à l'intelligence de la foi (*op. cit.,* 166).

Finally Boyer sums up very accurately the relationship between the two doctrines: D'autre part, tout en reconnaissant la prépondérance définitive de la foi chrétienne dan l'esprit d'Augustin, dès avant l'épisode des livres 'platoniciens,' nous avons laissé au néo-platonisme un rôle considérable dans la formation de la pensée augustinienne. . . . Saint Augustin est convaincu de la vérité de beaucoup d'idées néo-platoniciennes, telles qu'il les a comprises, et de leur accord avec la foi chrétienne. . . . Il les utilize pour comprendre sa foi (*op. cit.,* 193-194).

See also C. Boyer, *Essais sur la doctrine da saint Augustin* (G. Beauchesne, Paris, 1932), 4, where the author holds that the Saint was already a Christian when he read the *Enneads* of Plotinus: Mais les *Confessions*

Switalski shows that Augustine in his *Confessions* cites the *Enneads* almost literally in a very significant passage, even utilizing the literary structure of Plotinus (*Conf.,* 8, 8, 19). In the first section of this passage he shows that God cannot be reached by any material form of movement; and this corresponds to the first part of the similar passage in the *Enneads.* Likewise, in the second section Augustine copies both the style and the thought of Plotinus, declaring that God can be possessed only by an act of the will.[15]

Switalski, moreover, points out that Plotinus helped Augustine to form correct concepts of evil and of sin. But he stresses the fact that Augustine does not follow the Neoplatonic philosopher blindly. Even before conversion Augustine selected from the *Enneads* only those ideas which were not opposed to Christian Revelation. Thus he harmonized the philosophy of Plotinus with Christian thought and morals.[16]

In his study of the same relationship Henry points out that St. Augustine made *radical* transformations upon the teachings of Plotinus before he adopted them as his own. He shows that the *Enneads* are concerned with the God of the philosophers, while the work of St. Augustine is addressed to the living God of Supernatural Revelation; and that the spirit of humility found in the

---

attestent avec netteté qu'avant de recevoir d'un ami 'gonflé d'orgueil' les livres des platoniciens, Augustin avait déjà reconquis une foi assurée et ferme. . . . Augustin croyait, il ne comprenait pas. Les néo-platoniciens l'aidèrent à comprendre.

[15] See *infra,* ch. 3, 99, n. 103.

[16] See Switalski, *op. cit.,* 87-96: The author shows that the Saint abandoned his Manichean conceptions of evil under the influence of the *Enneads.* See also *ibid.,* 109: It is then evident that Augustine does not blindly follow the Neoplatonic philosopher, but judges his doctrine in the light of the authority of the Church, which authority, as infallible, was for him the criterion of truth and that he selected only those ideas from the writings of Plotinus which were not opposed to Christian revelation; C. Boyer, *op. cit.,* 130: Il faut reconnaître que, d'après les *Confessions,* son esprit s'était soumis à la foi chrétienne avant de s'ouvrer au néoplatonisme. See also *supra,* n. 14. In line with Boyer and Switalski, Vega adds that the doctrine of the Saint on virtues and vices reflects Neoplatonic influences but remains essentially Christian (*op. cit.,* 44).

Confessions is in direct contrast to the spirit of presumption characteristic of the *Enneads*.[17]

Another aspect of the *Confessions* is the informal teaching method of the Saint. After describing a particular incident, he draws a moral from it; and occasionally he develops the moral with more extensive applications. Even in the analysis of a trivial incident he shows how its basic motivations are common to other sins also. The manner in which he explores the motivations behind the looting of the pear tree, and the skill with which he portrays the rashness of Alypius in an occasion of sin are but two examples of his method of concrete presentation of moral questions.[18]

It should be noted that the completeness or perfection of his moral system is not to be sought in the *Confessions;* however, although its primary purpose was not didactic, one may find in this work practical applications of his moral teaching.

In the search for a basis of division of the thesis the writer found it more satisfactory to classify the moral matter culled from the *Confessions* according to the dynamic pattern of the book. Thus, at the very beginning of his work the Saint declares that the goal of man is God alone, and hence all human activity must be pointed towards its true fulfillment, or else it will lead to a frustrated soul. This much repeated concept suggested the first chapter of the thesis: God as the *goal* of man.

The idea of goal, in turn, connoted immediately the question of the road thither, and so the second chapter discusses the way to God. Herein is outlined the teaching of the *Confessions* on such topics as law, conscience, prayer, and the various virtues as paths leading man to God and happiness.

Along any road one may meet obstacles, and the path to God is no exception. Consequently, the third chapter takes account of the obstructions found on the road to heaven. These include ignorance, concupiscence, division of will, bad habit, defective education, and

[17] See P. Henry, *Plotin et L'Occident* (Louvain, 1934), 104-116. See also *infra,* ch. 3, 99, n. 103; Sister Mary Patricia Garvey, *St. Augustine: Christian or Neo-Platonist?* (Marquette U., Milwaukee, 1939), 53-60. This work contains an excellent comparison of Neoplatonism with Christianity.

[18] See *Conf.*, 6, 8-9, 13-14. See also *infra,* ch. 3, 119-120, 131-132.

sin in all its ramifications. This chapter is the longest in the thesis, because the major portion of the moral teaching of the *Confessions* is concerned with moral hindrances to perfection.

In his very analyses of such negative elements, however, the Saint suggests various concrete aids for the struggle against them. Thus, he stresses the interplay of Scriptural reading, group good example, humility, and Divine grace in his personal victory over the habit of impurity. For this reason *remedies* is the caption of the fourth chapter. Finally, the entire study brings into focus certain *important* moral contributions of the *Confessions,* which will be summarized in the conclusion.

CHAPTER I

God as the Goal of Man

"This is the happy life: to rejoice concerning thee, in approaching thee, and on account of thee. This it is, and there is no other."[1] God is the complete fulfillment of man's desire for happiness. This truth the *Confessions* repeat many times with varied richness. Thus, the very first chapter of this work affirms that the human heart is restless until it rests in God—a fact that St. Augustine had discovered, not from a textbook, but only after years of wasted living.[2] Bitter experience had taught him that all created values were empty by comparison.[3]

This personal, introspective viewpoint of the Saint sprang from an experiential knowledge of the human heart, so that he was able to state his teaching in terms that have found a response in all sincere searchers after truth. He speaks not about happiness, an abstract thing, but about the happy life, a concrete thing, which all men desire, and which no one does not want.[4]

Fundamentally, this happy life consists in the possession of truth, because the full possession of truth is the possession of God: "For a blessed life is a rejoicing in the truth; and this is a rejoicing in thee, who art Truth, O God, my light. . . . This blessed life all

[1] *Conf.*, 10, 22, 32: Et ipsa est beata vita, gaudere de te, ad te, propter te: ipsa est, et *non est altera* (italics mine).

[2] See *Conf.*, 1, 1, 1: Tu excitas, ut laudare te delectet, quia fecisti nos ad te et inquietum est cor nostrum donec requiescat in te.

[3] See *ibid.*, 10, 27, 38: Sero te amavi, pulchritudo tam antiqua, et tam nova, sero te amavi! Et ecce intus eras et ego foris; et ibi te quaerebam et in ista formosa, quae fecisti, deformis inruebam. Mecum eras et tecum non eram. Ea me tenebant longe a te, quae si in te non essent, non essent. . . . Tetigisti me, et exarsi in pacem tuam. See also *ibid.*, 10, 28, 39.

[4] See *ibid.*, 10, 20, 29: Nonne ipsa est beata vita, quem omnes volunt et omnino qui nolit nemo est. See J. Mausbach, *Die Ethik des heiligen Augustinus* (2. ed., Freiburg in Breisgau, 1929), 1.53. Mausbach points out that the desire for happiness is a psychological fact of the first importance, springing from self-love and the dynamic source of all effort.

men desire; . . . joy in the truth is the desire of all men. I have known many who were content to deceive others, but never any who would himself be glad to be deceived."[5]

One finds this happy life only in knowing the truth, which is God.[6] This concept of God as the desired truth of the human intellect is developed again by St. Augustine when he compares the knowledge of God with the knowledge of created things. A man who knows very much about creatures, but lacks the knowledge of God is miserable, whereas he who knows about God, but is ignorant of created things can be happy. It is not the additional knowledge of creatures, but the knowledge of God joined with His *glorification* which brings happiness to man.[7]

The joy of heaven is visualized by the Saint as an endless drinking-in of Divine Wisdom. Thus, the Saint conceives his dead friend, Nebridius, who had sought wisdom before his death, as now in heaven joyously slaking his thirst for truth at the fonts of Divine Wisdom.[8]

St. Augustine's concept of happiness is not, however, purely intellectual; he also teaches that the human will finds its peace in God, who draws the human heart unto Himself.[9] To explain this truth he uses a beautiful comparison: The elements of creation follow a certain pattern in seeking their proper place in the universe. Fire tends upward; a stone plumps downward. Oil poured beneath the water is drawn above the water; and water poured

---

[5] *Conf.*, 10, 23, 33: Beata quippe vita est gaudium de veritate; hoc est enim gaudium de te, qui veritas es, Deus, inluminatio mea, . . . Hanc vitam beatam omnes volunt; . . . gaudium de veritate omnes volunt. Multos expertus sum qui vellent fallere; qui autem falli, neminem.

[6] See *loc. cit.* See also *ibid.*, 10, 24, 35; E. Gilson, *Introduction à l'étude de saint Augustin,* 9, 134-137.

[7] See *ibid.*, 5, 4, 7.

[8] See *ibid.*, 9, 3, 6: Et nunc ille (Nebridius) vivit in sinu Abraham. . . . Ibi vivit, unde me multa interrogabat homuncionem inexpertum. Iam non ponit aurem ad os meum, sed spirituale os ad fontem tuum et bibit quantum potest sapientiam pro aviditate sua sine fine felix.

[9] See *ibid.*, 13, 9, 10: In *dono tuo* (Spiritu Sancto: Acts 2:38) requiescimus; ibi te fruimur. Requies nostra locus noster. Amor illuc attollit nos. . . . Dono tuo accendimur et sursum ferimur. . . . Igne tuo, igne tuo bono inardescimus et imus, quoniam sursum imus ad *pacem Jerusalem* (Ps. 121:6).

upon oil sinks beneath the oil. Each created thing has its peculiar tendency under whose pull it moves in a specific direction. This St. Augustine calls its gravitation; and the gravitation of the human heart is *love.*

By this force the heart is drawn to its proper place of repose in the Divinity. In its movement towards God, moreover, it is inflamed by the gift of Divine Love, infused by the Holy Ghost. Thus it is borne upward to the heavenly Jerusalem, where it finds complete satisfaction, desiring nothing except to remain there forever.[10]

In this sublime conception of the goal of man St. Augustine goes far beyond the pagan philosophers, who never thought of such things as Divine Love inflaming the will of man in his journey towards heaven. A full discussion of these supernatural elements will be presented later.[11]

In considering the qualities of the object of happiness St. Augustine stresses the immutability of God in contrast to the transient nature of creatures:

> And I beheld all other things that are beneath thee, and I saw that they had neither any absolute being, nor had they absolutely no being at all. They have a being because they are of thee; and they have no being, because they be not that which thou art. For that truly is, which doth unchangeably remain.[12]

---

[10] See *loc. cit.*: Corpus pondere suo nititur ad locum suum. Pondus non ad ima tantum est, sed ad locum suum. Ignis sursum tendit, deorsum lapis. Ponderibus suis aguntur, loca sua petunt. Oleum infra aquam fusum super aquam attollitur; aqua super oleum fusa infra oleum demergitur: Ponderibus suis aguntur, loca sua petunt. Pondus meum amor meus; eo feror quocumque feror. *Dono tuo* accendimur; et sursum ferimur. . . . Igne tuo, igne tuo bono inardescimus et imus, quoniam sursum imus ad *pacem Jerusalem*. . . . Ibi nos conlocabit voluntas bona ut nihil velimus aliud quam permanere illic in aeternum. (This passage also brings out the supernatural end of man, the peace of the heavenly Jerusalem; and the means leading thence: the graces of the Divine Gift, the Holy Spirit.) See also *infra,* ch. 2, 34, n. 114.

[11] See *infra,* ch. II, 23-30; ch. IV, 147-154.

[12] *Conf.,* 7, 11, 17: Et inspexi cetera infra te et vidi nec omnino esse nec omnino non esse: esse quidem, quoniam abs te sunt, non esse autem, quoniam id quod es non sunt. Id enim vere est, quod inconmutabiliter manet.

Augustine develops this notion in many other texts of the *Confessions.* The qualities of the Creator are contrasted with those of his creatures: God is immutable, necessary, eternal, and the fullness of being, while creatures are mutable, contingent, mortal, and dependent for their very being upon God.[13]

Again, the changing nature of creatures was impressed deeply upon his mind by the bitter grief which was occasioned by the death of a dear friend of his student days. In the narrative of his sorrow the Saint dwells upon the inadequacy of creatures to bring true happiness to the soul, inasmuch as they do not endure. Hence, the soul must detach itself from them and attach itself to God, in whom alone it finds rest and peace.[14]

The reason why the soul finds satisfaction in God is that the possession of Him includes the perfection of all other delights, even as it transcends them. This is the idea developed in one of the most beautiful passages in the *Confessions,* which begins with the question: "But yet, when I love thee, what is it that I love?"[15]

The Saint replies that it is not any beauty of the senses, however attractive,[16] and yet it includes "a kind of light, a kind of voice, a kind of odour, a kind of food, and a kind of embracing."[17] The

---

[13] See *ibid.,* 1, 4, 4: . . . immutabilis, mutans omnia. . . . See also *ibid.,* 4, 16, 29: Deus meus, mirabiliter simplicem atque incommutabilem . . . ; *ibid.,* 7, 20, 26: Certus . . . et vere te esse, qui semper idem ipse esses, ex nulla parte nulloque motu alter aut aliter, cetera vero ex te esse omnia, hoc solo firmissimo documento, quia sunt, certus quidem in istis eram . . . ; *ibid.,* 7, 21, 27: . . . et ut te, qui es semper idem; *ibid.,* 11, 31, 41; *ibid.,* 13, 16, 19.

[14] See *ibid.,* 4, 10, 15: Nam quoquoversum se verterit anima hominis, ad dolores figitur alibi praeterquam in te, tametsi figitur in pulchris extra te et extra se. Quae tamen nulla essent, nisi essent abs te. Quae oriuntur et occidunt et oriendo quasi esse incipiunt et crescunt, ut perficiantur, et perfecta senescunt et intereunt. . . . Sic est modus eorum. See also *ibid.,* 9, 4, 11.

[15] *Ibid.,* 10, 6, 8: Quid autem amo, cum te amo?

[16] See *loc. cit.*: Non speciem corporis nec decus temporis, non candorem lucis ecce istum amicum oculis, non dulces melodias cantilenarum omnimodarum, non florum et unguentorum et aromatum suavi violentia, non manna et mella, non membra acceptabilia carnis amplexibus: non haec amo, cum amo Deum meum.

[17] *Loc. cit.*: Et tamen amo quandam lucem et quandam vocem et quendam odorem et quendam cibum et quendam amplexum, cum amo Deum meum. . . .

object of his love is a light uncircumscribed by any place, a voice that is eternal, an odor that remains fragrant, a nourishment that remains unconsumed by eating, and an embrace that never becomes tiresome. In short, it is uncreated Beauty, ever ancient and ever new.[18]

In this description St. Augustine ascends from the diverse beauty of created objects to the uncreated Beauty. Hence, he does not say that one must despise created beauty. One should, indeed, praise God for it, but one should not allow it to enslave him; for the attractiveness of created things disturbs the human heart, which ends by desiring the impossible, namely, that these things should remain. Thus, the Saint concludes that one should turn from such things and seek his happiness in the Divinity.[19]

Reasoning, then, from the enduring goodness of the Word and its power to make the soul happy, he enunciates a practical norm of conduct: Instead of allowing carnal desires to rule him, man must rule them.[20] Further exploring the nature of sense pleasure, he shows how inadequate these pleasures are to satisfy the human heart. Such pleasures have a twofold limitation: They are transient; they satisfy only a part of man, and not the whole man. Better it is for man to seek Him who created both the senses and their pleasures, thus satisfying not a part of man, but the whole man, not according to the mode of time or succession, but all at once and completely. The possession of God is far above all these partial pleasures.[21]

St. Augustine's reflections on the inadequacy of sense pleasures to bring happiness to man were truths tested in the crucible of daily living. Probably this fact would give them an added appeal for

[18] See *loc. cit.* See also *Conf.*, 10, 27, 38: Sero te amavi, pulchritudo tam antiqua et tam nova, sero te amavi!

[19] See *ibid.*, 4, 10, 15. See also *ibid.*, 4, 11, 16.

[20] See *ibid.*, 4, 11, 17: Ut quid perversa sequeris carnem tuam? Ipsa te sequatur conversam.

[21] See *loc. cit.*: Quidquid per illam sentis in parte est et ignoras totum cujus hae partes sunt et delectant te tamen. . . . Ita semper omnia, quibus unum aliquid constat, et non sunt omnia simul ea quibus constat; plus delectant omnia quam singula, si possint sentiri omnia. . . . Sed longe his melior qui fecit omnia, et ipse est Deus noster, et non discedit, quia nec succeditur ei. See also *ibid.*, 6, 16, 26.

the modern mind that sets such a high value on empirical findings. His teaching becomes all the more cogent, because he himself had been afraid that he could not do without carnal pleasures. In fact, this fear was one of the factors that delayed his conversion.[22] Yet after his conversion he testifies to the great joy that he had found in his newly discovered love for God. God had ejected from his heart sensual delights and had Himself entered in.[23] Thereupon Augustine experienced the possession of God as sweeter than all sense pleasure and brighter than all earthly light, not according to the mode of such pleasures, but rather in a transcendent fashion.

So far it has been shown that the *Confessions* depict God as the Truth in whose possession man rejoices, and the Goodness towards which the will and heart of man gravitate. God fulfills the aspirations of the whole man in a transcendent manner. But the *Confessions* teach also that even when men sin they are seeking the happiness that is found only in God. The sinner strives for a kind of goodness, the reality of which is found in its perfection only in God.[24]

The proud seeking greatness, the tyrant seeking power, the lazy seeking peace, the sensual seeking voluptuous pleasures, all are striving for values found lasting, pure, and perfect only in God. Since only the goodness of God satisfies the heart of man, man seeks to imitate God, even as he turns away from Him. This is sin: man seeks to be God.[25]

---

[22] See *ibid.*, 8, 5, 11: Ego autem adhuc terra obligatus militare tibi recusabam et inpedimentis omnibus sic *timebam* expediri, quemadmodum inpediri *timendum* (italics mine) est. See also *ibid.*, 8, 5, 12: Non enim erat quod tibi responderam dicenti mihi: *Surge qui dormis et exsurge a mortuis, et inluminabit te Christus* (Ephes. 5:14), et undique ostendenti vera te dicere, non erat omnino, quid responderem, veritate convictus, nisi tantum verba lenta et somnolenta: 'modo,' 'ecce modum,' 'sine paululum,' . . .

[23] See *ibid.*, 9, 1, 1: Ejiciebas enim eas a me, vera tu et summa suavitas, ejiciebas et intrabas pro eis omni voluptate dulcior, sed non carni et sanguini, omni luce clarior, sed omni secreto interior, omni honore sublimior, sed non sublimibus in se.

[24] See *ibid.*, 2, 6, 13. See also Mausbach, *op. cit.*, 2.70.

[25] See *ibid.*, 2, 6, 14: Perverse te imitantur omnes qui longe se a te faciunt et extollunt se adversum te. Sed etiam sic imitando indicant creatorem te esse omnis naturae et ideo non esse quo a te omni modo recedatur. Even sin is an indirect avowal of the all perfect God.

This is possible for men, because, as St. Augustine points out, they may seek the one happiness in different objects.[26] Even those who pursue a false object still wish happiness.[27] Again, although all men desire happiness, many do not find it because weakness and division of will conspire with sensible pleasures to render them satisfied with something less than God:

> Or do not all men desire this, but because '*the flesh lusts against the spirit and the spirit against the flesh, so that they can not do what they would,*' they slip back into that which they can do, and become satisfied with it, because what they think themselves unable to achieve, they do not will so strongly as would be necessary to render them capable of accomplishing it.[28]

With deep intuition St. Augustine here puts his finger upon the factor of discouragement leading to the abandonment of the difficult ideal in favor of objects easily possessed. Special analysis will later be given to this problem of *strength of will.*[29]

God gives Himself as a reward to those who love Him by the goodness of their moral life. Indeed there is no other reward, no other true joy, except that of rejoicing in God.[30] This idea is repeated by the Saint quoting the Psalmist: *Mihi autem adhaerere Deo bonum est* (Ps. 72:28).[31] In the final chapter of the *Con-*

---

[26] See *ibid.*, 10, 21, 31: . . . Quod etsi alius hinc, alius illinc assequitur, unum est tamen quo pervenire omnes nituntur, ut gaudeant.

[27] See *ibid.*, 10, 22, 32: Qui autem aliam putant esse, aliud sectantur gaudium, neque ipsum verum. Ab aliqua tamen imagine gaudii voluntas eorum non avertitur.

[28] *Ibid.*, 10, 23, 33: An omnes hoc volunt, sed quoniam *caro concupiscit adversus spiritum et spiritus adversus carnem, ut non faciant quod volunt* (Gal. 5:17), cadunt in id quod valent eoque contenti sunt, quia illud quod non valent non tantum volunt, quantum sat est ut valeant?

[29] See *infra*, ch. III, 94-103.

[30] See *Conf.*, 10, 22, 32: Est enim gaudium, quod non datur inpiis sed eis qui te gratis colunt, quorum gaudium tu ipse est. . . . Et ipsa est beata vita, gaudere de te, ad te, propter te: ipsa est, et *non est altera* (italics mine).

[31] See *ibid.*, 7, 11, 17. See also Mausbach, *op. cit.*, 1.64, where it is shown that the Saint uses this verse to teach us that our very being must be rooted in God, or else it will be without support. Such an adherence of the will to God brings about an elevation of the intellect also.

fessions, moreover, the Saint expresses the hope that he will possess as his reward Him who has given man the power to do good works.[32]

Finally St. Augustine implicitly identifies his ultimate end with heaven. He relates that his conversations with the dying Monnica so inflamed them both with the desirability of heaven that the highest pleasure of the senses seemed as nothing compared with it.[33]

In short, the *Confessions* repeat the fundamental moral principle that the human soul tends to God as its happiness and perfection. As the Creator, God is the Source of all being; and, as the Supreme Good, He is the source of all conscious activity, of all volition. Morality, then, consists in directing our liberty towards God.[34] In his *Confessions* the Saint also discusses the *way* to the ultimate end, various aspects of which will be considered in the next chapter.

It should be noted that the *Confessions'* references to the goal of man are permeated with Scriptural thought. Thus, even though in the passages already considered the Saint does not make formal distinctions between the natural and the supernatural end of man, it is clear that he views the goal of man under the light of supernatural Faith rather than by reason alone. It is the God of the Psalms, the God of Revelation, whom he seeks.

---

[32] See *Conf.,* 13, 38, 53.

[33] See *ibid.,* 9, 10, 24. See also *ibid.,* 9, 10, 26.

[34] See E. Portalié, "Augustin," DTC (Paris, 1909), 1.2432: Toute la morale, implicitement ou explicitement, consistera à diriger vers Dieu notre liberté.

CHAPTER II

The Way to God

A. LAW

In the fragmentary references to law in the *Confessions* one finds neither a definition nor a formal division; still one can pick out passages that refer to various kinds of law and to special precepts given by God to the patriarchs and prophets of the Old Testament. One may discover, moreover, a few references to the purposes of law, and to its reward. First of all, the notion of Divine law will be considered.

All things are ordered by the Divine eternal law. Upon this all other laws must be based.[1] Thus, true internal justice is founded upon the most just law of God, to which human customs must be subordinate. Always and everywhere this law of God remains the same, yet at the same time it disposes the manners and customs of times and places in accordance with such times and places.[2] Obviously, here the Saint is speaking about the immutability of the eternal law. In the next passage he examines the actions of the patriarchs, actions that had puzzled him when he had read the Old Testament as a Manichean.

He insists that certain actions of the patriarchs should not be judged by the peculiar viewpoint of any given period but by the

[1] See *ibid.,* 1, 6, 9: Tu es et Deus es Dominusque omnium quae creasti et apud te rerum omnium instabilium stant causae et rerum omnium mutabilium inmutabiles manent origines et omnium inrationabilium et temporalium sempiternae vivunt rationes. See also *ibid.,* 1, 7, 12: . . . et lege tua ordinas omnia.

[2] See *ibid.,* 3, 7, 13: Et non noveram justitiam veram interiorem non ex consuetudine judicantem, sed ex lege rectissima Dei omnipotentis, qua formarentur mores regionum et dierum pro regionibus et diebus, cum ipsa ubique et semper esset, non alibi alia nec alias aliter, secundum quam justi essent Abraham et Isaac et Jacob et Moyses et David et illi omnes laudati ore Dei.

unchanging and eternal law of God, while he points out that man tends to judge the moral habits of the whole human race in terms that are valid only for his own time and place.[3] Here the Saint quotes the Pauline phrase *ex humano die* (I Cor. 4:3) to illustrate his point.[4]

The next point for study is St. Augustine's comparison between human laws changed to fit varying conditions and certain parts of the Divine Law (usually called Divine Positive Law) changed by God to serve His Wisdom. Men have different regulations for different conditions within their state; likewise, under special circumstances, God has allowed certain things as licit and has forbade others:

> Such are they that storm when they hear that it was lawful for holy men to do in one age that which is not lawful in this, or that God, for certain temporary reasons, commanded them one thing and these another, whereas both did observe the same rule of justice; or, when they observe that in one man and in one day, and in one house, different things are fit for different members, and that the same thing, which before was lawful, within an hour after will not be so, and that something is permitted or commanded in that corner, which is justly prohibited and punished in this other.[5]

[3] See *loc. cit.*: Numquid justitia varia est et mutabilis? Sed tempora quibus praesidet, non pariter eunt; tempora enim sunt. Homines autem quorum vita super terram brevis est, quia sensu non valent causas contexere saeculorum priorum aliarumque gentium, quas experti non sunt, cum his quas experti sunt, in uno autem corpore vel die vel domo facile possunt videre, quid cui membro, quibus momentis, quibus partibus personisve congruat, in illis offenduntur, hic serviunt.

[4] See *loc. cit.*: Sed eos (Abraham et Isaac, etc.) ab imperitis judicari iniquos, judicantibus *ex humano die* (I Cor. 4:3) et universos mores humani generis ex parte moris sui metientibus, tamquam si quis nescius in armamentis, quid cui membro adcommodatum sit, ocrea velit caput contegi et galea calciari et murmuret quod non apte conveniat.

[5] *Loc. cit.*: Sic sunt isti qui indignantur, cum audierint illo saeculo licuisse justis aliquid quod isto non licet justis, et quia illis aliud praecepit Deus, istis aliud pro temporalibus causis, cum eidem justitiae utrique servierint, cum in uno homine et in uno die et in unis aedibus videant aliud alii membro congruere et aliud iam dudum licuisse, post horam non licere, quiddam in illo angulo permitti aut juberi, quod in isto juste vetetur et vindicetur.

One must consider, therefore, the principles of God's law. Just as the principles of the art of writing verse remain a unity despite diverse applications, so also within the one Divine Justice are contained all the precepts that God made in different ages. The oneness of Divine Justice is not contrary to the gradual unfolding of the Divine Law, which does not command everything at once, but under changing circumstances selects and enjoins what is appropriate for each time and place.[6] Hence the principles of Divine Justice are immutable, while their special applications vary.

These applications refer to the purely positive precepts of the Divine Law, to the deeds of the patriarchs and of the prophets, and not to certain actions that are always sinful, because they are against nature. These are considered in the following paragraph.

Were all nations to commit the sins of Sodom, they would all stand guilty of the same crime before the law of God. When lust perverts the nature of man, it also upsets the due relationship of man to the Author of his nature.[7] To this example St. Augustine adds another to stress the immutable character of the Divine natural law. The Saint points out that the impudent and lawless students of Carthage committed injustices which were left unpunished, because they were protected by depraved custom. They escaped human sanctions; nevertheless, they must face Divine retribution, since they did things that will never be allowed by the natural law of God.[8]

---

[6] See *Conf.*, 3, 7, 14: Et ars ipsa qua canebam non habebant aliud alibi, sed omnia simul. Et non intuebar justitiam cui servirent boni et sancti homines longe excellentius atque sublimius habere simul omnia quae praecepit et nulla ex parte varie, tamen variis temporibus non omnia simul sed propria distribuentem et praecipientem. . . . Et reprehendebam caecus pios patres non solum, sicut Deus juberet atque inspiraret, utentes praesentibus verum quoque, sicut Deus revelaret, futura praenuntiantes. (See also B. Roland-Gosselin, *La morale de Saint Augustin,* Paris, Rivière, 1925, 50.)

[7] See *Conf.*, 3, 8, 15: Itaque flagitia, quae sunt contra naturam, ubique et semper destestanda atque punienda sunt, qualia Sodomitarum fuerunt. Quae si omnes gentes facerent, eodem criminis reatu divina lege tenerentur, quae non sic fecit homines, ut hoc se uterentur modo. Violatur quippe ipsa societas, quae cum Deo nobis esse debet, cum eadam natura, cujus ille auctor est, libidinis perversitate polluitur.

[8] See *ibid.*, 5, 8, 14. See also *infra,* ch. 3, 133-134.

Such an immutability does not pertain to human law, which develops from the particular customs and needs of each social group. Since human laws are made for the common good of the community, they may not be transgressed to please the lawless caprice of any native or visitor. Here then St. Augustine refers to the social norm in human law, namely, the common good of the group. He states it in a negative fashion: "Any part that harmonizes not with the whole is offensive."[9]

The next question considered by St. Augustine is that of conflicts between Divine and human laws. In such cases the Divine Law always takes precedence: "But when God commandeth anything which is against the custom or compact of any people, although it were never done there before, it must then be done; and if it were discontinued it must be restored, or if before it were not instituted, it must be so then."[10]

In human society, kings rule by common consent. It is their right to make the laws, and it is the citizens' duty to obey them. This is for the common good of society. With all the more reason, then, are creatures bound to obey God who is the King of the universe. Unhesitatingly He must be obeyed. Just as in human society, wherever there exists a hierarchy of authority, in which the person of lesser authority is subject to the person of greater and so on up the scale to the supreme authority of the king, so also must God be obeyed before all kings, for they bear a relationship of subordination to Him, similar to that of their officials to themselves. God is King of Kings.[11] Thus, a Divine command must take first

---

[9] See *ibid.*, 3, 8, 15: Quae autem contra mores hominum sunt flagitia pro morum diversitate vitanda sunt, ut pactum inter se civitatis aut gentis consuetudine vel lege firmatum nulla civis aut peregrini libidine violetur. Turpis enim omnis pars universo suo non congruens. (See also Roland-Gosselin, *op. cit.*, 54.)

[10] *Loc. cit.*: Cum autem Deus aliquid contra morem aut pactum quorumlibet jubet, etsi numquam ibi factum est, faciendum est, et si omissum, instaurandum, et si institutum non erat, instituendum est.

[11] See *loc. cit.*: Si enim regi licet in civitate cui regnat jubere aliquid, quod neque ante illum quisquam nec ipse umquam jusserat . . . generale quippe pactum est societatis humanae oboedire regibus suis—quanto magis Deus regnator universae creaturae cui ad ea quae jusserit sine dubitatione serviendum est! Sicut enim in potestatibus societatis humanae major potestas minori ad oboediendum praeponitur, ita Deus omnibus.

place, even though its reason be hidden in Divine Wisdom, or is contrary to custom.[12]

After establishing the supremacy of Divine Law, St. Augustine considers the problem of certain actions that have the appearance of sin, but are not such in reality: "Again there are some things, resembling sins of inordinate passion or of violence, which yet are not sins, because they neither offend thee, our Lord and God, nor human society."[13] Here the Saint is referring to events like the command of God to slay Isaac (Gen. 22:2 ff.), to the spoliation of Egypt, and to the adultery of Osee (Osee 1:2). In all these situations men were obliged to carry out explicit commands of God, even though their fulfillment seemed to be sinful.[14]

---

[12] See *Conf.*, 3, 9, 17: Cum vero aliquid tu repente inusitatum et improvisum imperas, etiamsi hoc aliquando vetuisti, quamvis causam imperii tui pro tempore occultes et quamvis contra pactum sit aliquorum hominum societatis, quis dubitet esse faciendum quando ea justa est societas hominum quae servit tibi? See also *Contra Faustum*, 22.71 (ML 42.445): Fieri autem potest ut sint aliae causae occultissimae, cur hoc illi populo divinitus dictum sit; sed divinis imperiis cedendum obtemperando, non resistendum est disputando. See also *De civ. Dei*, 1, 26 (Dombart-Kalb, Leipzig: Teubner, 1928, 4th edit., 1.41): Cum autem Deus jubet seque jubere sine ullis ambagibus intimat, quis obedientiam in crimen vocet? Quis obsequiem pietatis accuset?

[13] *Conf.*, 3, 9, 17: Et sunt quaedam similia vel flagitio vel facinori et non sunt peccata, quia nec te offendunt Dominum Deum Nostrum nec sociale consortium.

[14] In other works of St. Augustine one may find references to:

(A) *The Divine Command to Abraham*: See *Quaestiones in Heptateuchum*, 7, 49, sect. 4 (ML 34.811).

(B) *The Divine Command to Moses:* See *Contra Faust.*, 22.71 (ML 42.445. See also *De doct. Christ.*, 2, 40, 61 (ML 34.63), in which the spoliation of Egypt is considered as a symbol of the profitable use of pagan learning by Christianity.

(C) *The Divine Command to Osee*: See *Contra Faust.*, 22.89 (ML 42.459-461): De Osee autem propheta, non a me opus est dici quid illa jussio factumve significet, quod dixit Dominus ad Osee, *Vade et accipe tibi uxorem fornicationis et fac filios de fornicatione* (Osee 1:2); cum satis hoc ipsa Scriptura demonstret unde et quare sit dictum. (Then he explains Osee 1:2, 10 in terms of St. Paul: Rom. 9:23; Gal. 3:29; Acts 2:41, 44; Gal. 1:22; Ephes. 2:14). . . . He concludes: (42.461) Huic ergo prophetiae tam manifeste ipso rerum affectu declaratae, quisquis contradicit, non solum propheticis, verum etiam apostolicis litteris; nec solum

Indeed it may be stated as a general principle that all the deeds that were done by the patriarchs and prophets were performed either to teach what was necessary at that time or to symbolize the coming of Christ and of His Church. Not only in what these men said, but also in what they did, and in what happened to them, is Christ foreshadowed.[15]

Thus, many actions disapproved by men are approved by God's testimony, and many approved by men are condemned by God. There are several reasons for this discrepancy between human and Divine norms. Often the external appearances of the action are very different from the intimate dispositions of its author; frequently circumstances in the situation, which may be known only by a few, must be considered. For example, actions not sinful in themselves may be done through a reprehensible motive. One man may seek some necessary temporal possession from a motive of greed. Another man who is duly constituted in authority may administer a warranted correction to someone whom he wishes merely to annoy.[16]

---

quibuslibet litteris, verum etiam rebus impletis, et clarissima luce perfusis, impudentissime contradicit. Aliquid ergo fortassis diligentioris requirebat intentionis Judae factum, ut haec fornicaria, quae significat Ecclesiam de gentibus superstitionum prostitutione collectam, in habitu mulieris illius, quae Thamar appellata est, posset agnosci.

Although St. Augustine refers to the *adultery* of Osee, it is not certain whether Osee 1:2 denotes an unmarried harlot or an adulteress. See A. Van Hoonacker, *Les Douze Petits Prophètes* (Paris, J. Gabalda, 1908), 13-14, who in his review of the problem favors the interpretation that the woman became an adulteress after her marriage to Osee: La nation d'Israël, l'épouse de Jahvé, a été infidèle; elle a engendré des enfants adultérins que Jahvé refuse de reconnaître pour siens: de même l'épouse d'Osée sera une femme adultère, elle engendrera des enfants adultérins. C'est à ce titre, évidemment, que les enfants en question représentent les membres de la nation infidèle.

The question remains an unsolved one for the exegetes.

[15] See *Conf.*, 3, 9, 17: Fiunt enim omnia a servientibus tibi vel ad exhibendum quod ad praesens opus est, vel ad futura praenuntianda. See also *Contra Faust.*, 22.24 (ML 42.417). See also *Serm.* 2, sect. 7 (ML 38.31).

[16] See *Conf.*, 3, 9, 17: Multa itaque facta, quae hominibus inprobanda viderentur, testimonio tuo adprobanda sunt et multa laudata ab hominibus te teste damnantur. . . . Cum saepe se aliter habet species mali et aliter facientis animus atque articulus occulti temporis. . . . Cum conciliantur aliqua

In regard to the *purpose* of law the Saint points out that from childhood onwards it exercises a salutary restraint on the use of freedom, tempering pleasures and preventing their deadly allurements from drawing men away from God.[17] This protective function of law may be drawn, moreover, from reflection upon the self-destructive nature of sin. In transgressing the commandments of God man does not injure God, who is beyond all injury, but man injures himself alone. By sin man acts against his own welfare.[18]

On the other hand, man remains on the road to happiness by the observance of the commandments of God. This follows from the positive purpose of the law, which is to foster charity in the heart, since Jesus Christ reduced all law to the twofold love of God and of neighbor.[19]

As a *reward* for those who fulfill this Divine precept of charity, God reveals Himself to them, and He becomes their happiness, so that they do not turn away from Him. This reward belongs, however, to doers of the law rather than to judges of it.[20]

B. CONSCIENCE

Although St. Augustine does not define conscience in his *Confessions,* one may find scattered throughout this work many passages which shed light upon the manifold and intertwining relationships of this act of practical moral judgment. First he affirms that the basis of conscience is inscribed in the heart before literary culture: "And surely no science of letters is more innate to man than

---

in usum vitae congrua et tempori et incertum est an libidine habendi, aut puniuntur corrigendi studio potestate ordinata et incertum est an libidine nocendi. . . .

[17] See *Conf.,* 1, 14, 23: Huc satis elucet majorem habere vim ad discenda ista (the rudiments of Latin) liberam curiositatem quam meticulosam necessitatem. Sed illius fluxum haec restringit legibus tuis, Deus, legibus tuis, a magistrorum ferulis usque ad temptationes martyrum, valentibus legibus tuis miscere salubres amaritudines revocantes nos ad te a jucunditate pestifera, qua recessimus a te.

[18] See *ibid.,* 3, 8, 16.

[19] See *ibid.,* 12, 18, 27.

[20] See *Conf.,* 12, 15, 19. See also *ibid.,* 13, 23, 33.

the record of conscience teaching that one should not do to another what he would be unwilling to suffer from another."[21] Thus one possesses the knowledge of the obligation of justice before the knowledge of letters.

Following St. Paul (Rom. 2:15), St. Augustine repeats the word *scripta* in another passage, stating that not even iniquity can delete this law written in the hearts of men.[22] That is why conscience will condemn a man who does not reciprocate due love.[23]

Aside from these references to conscience, the Saint in his autobiography stresses two related truths, namely, the difficulty of attaining an adequate knowledge of self and the light of supernatural grace, which leads man onwards to the knowledge of himself, despite rationalization, spiritual blindness and other obstacles. First, the difficulty of self-knowledge will be considered; then, the light of God's grace goading the Saint on to a deeper understanding of himself will be studied; and, finally, conversion will be shown as the climax of this development in self-knowledge.

Concerning self-knowledge St. Augustine says that man is a great depth known only to God and that it is easier to number the hairs on his head than to enumerate the diverse motivations of his heart.[24] He stood apart from himself as from an unsolved puzzle.[25] The spirit of man does not know a certain portion of himself; whatever he does know about himself, he knows under the light

---

[21] *Ibid.*, 1, 18, 29: Et certe non est interior litterarum scientia quam *scripta* conscientia (italics mine), id est se alteri non facere quod nolit pati. See also Aertnys-Damen, *Theologia Moralis* (Marietti, 1944), 1.70, sect. 64b, where the author distinguishes *synderesis* from *conscientia* in the strict theological sense. In the above text St. Augustine uses the term *conscientia* in the sense of what later came to be called *synderesis,* inasmuch as he states that *conscientia* is an innate principle of reality, whereas the *act* of conscience is a judgment deduced from the principle of *synderesis.*

[22] See *ibid.*, 2, 4, 9: Furtum certe punit lex tua, Domine, et lex *scripta* in cordibus hominum, quam ne ipsa quidem delet iniquitas.

[23] See *ibid.*, 4, 9, 14.

[24] See *Conf.*, 4, 14, 22: Grande profundum est ipse homo, cujus etiam capillos tu, Domine, numeratos habes . . . et tamen capilli ejus magis numerabiles quam affectus ejus et motus cordis ejus. See also *ibid.*, 13, 12, 13.

[25] See *ibid.*, 10, 33, 50: Mihi quaestio factus sum et ipse est languor ejus.

of Divine grace. "Because that which I know of myself, I know by thy light shining upon me."[26]

Here the Saint attributes his growth in self-knowledge to Divine enlightenment. Without this guidance the soul is helpless: "Behold where the weak soul doth lie, which adhereth not yet to the solidity of Truth."[27] From the viewpoint of temptation, moreover, man does not know how he will react to it; but this aspect of self-knowledge will be studied under *Temptation*.[28]

This teaching of the *Confessions* serves as a background for the consideration of the Saint's theocentric viewpoint on conscience. God enlightens the conscience of men, being within their hearts. Since men have strayed away from their own hearts and from truth,[29] they must return to themselves and to God. "Return, ye sinners, into your own heart (Is. 46:8), and be united unto him that made you."[30] A similar idea is found in his commentary on Psalm Fifty-seven where the Saint teaches that after man had become a stranger to himself, the *written* law also was given him.[31] Man had strayed from the law already written in his heart, i.e., his conscience. From his own experience St. Augustine warns that

---

[26] *Ibid.*, 10, 5, 7: Et quod de me scio te mihi lucente scio. See also Mausbach, *Die Ethik des heiligen Augustinus*, 1.20, where the author says that only by God's help can the darkness of self be penetrated by the sunlight of knowledge.

[27] *Ibid.*, 4, 14, 23: Ecce ubi jacet anima infirma nondum haerens soliditate veritatis. See also *ibid.*, 13, 16, 19.

[28] See *infra*, ch. 3, 128-131.

[29] See *ibid.*, 4, 12, 18: Non enim fecit atque abiit, sed ex illo in illo sunt. Ecce ubi est, ubi sapit veritas? Intimus cordi est, sed cor erravit ab eo.

[30] *Loc. cit.*: *Redite, praevaricatores, ad cor* (Is. 46:8) et inhaerete illi qui fecit vos.

[31] See *Enar. in Ps. 57*, sect. 1 (ML 36.673-674): Sed quia homines appetentes ea quae foris sunt, etiam a seipsis exsules facti sunt, data est etiam conscripta lex: non quia in cordibus scripta non erat; sed quia tu fugitivus eras cordis tui, ab illo qui ubique est comprehenderis et ad teipsum intro revocaris. Propterea scripta lex quid clamat eis qui deseruerunt legem *scriptam in cordibus suis* (Rom. 2-15)? *Redite, praevaricatores, ad cor* (Is. 46:8).

the forsaking of conscience had plunged him into error and brought him to the brink of despair.[32]

Admonished by the writings of Plotinus to seek self-knowledge, St. Augustine did so with the help of God's grace.[33] The result was a spiritual earthquake. Under the strong light of God's grace the Saint saw his sinful self, and he trembled with love and with terror, realizing how far away he was from God.

This same light of grace made him realize that God was punishing him for his sins. Not merely in the moral sphere did this light shine. Together with the penetrating perception of self and of sin came the concept of a *spiritual* God.[34] The importance of this concept will be seen in the subsequent analysis of *Ignorance*.[35] Here

---

[32] See *Conf.*, 6, 1, 1: Et ambulabam per tenebris et lubricum et quaerebam foris a me, et non inveniebam Deum cordis mei, et veneram in profundum maris et diffidebam et desperabam de inventione veri.

[33] See *ibid.*, 7, 10, 16: Et inde admonitus redire ad memet ipsum intravi in intima mea, *duce te* (italics mine) et potui, quoniam factus es adjutor meus. . . . Intravi et vidi qualicumque oculo animae meae supra eundum oculum animae meae—supra mentem meam lucem inconmutabilem.

[34] See *loc. cit.*: Et reverberasti infirmitatem aspectus mei radians in me vehementer, et contremui amore et horrore: et inveni longe me esse a te in regione dissimilitudinis, tamquam audirem vocem tuam de excelso: 'cibus sum grandium: cresce et manducabis me. . . .' Et cognovi quoniam *pro iniquitate erudisti hominem et tabescere fecisti sicut araneam animam meam* (Ps. 38:12), et dixi: 'Numquid nihil est veritas, quoniam neque per finita neque per infinita locorum spatia diffusa est?' Et clamasti de longinquo: *Ego sum qui sum* (Ex. 3:14). Et audivi, sicut auditur in corde, et non erat prorsus unde dubitarem faciliusque dubitarem vivere me quam non esse veritatem, quae *per ea quae facta sunt, intellecta* (Rom. 1:20) conspicitur. See also P. Henry, *Plotin et l'Occident,* 114: After pointing out that the above text of the *Confessions* is very similar to *Enneads,* 1, 6, Henry adds: Augustin, de plus, a complètement lavé le texte de Plotin de sa couleur panthéiste, et les mêmes mots n'ont plus tout à fait la même nuance. Cette éclatante lumière spirituelle, objet de la contemplation, qui paraît s'identifier chez Plotin, au moins en partie, avec l'intelligence humaine, symbolize clairement dans les *Confessions* Dieu lui-même.

[35] See *Conf.*, 7, 17, 23: . . . et abduxit cogitationem a consuetudine, subtrahens se contradicentibus turbis phantasmatum, ut inveniret, quo lumine aspargeretur, cum sine ulla dubitatione clamaret inconmutabile praeferendum esse mutabili. . . . See also C. Boyer, *Christianisme et Néo-Platonisme dans la formation de saint Augustin,* 95: Mais quelle voie connaissait alors Augustin, qui menât à la vision de la Vérité? *Confessions* et *Dialogues* font une response identique: la purification.

it suffices to point out that when St. Augustine began to change himself on the moral level, his intellect was enlightened and false notions as to the nature of God and of evil were dissipated.

Another example may be given to show how Divine grace aided the Saint to know himself. The reader does well, however, in studying such instances to remember that his growth in self-knowledge under the light of grace was a gradual process, in which certain incidents stand out. Thus, while Augustine was listening to the story of Pontitianus, he was forced to turn round to face himself as he really was, even though he shrank from such introspection. Divine grace made him see how foul he was; and he tried to turn his thoughts into another channel, but the same power again thrust his inner self before his conscience, so that he might see his sins and hate them. Indeed Augustine knew his state of soul already, but he had been trying to make believe that he did not know it. He wanted to forget his guilt, but Divine grace was too active.[36]

Thus, good example and God's grace broke through the coating of rationalization that had formed around his conscience. No longer did he excuse himself. Even though he still found it difficult to rise from a life of sin, at least he was now honest in admitting his guilt.[37] Spiritually, this was progress. Again, at this stage in his conversion one notes salutary confusion and internal dissatisfaction,[38] characteristics usually found in a reactivated conscience. While it is true that such inner turmoil is part of the punishment for sin,[39] it is equally true that this same unrest may be the beginning of repentance and conversion, as it was in the case of the Saint. At the period of this mental anguish, however, he did not foresee its good effects.[40] Here then one notes a *salutary* disturbance of conscience leading to God.

In this inner conflict, moreover, love plays a part. For St. Augustine testifies that even while living in sin, he remembered God,

---

[36] See *Conf.*, 8, 7, 16.

[37] See *ibid.*, 8, 7, 18.

[38] See *ibid.*, 8, 7, 19: Sed tantum insaniebar *salubriter* (italics mine) *et* moriebar vitaliter, gnarus quid mali essem et ignarus quid boni post paululum futurus essem. See also *ibid.*, 8, 7, 18: Et increparet in me conscientia mea.

[39] See *ibid.*, 1, 12, 19: Jussisti enim et sic est ut poena sua sibi sit omnis inordinatus animus.

[40] See *ibid.*, 8, 7, 19.

heard His voice calling amidst tumult, loved Him, and finally returned in sorrow.[41]

From the study of St. Augustine's conflicts at this period, then, one may form observations of a moral nature. Beneath compunction in the soul is the fact of sin. In Augustine's case the recognition of sin created a healthy dissatisfaction which, in turn, led to the repudiation of dishonest motivation and to the choice of God.[42] On the other hand, rationalization and the refusal to admit moral guilt cause spiritual blindness.

One can hide God from himself, but he cannot hide himself from God.[43] Indeed dissatisfaction with self is confession unto God;[44] and to hear from God about self is the same thing as the attainment of self-knowledge.[45] Hence there is an intimate connection between the light of God's grace and growth in self-knowledge. This relationship is exemplified very vividly in the garden scene.[46] There the grace of conversion is ushered in by most in-

---

[41] See *ibid.*, 12, 10, 10: Defluxi ad ista (Manichean errors) et obscuratus sum, sed hinc, etiam hinc adamavi te. *Erravi et recordatus sum tui* (Ps. 118:176). *Audivi vocem tuam post me* (Ezech. 3:12), ut redirem et vix audivi. . . . Et nunc ecce redeo aestuans et anhelans ad fontem tuum (Divine truth).

[42] See *Conf.*, 10, 2, 2.

[43] See *loc. cit.*, 10, 2, 2,

[44] See *loc. cit.*: Cum enim malus sum, nihil est aliud confiteri tibi quam displicere mihi.

[45] See *Conf.*, 10, 3, 3: Quid est enim a te audire de se nisi cognoscere se.

[46] See *ibid.*, 8, 12-28, 29, 30 (the entire chapter): Inasmuch as the garden-scene is linked with the controversy concerning the conversion of St. Augustine, see C. Boyer, *Christianisme et Néo-Platonisme dans la formation de saint Augustin,* 1-18; 189-195, for a summary of the problem. See also Campbell and McGuire, *Confessions,* 55: A large controversial literature has been devoted to the subject, with scholarship tending latterly to accept the historicity of the *Confessions* as well as of the *Dialogues.* The initial fact of Augustine's scrupulosity as a writer could not lightly be cast aside, and it has gradually become evident to many that the two Augustines are psychologically possible in the same personality, that the one is in fact a supplement of the other, that the apparent contradictions between these writings arise because of the very special purpose which called each forth, that the *Dialogues* contain statements and references that clearly show Augustine a Christian in thought and in practice at the time of their composition, de-

tense self-penetration, full of all the soul-agony that comes to one who has arrived at long last at a clear perception of his own sinfulness and misery. The full weight of moral guilt, clearly seen and admitted, crushes all his scale of values.[47] His prayer for God's grace is heard; he picks up and reads St. Paul; and then he forms an efficacious resolution to turn completely to the Faith of Monnica and to Christ.[48] This is conversion, a new scale of values, a new outlook. But it was the *consummation* of a *gradual* growth in self-knowledge under the light of God's grace.

Later in the *Confessions* the Saint describes how he applied Psalm Four to himself in prayerful meditation and derived thence resolutions for the renewal of his moral life:

> I read on, '*Be angry and sin not*' (Ps. 4:5); and how was I moved, O my God—I who had now learned to be angry with myself in the past, that I might not sin in the time to come. . . . Nor was the good that I sought for any longer in external things, nor did I seek them with the eyes of flesh and blood in this visible world. For they who seek their delight in such visible things, do easily vanish away like the smoke, and are poured out upon those things which are seen and are temporal, and in the starvation of their thoughts they do lick the very shadows thereof. O that they might grow wearied for very hunger, and say, 'Who will show us good things?' (Ps. 4:6). . . And I cried out, reading these things in the letter, and finding them to be verified in the spirit.[49]

From the above passage, from the garden-scene narration, and from the various references to conscience already discussed one

---

spite the Neoplatonic language, which, as a comparative stranger to the Scriptures and as a deep lover of Neoplatonism, he used as the vehicle of his thought.

[47] See *ibid.*, 8, 12, 28.

[48] See *ibid.*, 8, 12, 29.

[49] *Ibid.*, 9, 4, 10: *Irascimini et nolite peccare* (Ps. 4:5) et quomodo movebar, Deus meus, qui jam didiceram irasci mihi de praeteritis, ut de cetero non peccarem. . . . Nec jam bona mea foris erant nec oculis carneis in isto sole quaerebantur. Volentes enim gaudere forinsecus facile vanescunt et effunduntur in ea, quae videntur et temporalia sunt, et imagines eorum famelica cogitatione lambiunt. Et o si fatigentur inedia et dicant: *quis ostendet nobis bona?* (Ps. 4:6) . . . Et exclamabam legens haec foris et agnoscens intus. . . .

may deduce that St. Augustine's concept of conscience is not purely philosophic but theocentric and dynamic. For him the judgments of conscience are not isolated phenomena, but complicated operations of the whole person in the varying situations of life—operations done under the influence of Divine Grace, or hardened by the rejection of it, as in the case of those who attempt to hide God from themselves. Thus, in the Saint's idea of conscience the sinner forms an honest judgment of guilt upon himself with the aid of Divine Light, but he is also capable of blinding himself, and the fact that he does so will be considered under *Ignorance*.[50]

St. Augustine also mentions in his *Confessions* a few problems that reveal his own delicacy of conscience. Speaking of the various forms of temptation, he narrates his own *perplexity*: He enjoyed listening to the chanting of the psalms, but he feared that in the enjoyment he might be indulging excessively in sensual pleasure. Consequently, he fluctuated between his desire to hear this sacred music and his fear of possible sin in the very hearing.[51] The same fine discernment of even the shadows of sin is found in the inquiry into the morality of eating for pleasure.[52] In both instances he is striving to avoid even the less harmful forms of inordinate concupiscence.

He calls his pleasure in the music of the chants a sin, but it can hardly have been a formal sin, since the awareness of guilt came only after listening to the music. It is curious, moreover, to note that previously, speaking of the period immediately after his conversion, he had experienced nothing but joy in hearing the chanting of the Psalms. Then he perceived no temptation in the sweetness of the music.[53]

This delicacy of conscience in the Saint is the expression of his desire to love God purely.[54] Hence he is careful to preserve his heart free from attachments such as those engendered by beautiful forms and colors. This also explains his annoyance at the dis-

---

[50] See *infra*, ch. 3, 62-77.

[51] See *Conf.*, 10, 33, 50.

[52] See *ibid.*, 10, 31, 44. See also *infra*, ch. 3, 86-87.

[53] See *ibid.*, 10, 33, 49: Ita in his pecco, non sentiens, sed postea sentio. See also *ibid.*, 9, 6, 14; *infra*, ch. 3, 88.

[54] See *ibid.*, 10, 34, 51.

tractions that prevented him from concentrating his thoughts on the object of his love.[55] At the end of this complaint, however, he expresses his confidence in God's mercy.[56] Similarly at the conclusion of his inquiry into the morality of his grief over his mother's death he advises that one should not inquire too narrowly into one's sins, but should place his hope in God.[57] Again, in treating the question of nocturnal pollution he says that provided one has resisted the temptation, he should return to peace of conscience.[58]

In these passages, then, one notes both love of God and trust in His mercy. These virtues are found in delicate consciences, but hardly in scrupulous ones. Yet the Saint's restraint of grief at the funeral of his mother had a touch of rigorism.[59]

C. PROVIDENCE AND GRACE

So far, law and conscience have been viewed as indicating the way to God. In the *Confessions'* references to conscience, moreover, the influence of Divine grace has been pointed out. For the sake of completeness, however, and at the same time to illustrate the intimate dependence of Moral upon Dogmatic Theology, it will be beneficial at this juncture to summarize the teaching of the *Confessions* on Providence and Divine grace. The aim will be, not to give a detailed analysis of all the passages referring to these two factors, but simply to note their general influence in the *moral* life of St. Augustine.

---

[55] See *ibid.,* 10, 35, 57.

[56] See *loc. cit.*: Et talibus vita mea plena est, et *una spes mea* magna *valde misericordia* tua. (Italics mine.)

[57] See *Conf.,* 9, 13, 34.

[58] See *ibid.,* 10, 30, 41: Sed adhuc vivunt in memoria mea, de qua multa locutus sum, talium rerum imagines, quas ibi consuetudo mea fixit, et occursantur *mihi vigilanti* (italics mine) quidem carentes viribus, in somnis autem non solum ad delectationem sed etiam ad consensionem factumque simillimum. . . . Et tamen tantum interest ut cum aliter accidit, evigilantes ad conscientiae *requiem* redeamus ipsaque distantia reperiamus nec non fecisse, quod tamen nobis quoque modo factum esse doleamus. (One may have peace of conscience and at the same time regret that the action took place in him even without his consent.)

[59] See *infra,* ch. 3, 92-93.

Although for a long time the Saint clung to a false notion of God, he always believed in the existence of God and in His care for men.[60] He conceived Providence as dealing with him in mysterious and wondrous ways in response to the prayers of his mother.[61] Again, he visualized it as a most kind hand, gently persuading his heart, or correcting him for sin and goading him on to repentance,[62] or leading him all unawares to St. Ambrose,[63] or using him as the unwitting instrument of correction in the case of Alypius.[64]

Not only in his own life and in those of Alypius and of St. Monnica, but in the lives of all men Providence is at work.[65] For the entire human race it provided a Mediator, Jesus Christ;[66] and it established a Church to be a universal light of salvation.[67] Thus God exercises His loving care for men both through the external medium of the Church and through the interior ways of Divine grace.

Since St. Augustine viewed Divine grace in many different passages in the *Confessions,* it seems best to distinguish passages

---

[60] See *Conf.*, 6, 5, 8: Semper tamen credidi et esse te et curam nostri gerere.

[61] See *ibid.*, 5, 7, 13: *Manus* enim tuae, Deus meus, *in abdito* (italics mine) providentiae tuae non deserebant animam meam; et sanguine cordis matris meae per lacrimas ejus diebus et noctibus pro me sacrificabatur tibi.

[62] See *ibid.,* 6, 5, 7: Deinde paulatim tu, Domine, *manu* (italics mine) mitissima et misericordissima pertractans et componens cor meum persuasisti mihi. . . . See also *ibid.,* 5, 2, 2: Sed fugerunt ut non viderent te videntem se atque excaecati in te offenderent, quia non deseris aliquid eorum, quae fecisti. . . .

[63] See *ibid.*, 5, 13, 23.

[64] See *ibid.*, 6, 7, 12.

[65] See *Conf.*, 9, 8, 18.

[66] See *ibid.*, 10, 43, 68. See also *ibid.*, 10, 43, 69 et 70; and *ibid.*, 4, 12, 19.

[67] See *ibid.*, 6, 5, 8: Ideoque cum essemus infirmi ad inveniendum liquida ratione veritatem et ob hoc nobis opus esset auctoritate sanctarum litterarum, iam credere coeperam nullo modo te fuisse tributurum tam excellentem illi scripturae per omnes iam terras auctoritatem, nisi et per ipsam tibi credi et per ipsam te quaeri voluisses. See also C. Boyer, *Essais sur la doctrine de saint Augustin* (Paris: G. Beauchesne, 1932), 16-17: Le lien entre la croyance à la Providence et la croyance à un secours préparé pour l'intelligence est marqué dans le récit des Confessions par un 'ideoque.' From his analysis of this section of the *Confessions* Boyer understands the Saint as arriving at this conclusion: Ou l'Église possède la vérité, ou il n'y pas de Providence.

treating it in general from those describing its power as a remedy for a specific vice. Here, only those passages considering the general notions of Divine grace will be mentioned; later the effects of such help will be shown as remedies against specific sins.[68]

From the reading of St. Paul the Saint gained an insight into the secrets of grace. By the power of grace man who is admonished to seek God is made strong to possess Him. Thus God not only points out the moral ideal, but He also strengthens human nature from within so that it can attain the goal for which it strives. Even he who is afar off and cannot see the way will find it and hold fast to it. Hence, not in himself, but in God's grace should man glory, and not merely for what he knows, but for the very power of knowing.[69]

In the very same passage St. Augustine compares the pagan philosophers to men standing on a hilltop, viewing the land of peace from afar, but unable to reach it:

> For it is one thing from some wooded mountain top to see the land of peace, without being able to find the way thither, and to strive towards it in vain through certain impenetrable ways, beset round about with those fugitive spirits, deserters of their God, lying in ambush with their prince, the lion and the dragon; and another to keep on the way thither, secure in the care of that heavenly leader, where there are none that have deserted from the heavenly army lying in wait to rob, for they shun that way no less than their very torment.[70]

By natural reason these men could, and did, know that God exists, but they were ignorant of the necessity of Divine grace

---

[68] See *infra*, ch. 4, 147-154.

[69] See *Conf.*, 7, 21, 27.

[70] *Loc. cit.*: Et aliud est de silvestri cacumine videre patriam pacis et iter ad eam non invenire et frustra conari per invia circum obsidentibus et insidiantibus fugitivis desertoribus cum principe suo leone et dracone, aliud tenere viam illuc ducentem cura caelestis imperatoris munitam, ubi non latrocinantur qui caelestem militiam deseruerunt; vitant enim eam sicut supplicium.

and of the virtue of humility.[71] In sharp contrast the Saint attributes the work of his conversion to Divine grace.[72] This does not mean, however, that his description of his gradual advance to conversion excludes natural influences. Indeed he shows how nature prepared the way for grace. Thus, his discovery of the spiritual nature of God in the *Enneads* of Plotinus prepared his soul for conversion, but only meditation on the words of St. Paul converted him.[73] The work begun by Plotinus was completed by St. Paul.[74]

The human intellect, moreover, has no claim upon God to receive the light of Divine grace; and, if it has been enlightened and elevated, it should attribute it solely to God's grace.[75] It is the Holy Spirit who gives the soul knowledge of supernatural truth:

> But so many as by the Spirit do see these things, it is thou that seest in them. When therefore they see that these things are good, it is thou who seest in them that

---

[71] See *Conf.*, 7, 20, 26: Et cum postea in libris tuis mansuefactus essem, et curantibus digitis tuis contrectarentur vulnera mea, discernerem atque distinguerem quid interesset inter *praesumptionem* et *confessionem;* inter videntes *quo* eundum sit nec videntes *qua* (italics mine), et viam ducentem ad beatificam patriam, non tantum cernendam, set et habitandam.

[72] See *ibid.*, 9, 1, 1: Et hoc erat totum nolle, quod volebam, et velle quod volebas.

[73] See *supra,* ch. 2, 18-19, nn. 34-36. See also *Conf.*, 8, 12, 28-30; Henry, *Plotin et l'Occident,* 143: La lecture des *Ennéades* a préparé sa conversion et l'a rendue possible, mais seule la méditation des lettres de saint Paul l'a converti.

[74] See Henry, *op. cit.*, 116: Oui, c'est le Dieu vivant qui s'est montré à Augustin et qui lui a dit: 'Me voici,' le Dieu des chrétiens bien plus que le Dieu des philosophes. Thus Augustine admitted his debt to Plotinus, but not that Plotinus had made him a Christian: L'oeuvre que Plotin avait commencée, saint Paul allait devoir l'achever.

[75] See *Conf.*, 13, 3, 4: Sed sicut non te promeruerat ut esset talis vita, quae inluminari posset, ita nec cum iam esset promeruit te, ut inluminaretur. Neque enim ejus informitas placeret tibi, si non lux fieret non existendo, sed intuendo inluminantem lucem eique cohaerendo, ut et quod utcumque vivit et quod beate vivit, non deberet *nisi gratiae tuae* (italics mine), conversa per conmutationem meliorem ad id, quod neque in melius neque in deterius mutari potest.

> they are good; and what things soever for thy sake are pleasing, it is thou who pleasest in them; and what things through thy Spirit please us, do please thee in us. *For what man knoweth the things of a man, but the spirit of a man, which is in him? Even so, no one knoweth the things of God, but the Spirit of God. Now we,* saith he, *have received not the spirit of this world, but the Spirit which is of God, that we might know the things which are freely given unto us of God* (I Cor. 2, 11, ff.).[76]

In another passage St. Augustine calls God the teacher of all truth. Here he refers to truths of both the natural and the supernatural orders: "Neither is there any other teacher of truth but only thou wheresoever and whencesoever it may shine."[77] God is

[76] *Ibid.*, 13, 31, 46: Qui autem per spiritum tuum vident ea, tu vides in eis. Ergo cum vident, quia bona sunt, tu vides quia bona sunt, et quaecumque propter te placent, tu in eis places, et quae per spiritum tuum placent nobis, tibi placent in nobis. *Quis enim scit hominum, quae sunt hominis, nisi spiritus hominis, qui in ipso est? Sic et quae Dei sunt nemo scit nisi spiritus Dei. Nos autem,* inquit, *non spiritum hujus mundi accepimus, sed spiritum, qui ex Deo est, ut sciamus quae a Deo donata sunt nobis* (I Cor. 2, 11 ff.).

[77] *Ibid.*, 5, 6, 10: Nec quisquam praeter te alius doctor est veri ubicumque claruerit. In the *Confessions* one does not find any formal distinction between the light of reason and the light of Faith. For a complete discussion of the notion of truth in the writings of St. Augustine, see E. Portalié, "Saint Augustin," DTC, 1.2334-2339; 2389; and C. Boyer, *L'idée de vérité dans la philosophie de saint Augustin,* Paris: G. Beauchesne, 1920, 1-4; 156-220; 251-252.

Portalié points out that St. Augustine's theory of knowledge is not an isolated problem, but one aspect of a more universal mystery, namely, our dependence upon God. Then he adds: Pour Augustin, l'intelligence a besoin de la lumière de Dieu, son soleil, pour la vérité, comme la volonté de la grâce de Dieu, bien suprême, pour la vertu (c. 2334). In another section (c. 2389) Portalié summarizes the Saint's conception a propos of the manner in which Divine grace acts upon the intellect: Saint Augustin a remarqué cette vérité d'expérience universelle que *l'homme n'est pas maître de ses premières pensées*: il peut influer sur le cours de ses réflexions, mais il ne peut déterminer lui-même les objets, les images, et par conséquent *les motifs* qui se présentent à son esprit. *Nemo habet in potestate quid ei veniat in mentem,* dit-il, *De spiritu et litt.*, c. 34, n. 60, PL., t. 44, col. 240, *sed consentire vel dissentire propriae voluntatis est.* Or le hasard n'étant qu'un mot, c'est Dieu qui détermine à son gré ces perceptions premières des hommes, soit par

able to lead men to the knowledge of immutable truth even through the corrections administered by changeable creatures.[78] By wondrous ways he made the sinner Augustine see and hate his errors.[79]

In these passages and in those concerning the virtue of Faith, which will be considered later,[80] St. Augustine teaches that Divine grace sheds light upon the intellect and that it exercises its influence over the will and penetrates the practical, moral life of man.[81]

These teachings of the Saint find exemplification in the story of his conversion, and especially in his own description of his fierce struggle against lust, wherein he develops the operation of Divine grace healing the ravages of sin and restoring order in the soul.[82]

In Book 13, the Saint compares the primordial physical chaos with the moral chaos of sin: As the Holy Spirit hovered over the dark waters and brought peace and order out of chaos, so also He hovers over the chaotic soul and pulls it out of the abyss of sin.[83] The grace of the Holy Spirit lifts the soul of man upwards even as inordinate affections drag him down.[84] It is the spiritual

---

l'action providentiellement préparées des causes extérieures, soit intérieurement par le ministère des anges ou même par une illumination divina envoyée à l'âme.

Boyer shows how knowledge is called *light* by St. Augustine: Une connaissance est une lumière. Le soleil n'est objet pour l'oeil que parce qu'il est lumière matérielle. Ainsi la vérité n'est perçue par l'esprit que parce qu'elle est lumière intellectuelle. . . . Saisir une vérité c'est percevoir une lumière. . . . La créature raisonnable s'illumine dans la vérité de Dieu, tout comme elle se réjouit dans la bonté de Dieu, tout comme elle subsiste dans l'éternité de Dieu. (*Ibid.*, 185.)

[78] See *Conf.*, 11, 8, 10: Quia et per creaturam mutabilem cum admonemur ad veritatem stabilem ducimur.

[79] See *ibid.*, 5, 6, 10-11: Me autem iam docueras, Deus meus, miris et occultis modis et propterea credo quod tu me docueris, quoniam verum est, . . . Qui mecum tunc agebas abdito secreto Providentiae tuae et inhonestos errores meos jam convertebas ante faciem meam ut viderem et odissem.

[80] See *infra*, ch. 2, 47-51.

[81] See *infra*, ch. 3, 98-103; ch. 4, 147-154.

[82] See *infra*, ch. 3, 79-86; ch. 4, 147-154.

[83] See *Conf.*, 13, 7, 8.

[84] See *loc. cit.*

counterbalance. Grace, then, is not only light for the intellect, but strength for the will. It is buoyancy against concupiscence; it causes love's gravitation towards God.[85]

All these Divine graces issue from the fullness of God's goodness. After creation God has perfected the life of man by means of Divine graces to render it more full, more beautiful, and more perfect.[86] This is God's gift, in no way due to man. Grace is gratuitous, but it is also necessary if man is to reach heaven and the God of the Psalms and of St. Paul. Thus, under the symbolisms of light and water, the *Confessions* teach that Divine grace is necessary for the supernatural life of man.[87]

Light and water are very necessary elements of human existence; and so also are their spiritual counterparts in the supernatural life of the soul. In the moral sphere, therefore, Divine grace is necessary. The human soul is like a parched land when left to itself. By its own powers it cannot enlighten itself, it cannot nourish itself. So the power by which it must see is Divine Light; and the fountain of its sustenance must be God.

Such are a few general notions concerning Divine grace found in the *Confessions*. Later, when the remedies against concupiscence will be considered, the specific and concrete activity of God's grace will be considered.[88] From this brief discussion, however, it is clear that the *Confessions* are concerned, not with the purely natural man of ethics, but with the supernatural man of Moral Theology, not with man in the abstract, but with man in the concrete, full of the conflict between Divine grace and sin.

This theocentric view of man flows from the very nature of the work; for "the *Confessions* are first and foremost a prayer. God is the author whom Augustine has first and chiefly in mind. . . . But the freedom of prayer is its outstanding and appropriate characteristic."[89]

---

[85] See *supra,* ch. 1, 3, n. 10.

[86] See *Conf.*, 13, 4, 5.

[87] See *Conf.*, 13, 16, 19: Ideoque *anima mea tamquam terra sine aqua tibi* (Ps. 142:6) quia sicut se inluminare de se non potest, ita se satiare de se non potest. Sic enim apud te *fons vitae,* quomodo *in lumine tuo videbimus lumen* (Ps. 35:10). See also *supra,* ch. 2, 27, n. 76.

[88] See *infra,* ch. 4, 147-154.

[89] J. Campbell and M. McGuire, *The Confessions of St. Augustine* (New York: Prentice Hall, 1936), 17.

Indeed the Saint uses the title *Confessiones* to connote praise of God as well as self-accusation:

> The work, therefore, begins appropriately on the note of praise and more appropriately with words inspired by Him in whose praises the *Confessions* were written. Augustine, with piety as well as philosophic insight, ascribes even his desire to praise God to God Himself and acknowledges his inability to praise God rightly without God's guidance. . . . The three elements of prayer—praise, petition, thanksgiving—are in this chapter. The entire first chapter—in fact, the first five chapters—is a prayer. It is thus a foretaste of a work that in its totality is a prayer, a *confessio,* a prayer of praise and thanksgiving.[90]

The moral value of prayer as a *means* of Divine grace needs no elaboration. Well did St. Augustine know the power of prayer. He believed that his mother's prayers kept him from dying in the state of sin, and so saved him from hell.[91] Among the manifold delineations of his mother, one virtue is characteristic: her perseverance in prayer.[92] Here one may note that St. Augustine prayed for self-knowledge amidst the anguish of doubt and indecision.[93] He prayed also for love, and *repeatedly for continence.*[94] He even prayed, and he asked his friends to pray, that he be relieved of a toothache; and his prayer was heard.[95] Certainly this petition for a purely natural favor reveals the human side of the Saint. He could pray for little things too.

---

[90] *Ibid.,* 65. See also *Conf.,* 1, 1, 1.

[91] See *Conf.,* 5, 9, 16.

[92] See *ibid.,* 5, 9, 17.

[93] See *Conf.,* 7, 7, 11: Tu sciebas quid patiebar et nullus hominum. . . . Totum tamen ibat in auditum tuum. See also *ibid.,* 8, 4, 9; and *ibid.,* 10, 37, 62: Obsecro te, Deus meus, et me ipsum mihi indica ut confitear oraturis pro me fratibus meis quod in me saucium conperero.

[94] See *ibid.,* 10, 29, 40: Continentiam jubes: da quod jubes et jube quod vis. See also *ibid.,* 10, 31, 45: *Nemo enim potens esse continens, nisi tu des* (Sap. 8:21). Multa nobis orantibus tribuis, et quidquid boni antequam oraremus accepimus, a te accepimus; et ut hoc postea cognosceremus, a te accepimus. . . . Da quod jubes, et jube quod vis.

[95] See *ibid.,* 9, 4, 12.

Again, the Saint points out the spiritual profit to be derived from self-accusation in the presence of God. Then the sinner bares his affections to the brightness of Divine light, admits his weakness and sin, and implores the Divine mercy to complete the work of purification that it has begun.[96] Thus purified, the soul finds happiness in God.

The spirit of prayer found in the *Confessions* transforms even the recital of sins into a labor of love: "For the love of Thy love do I make this confession."[97] Hence in the moral life of St. Augustine prayer is a most powerful source of grace.

Another means of grace mentioned in the *Confessions* is Baptism, concerning which Augustine relates a significant experience: As a young man, he had begun to teach rhetoric in his native town, and he had formed an intimate friendship with another youth, who was poorly instructed in the Faith. Subsequently, the clever rhetorician had led his friend into Manicheanism. Shortly thereafter his friend was taken seriously ill, and, while he lay senseless and dying, he was baptized.[98] Thereupon he recovered. Meanwhile, Augustine, confident that his friend would regard his Baptism as a joke, tried to jest with him about it. He met, however, a *new* person with a new found freedom, who rebuked the unbelieving Augustine and insisted that he refrain from such mockery, or else they would be friends no longer. This astonished the would be seducer.[99]

In this incident one may note a twofold contrast: first, between the youth before Baptism, who was easily led astray, and the same youth after Baptism, who resisted false teaching; and, secondly, between the baptized youth, possessed of a newly found strength, and the unbaptized Augustine, still wallowing in sin. Clearly, all this underscores the effects of Baptism in practical, moral life.

---

[96] See *ibid.*, 11, 1, 1. See also *ibid.*, 2, 3, 5.

[97] *Ibid.*, 11, 1, 1: Cur ergo tibi tot rerum narrationes digero? Non utique per me noveris ea, sed affectum meum excito in te et eorum, qui haec legunt, ut dicamus omnes: *Magnus Dominus et laudabilis valde* (Ps. 95:4). Jam dixi et dicam: Amore amoris tui facio istuc.

[98] See *Conf.*, 4, 4, 7-8.

[99] See *ibid.*, 4, 4, 8.

In his other references to Baptism, moreover, St. Augustine shows the direct relationship of this sacrament to moral goodness. It is a necessity demanded by man's misery;[100] it is a washing from sin;[101] it is a buttress against the manifold temptations of the world.[102] Again, it is conceived as the beginning of the spiritual life;[103] and, finally, it is pictured as dividing the darkness from the light, that is, it is the means whereby the Holy Spirit restores order within the chaotic soul. Quoting St. Paul to the effect that we were once darkness but are now light (Ephes. 5:8), St. Augustine teaches that Baptism brings the light of grace and dispels the darkness of ignorance.[104] Hence Baptism both enlightens the intellect and strengthens the will.

D. THE VIRTUE OF CHARITY

"'Oh, Lord,' he wrote in his *Confessions*, 'Thou didst knock at my heart with Thy word, and I have loved Thee.' St. Augustine's whole moral system is contained in that sentence: 'Lord, I have loved Thee.'"[105]

After a long search St. Augustine had heard the voice of the living God of the Gospels. He had found the basis of all moral striving in the doctrine of Christ, who as the God-man, is the perfect Mediator between God and man. Moral perfection, which is one and the same as the perfection of love, always leads the soul back to Christ. Thus the twofold commandment to love God

---

[100] See *ibid.*, 13, 20, 27.

[101] See *ibid.*, 13, 19, 24: Sed prius *lavamini, mundi estote, auferte nequitiam ab animis vestris* (Is. 1:16). See also E. Pusey, *The Confessions of St. Augustine* (Everyman's Library, New York: Dutton, 1936), 327, n. 2. Pusey notes that the words of Is. 1:16 are thus understood in the ancient Liturgies and in the Fathers as a group.

[102] See *ibid.*, 13, 20, 26.

[103] See *ibid.*, 13, 20, 28.

[104] See *ibid.*, 13, 12, 13.

[105] B. Roland-Gosselin, "St. Augustine's System of Morals" (translated by Fr. Leonard), *A Monument to St. Augustine*, London: Sheed and Ward, 1930, 228. See also *Conf.*, 10, 6, 8; Portalié, "Augustin," DTC, 1.2433: Toute la morale chrétienne se résumera donc dans la victoire de la charité, qui est l'amour de Dieu jusqu'au mépris de soi sur la cupidité qui est l'amour de soi jusqu'au mépris de Dieu.

and to love neighbor finds its fulfillment in the one love for Him who is both God and man.[106] This love is charity. All creation reminds man constantly of his obligation to love God so that he who fails in this obligation is without excuse.[107]

In connection with this obligation of charity, there is the duty to form a pure intention in the practice of virtue. Thus, the Saint says that he rejected a sinful overture, but not out of a pure love for God.[108] This need for purity of intention is stressed in other works of the Saint, and particularly in his commentary on Psalm 72. There he teaches that God has no reward except Himself, and that in wishing for anything else in place of God one esteems a creature above the Creator.[109] In accord with this principle the Saint dedicates *all* his work to God.[110]

Essentially, this purity of intention consists in the complete submission of the will to God. Action rather than mere thought is its mode of expression. The man who has been renewed in grace ought to be a doer of the law, and not its judge.[111]

After his conversion St. Augustine himself made an act of complete submission to the will of Christ,[112] an act of virtue which brought with it not merely a revolution in his scale of values, but also great peace of soul. The new object of his love, Christ,

---

[106] See J. Mausbach, *op. cit.*, 2.369: Auch die sittliche Vollendung im engeren Sinne, die Vollkommenheit der Liebe, führt uns immer wieder zu Christus hin; das doppelte Gebot, Gott und den Nächsten zu lieben, ist vollkommen eines in der Liebe zu ihm, der Gott und Mensch zugleich ist. See also *Conf.*, 10, 43, 68-69.

[107] See *Conf.*, 10, 6, 8: Percussisti cor meum verbo tuo, et amavi te. Sed et coelum et terra et omnia quae in eis sunt, ecce undique mihi dicunt, ut te amem, nec cessant dicere omnibus, ut *sint inexcusabiles* (Rom. 1:20).

[108] See *ibid.*, 4, 2, 3: Sed hoc quoque malum non ex tua castitate repudiavi, *Deus cordis mei* (Ps. 72:26).

[109] See *Enar. in Ps.* 72, 32 (ML 36.928): Qui aliud praemium petit a Deo, et propterea vult servire Deo carius facit quod vult accipere, quam ipsum a quo vult accipere. Quid ergo? Nullum praemium Dei? Nullum praeter ipsum. Praemium Dei ipse Deus est. Hoc amat, hoc diligit; si aliud dilexerit, non erit *castus* amor. . . . See also *Serm.* 137, sec. 10 (ML 38.760) and *De Beata Vita*, sect. 18 (CSEL 63.103-104).

[110] See *Conf.*, 1, 15, 24.

[111] See *ibid.*, 13, 23, 33. See also *ibid.*, 13, 22, 32.

[112] See *ibid.*, 9, 1, 1,

transcended the totality of sensual pleasures. Thus, as soon as the Saint had made the decision to submit his will to Christ, Divine grace brought light to his intellect and strength to his will. What a contrast there is between the man before and the man after conversion. While he had remained in the state of indecision, he had groped in darkness and had remained a slave to carnality; but after his conversion he was so powerfully drawn by Christ that his former desires had no more hold upon him.[113]

The Saint stresses the truth that the love of God is a gift: "By thy gift we are kindled and carried upwards, we burn within, and we go forward."[114] Because the Holy Ghost has infused the love of God into our hearts, we are able to love the Divine goodness reflected in his creatures. Without the help of the Holy Spirit, this would be impossible.[115]

Since this love, moreover, inflames reason and deepens Faith,

---

[113] See *loc. cit.*: Ejiciebas enim eas a me, vera tu et summa suavitas, ejiciebas et intrabas pro eis omni voluptate dulcior, sed non carni et sanguini, omni luce clarior, sed omni secreto interior, omni honore sublimior, sed non sublimibus in se.

[114] *Conf.*, 13, 9, 10: Dono tuo accendimur et sursum ferimur; inardescimus et imus. The notion of charity as a supernatural gift is found frequently in the writings of St. Augustine, especially in his exegesis of Rom. 5:5. See P. Platz, *Der Römerbrief in der Gnadenlehre Augustins* (Würzburg, 1937). In this study devoted to the use of Romans by St. Augustine in his doctrine on grace the author points out (136-137) that the Saint uses Rom. 5:5 over 150 times in his writings, and then he adds: Sehr häufig finden wir Rom. 5, 5, um den göttlichen Ursprung der Liebe zu bezeichnen: 'caritas Dei, non per nos ipsos, sed per Spiritum Sanctum.' Er selbst sagt, dass man nicht oft genug darauf zurückkommen kann (de perf. just. hom. 10, 21) (44.302).

Besides considering charity as a gift the *Confessions* also place emphasis on the dynamic aspects of this virtue: Charity is motion towards the Beloved: Pondus meus, amor meus (*Conf.*, 13, 9, 10). The possession of the Beloved, moreover, is conceived as the final peace and repose of the human will: In dono tuo requiescimus, ibi te fruemur: requies noster, locus noster (*loc. cit.*). Already it has been shown that Augustine describes the human heart gravitating towards God as its love (ch. 1, 2-3). This dynamic notion of charity found in the *Confessions* is incorporated into one of the Saint's definitions of charity: Caritatem voco motum animi ad fruendum Deo propter ipsum et se atque proximo propter Deum (*De doc. Christ.* 3, 10, 16; ML 34.72).

[115] See *Conf.*, 13, 31, 46.

the love of God leads to a deeper knowledge of God: "Charity knoweth it (the unchangeable light of the Lord)."[116] Indeed there is a reciprocity between knowledge and love, love deepening understanding, and understanding fostering love.

In regard to the exercise of fraternal charity St. Augustine is concerned mainly with the problem of human friendship. His thoughts on this subject were molded by his own bitter experience. Accordingly, it seems best to explain his moral teaching on friendship in the light of this background.

At Tagaste he had formed an intimate friendship with a youth the same age as himself, and soon he had led his friend into the heresy of Manicheanism. Then the sudden death of his friend plunged Augustine into a state of bitter grief. Having no true God to turn to for consolation, he sought a vicarious and morbid pleasure in tears. His grief had no hope, since he considered his friend as utterly lost, and himself as one without the support of solid trust in God.[117]

It should be recalled that during this period his mind possessed only a materialistic, anthropomorphic conception of God. For example, while grief-stricken by the loss of his friend and groping for consolation, he found scant comfort in the shadowy conception of God learned from the Manicheans. Compared to the crushing concreteness of his grief, his God was truly a nebulous phantasm.

---

[116] *Ibid.*, 7, 10, 16: Charitas novit eam (lucem inconmutabilem). See also C. Boyer, *L'idée de vérité dans la philosophie de saint Augustin,* 251-2: La théorie de la foi résout une antinomie que fait surgir la dépendance réciproque de la connaissance et de l'amour. Pour contempler, il faut avoir l'oeil purifié. On ne se purifie que par une volonté droite, en vivant bien. Mais pour vivre bien, il faut aimer ce qui doit l'être, et comment l'aimer, si l'on n'est point en état de le connaître? Si l'intellection est la seule connaissance possible, le problème, dans l'état présent de l'humanité, est vraiment insoluble. Mais il y a la connaissance de foi. . . . Avec la connaissance de foi, la charité devient possible, et par la charité, le salut.

[117] See *Conf.*, 4, 4, 7: Conparaveram amicum societate studiorum nimis carum, coaevum mihi. . . . See also *ibid.*, 4, 4, 9: Quo dolore contenebratum est cor meum. . . . Et si dicebam: 'spera in Deum' juste non obtemperabat, quia verior erat et melior homo, quem carissimum amiserat, quam phantasma, in quod sperare jubebatur. Solus fletus erat dulcis mihi et successerat amico meo in deliciis animi mei.

It is not surprising then that such a God would have no part in his friendships of this period, or that his love for fellow humans should become inordinate.[118]

Accordingly, one factor in the remedy for such a situation would be a correct concept of the role of God in human friendships. Thus, Augustine was led to state the guiding principle of all human friendships: A true friendship does not exist unless God Himself be the bond of union between the friends.[119]

Failure to recognize God's role in human friendship leads to despair upon the loss of the loved one, whom one has loved as if he were God, and now has lost forever. Such a thing happened to Augustine, who stresses the misery of the soul enslaved in the friendship of perishable things.[120] He is torn asunder when he loses them. Thus, after the death of his friend, he could find rest in neither pleasures nor occupations. The depth of his grief was so shattering because he had loved someone mortal, as if he were immortal. This occasions him to exclaim: "O madness, which knoweth not how to love men, as men should love."[121]

[118] See *ibid.*, 4, 7, 12: Ad te, Domine, levanda erat et curanda, sciebam, sed nec volebam nec valebam, eo magis, quod mihi non eras aliquid solidum et firmum, cum de te cogitabam. Non enim tu eras, sed vanum phantasma et error meus erat Deus meus. Si conabar eam ibi ponere, ut requiesceret, per inane labebatur et iterum ruebat super me, et ego mihi remanseram infelix locus, ubi nec esse possem nec inde recedere. Quo enim cor meum fugeret a corde meo? See also *ibid.*, 4, 4, 9, quoted in preceding footnote; Campbell and McGuire, *Confessions*, 121, n. 53; 123, n. 16, n. 22. These notes explain the full connotation of the term *phantasma*. It is of interest to note, moreover, that, after his emancipation from his materialistic conception of God, the Saint wondered at himself for having possessed so false a concept of God: See *Conf.*, 7, 17, 23: Et mirabar, quod iam te amabam, non pro te *phantasma* (italics mine). See *infra*, ch. 3, 64 ff., where the moral consequences of Augustine's materialistic conception of God are discussed.

[119] See *ibid.*, 4, 4, 7: Sed nondum erat sic amicus, quamquam ne tum quidem sic, uti est vera amicitia, quia non est vera, nisi cum eam tu agglutinas inter haerentes sibi caritate diffusa in *cordibus nostris per spiritum sanctum, qui datus est nobis* (Rom. 5:5).

[120] See *ibid.*, 4, 6, 11.

[121] *Ibid.*, 4, 7, 12: O dementiam nescientem diligere homines humaniter. See also *ibid.*, 4, 8, 13: Nam unde me facillime et in intima dolor ille penetraverat, nisi quia fuderam in harenam animam meam diligendo moriturum acsi non moriturum?

Hence, in describing his own errors and excesses St. Augustine insinuates two remedies against morbid grief over the death of a friend. One must keep in mind that the person he loves is mortal; and, again, upon the death of the beloved, one must put his trust in God, who has been the very bond of the friendship.

The Saint, moreover, enlarges upon the notion of God as the bond of human friendship when he says: "Blessed is the man that loves thee, and his friend in thee, and his enemy for thee. For he alone never loses a dear friend, to whom all men are dear for His sake who is never lost. And who is this but our God?"[122]

Thus, the solution of the problem of human friendship lies in the integration of the love of man with the love of God. One loves his friend as the image of God; one loves his enemy, because God has commanded it, and because the sinful soul still retains the Divine image, however blurred, as well as a capacity for Divine grace. Furthermore, one has the happiness of knowing that nothing is loved in vain that is loved *in* God.

It must not be forgotten that the goodness one loves in his friend comes from God and must be referred back to Him. Souls must be loved in God. One presents, as it were, his friend to God. Filled with love, one exhorts his friend to love God, realizing that whatever is beautiful in his friendship is a Divine gift. On the other hand, he who abandons God in his quest for human love will suffer the bitterness of a false friendship.[123] An inordinate friendship carries with it its own punishment.[124]

Already several elements in this punishment have been described. One notes turbulence over the physical absence of the beloved, and despair upon his death.[125] To these may be added *spiritual blindness*. Thus, although man can draw the conclusion

---

[122] *Ibid.*, 4, 9, 14: Beatus qui amat te et amicum in te et inimicum propter te. Solus enim nullum carum amittit, cui omnes in illo cari sunt, qui non amittitur. Et quis est iste nisi Deus noster? . . .

[123] See *Conf.*, 4, 12, 18.

[124] See *ibid.*, 4, 9, 14: Quo it aut quo fugit nisi a te placido ad te iratum? Nam ubi non invenit legem tuam in poena sua?

[125] See *infra*, ch. 3, 132-134. See also *ibid.*, 4, 4, 9: Expetebant eum undique oculi mei, et non dabatur; et oderam omnia, quod non haberent eum. . . .

that God exists from visible creation itself, inordinate affections sometimes prevent his judgment from making that inference.

It is not that the affections by which man binds himself to creatures rebel directly against God; they blind the intellect so that it does not understand that God must be sought and loved. Hence inordinate love of creatures can lead to ignorance concerning the existence and worship of God. Such was the culpable ignorance of the pagan philosophers who were blinded by the depravity of their hearts.[126]

The Saint in his *Confessions* gives other scattered references to friendship. He describes the great admiration that Alypius had for Augustine himself, an admiration that made Alypius ready to follow him into the service of the flesh, even though Alypius was not addicted to this vice. This tendency in Alypius may be termed the danger of *idolization* in friendship, for he was willing to imitate even the bad habits of his friend.[127] On the contrary, in a good friendship one imitates the virtues of his friend, as St. Augustine imitated the apostolic virtues of St. Ambrose. Finally, Augustine gives an example of virtuous friendship, relating how Nebridius joined Alypius and himself in their ardent search after truth and wisdom.[128] This common aim ennobled their bond of union.

Besides the question of friendship the *Confessions* also mention other duties of fraternal charity. In his explanation of Gen. 1:29 the Saint interprets "fruits of the earth" to mean works of mercy. He points out that Onesiforus practiced hospitality towards St. Paul, of whose chains he was not ashamed. Later, however, when St. Paul was a prisoner at Rome, others failed to fulfill this duty of hospitality towards him; whereupon St. Paul prayed that this failure might not be imputed to his neglectors. But, reasons St. Augustine, the Apostle would not have prayed that they be free of this neglect, unless it were truly their charge. It is interesting to note that in the same passage St. Augustine teaches that the faithful have the duty to support those who preach the Gospel.

---

[126] See *ibid.*, 10, 6, 10. See also *ibid.*, 10, 6, 8 and *infra*, ch. 2, 40, n. 136.
[127] See *ibid.*, 6, 12, 21-22.
[128] See *Conf.*, 6, 10, 17.

This obligation stems from the virtue of justice rather than from that of mercy.[129]

The Saint makes a few references to fraternal charity in thought and in speech. The spiritual man does not assume the right to judge of his neighbor's spiritual condition. God alone sees the heart of man. Nor does he judge those who are living outside the Church according to the fashion of the world. For how is he to know which of these God will later call into the sweetness of His grace? Man cannot judge the possibilities of another man's salvation.

The spiritual man, however, can and should judge in those matters falling within his power of correction, that is, in external matters of morality.[130] The preacher should endeavor to draw the rebellious back to Christ; this, however, he must do, not in a spirit of condemnation, but in one of *ardent charity*.[131] Such a reprimand is quite removed from the usual flattery of friends, whose words tend more towards perversion than towards conversion; on the other hand, the reproaches of one's enemies tend very often to correct one.[132]

In the exercise of fraternal charity one gains merit, provided that he has the right intention. Such is the teaching of Scripture. In his letter to the Philippians St. Paul rejoiced in their charity towards him, not because he was receiving a *gift,* but because they were once again flourishing in the *fruit* of good works, like a fruitful field green with promise. This passage inspires St. Augustine to distinguish between a *gift* and a *fruit.* A *gift* is the thing one gives to fulfill the needs of his neighbor, such as money, food, and clothing. The *fruit* is the good and right will of the giver; and this is what is necessary to render our acts of kindness

---

[129] See *ibid.,* 13, 25, 38.

[130] See *ibid.,* 13, 23, 33. See also *ibid.,* 13, 23, 34: Judicat enim spiritalis approbando quod rectum, inprobando autem quod perperam invenerit in operibus moribusque fidelium . . . in cogitationibus piis de his, quae per sensum corporis percipiuntur. De his enim judicare nunc dicitur, in quibus et potestatem corrigendi habet.

[131] See *ibid.,* 4, 12, 19.

[132] See *ibid.,* 9, 8, 18: Sicut amici adulantes pervertunt, sic inimici litigantes plerumque corrigunt.

towards our neighbor meritorious. Thus Our Lord promised a reward to the one who receives a prophet *in the name of a prophet*; and, again, he does not merely say: *And whosoever shall give to drink to one of these little ones a cup of cold water only,* but He adds: *in the name of a disciple,* thereby stressing the intention of directing the action towards Him, so that the action may possess the *fruit* of supernatural reward.[133]

Another aspect of the virtue of charity found in the *Confessions* is the moderate use of creation's bounty. Just as the love of human friendship must be centered in God, so also must other created goods be used for his glory; and just as human friendship becomes evil when man substitutes his friends for God, so also an inordinate desire for material possessions can cause the soul to forget God. One avoids this danger, however, if he makes corporeal beauty the occasion for lifting his heart up to God.[134] Unfortunately, this is not the case with many men who are carried by their greed far beyond the limits of moderate use of creatures.

These tempt the eyes with innumerable toys in the way of apparel, shoes, utensils, pictures, and images. Going far beyond the necessary in their acquisitiveness, they become so immersed in their own creations that they forsake their God, blindly seeking outside of themselves the Creator who is found within their very souls.[135] Their concentration on *this* world, their forgetfulness of God, and their neglect of their own destiny are qualities of an attitude that may be termed *renaissance.* The renaissance period was characterized by a similar worldliness.[136]

---

[133] See *ibid.,* 13, 26, 40-41.

[134] See *ibid.,* 4, 12, 18: Si placent corpora, Deum ex illis lauda et in artificem eorum retorque amorem, ne in his quae tibi placent, tu displiceas. See also C. Boyer, "De fundamento moralitatis secundum Sanctum Augustinum," in *Acta Hebdomadae Augustinianae-Thomisticae,* Turin, 1931, 105 ff.

[135] See *ibid.,* 10, 34, 53.

[136] See P. Hughes, *A History of the Church,* vol. 3 (New York: Sheed and Ward, 1947), 361-385, in which the author describes the Renaissance as the return of the ancient world of paganism: (365) "Almost from the beginning the movement affected important—if as yet concealed—apostasies from the Christian standard of morals . . ." (380): "To the Christian doctrine of the fall and its effects on human nature, of all men's need of healing grace, there is opposed the new, more elegantly stated, cult of man as he

In opposition to this spirit the Saint points out that man should use material things to satisfy his needs, but that he should not set his affections on them. Too little does he love God who loves anything along with God, but not for His sake.[137]

What does St. Augustine mean by loving God "too little"? Does he mean that in loving anything apart from God, and not for His sake, one proves that he does not love God at all? Or does he mean that such a one does love God, does fulfill the moral law in its minimum, but fails to fulfill the law of charity in all its fullness and perfection? Mausbach poses these questions and adopts the view that "minus enim te amat" means that one possesses charity in his heart, but allows attachments to creatures to restrict its full blossom.[138] This opinion seems to agree best with the general pattern of thought in the *Confessions,* which stresses an ideal of love beyond the moral minimum. Furthermore, as will be shown later

---

is, meditations on a way of life unfettered by sobering thoughts of man as he ought to be. The new man is to be made perfect by the full freedom to indulge his every impulse, to satisfy his every desire; for this alone is life. Man is simply an animal endowed with the power to think . . . to whom all that is possible is lawful. . . ."

[137] See *Conf.,* 10, 34, 53: Sed pulchritudinum exteriorum operatores et sectatores inde trahunt adprobandi modum, non autem inde trahunt *utendi modum.* See also *Conf.,* 10, 29, 40: Minus enim te amat qui tecum aliquid amat, quod non propter te amat. See also *De Trinitate,* 8, 13 (ML 42.968): Non quod sit amanda creatura; sed si ad Creatorem refertur ille amor, non iam cupiditas, sed charitas erit. Tunc enim est cupiditas cum *propter se amatur creatura;* and *De Moribus Ecclesiae,* 1, sect. 39 (ML 32.1328): Habet igitur vir *temperans* in hujuscemodi rebus mortalibus et fluentibus, vitae regulam utroque Testamento firmatam ut . . . nihil per se appetendum putet, sed ad vitam hujus atque officiorum necessitatem quantum sat est usurpet, *utentis* modestia, non *amantis affectu* (all italics mine).

[138] See Mausbach, *Die Ethik des heiligen Augustinus,* 1.262-263: Demnach können wir nun auch das berühmte Wort Augustins würdigen: 'Minus enim te amat, qui tecum aliquid amat, quod non propter te amat.' . . . Augustin redet an der Stelle von der Enthaltsamkeit, von der inneren Konzentration auf Gott; wir werden daher das 'propter te' im engeren Sinne einer positiven, treibenden Motivation fassen. Wer Geschöpfliches nicht wegen Gott, d.h., aus dem Interesse und Impulse der caritas liebt, hat eine geringere Liebe als derjenige, der es aus inneren Sammlung und Kraft jener höchsten Liebe liebt und besorgt. Dieses Mehr und Weniger ist es, bei dem die Lehre von den evangelischen Räten einsetzt. . . .

in the study of sin, the Saint does not consider even a lesser degree of love when he describes sin. For him sin is the antithesis of love.[139] It seems, then, that in this passage one does not find a reference to mortal sin, but only, at most, to venial sin.

E. THE VIRTUE OF HUMILITY

After charity the virtue most stressed by the *Confessions* is humility. Just as God's grace is given to the humble, so is charity built upon humility. Indeed the Incarnation of Christ and His entire life provide man with a very beautiful pattern of this virtue.[140] Its importance is seen in the sharp contrast between the smug pride of the Neoplatonists and the humility of the Incarnate Word, a contrast which St. Augustine develops from the depths of his own experience, having shared both the pride and the blindness of this school of thought. He shows that Christ is the model *par excellence* of this all important virtue.[141]

The Word became flesh to provide milk for our infant state. Thus God adapted Himself to the weakness of man. Just as one feeds infants milk, because it is the only kind of food that they can readily digest, so also Divine Wisdom has sought to teach feeble human minds concrete truths within their grasp. This it has

---

[139] See *infra*, ch. 3, 124-125.

[140] See *Conf.*, 4, 12, 19: Et descendit huc ipsa vita nostra et tulit mortem nostram et occidit eam de abundantia vitae suae et tonuit clamans, ut redeamus hinc ad eum in illud secretum, unde processit ad nos in ipsum primum virginalem uterum, ubi ei nupsit humana creatura, caro mortalis. . . . Non enim tardavit, sed cucurrit clamans dictis, factis, morte, vita, descensu, ascensu, clamans, ut redeamus ad eum. . . . Descendite ut ascendatis, et ascendatis ad Deum. Cecidistis enim ascendendo contra Deum. See also *ibid.*, 7, 20, 26: Iam enim coeperam velle videri sapiens plenus poena mea et non flebam, insuper autem inflabar scientia. Ubi enim erat illa aedificans caritas a *fundamento humilitatis,* quod est Christus Jesus? (italics mine.) See also R. Ottley, *Studies in the Confessions of St. Augustine* (London: Scott, 1918), 76: For him the significance of the Incarnation lies in the fact that it is a Divine object-lesson, bringing home to the heart of humanity, in a way that cannot be misunderstood, its need of unbroken and entire dependence on God Himself as the only giver of grace and salvation: in other words, the supreme significance of humility as the gate of entrance to the kingdom.

[141] See *ibid.*, 7, 9, 13. See also *ibid.*, 7, 18, 24. See also *ibid.*, 7, 21, 27.

done through Jesus Christ, who assumed the weakness of human flesh to teach mankind. By the practice of humility He draws the lowly out of themselves and lifts them up unto Himself. At the same time He condemns smug self-confidence and boasting, and bids men to recognize their own misery and to put their trust in Him.[142] *Confidence* in God, then, is the *positive* aspect of humility.

Men must consent to be weak with the weakness of Christ so that His grace may dwell in them. This correspondence between human weakness and Divine grace was discovered by St. Augustine in the writings of St. Paul, and *not* in those of the Neoplatonists. Presumption and pride are characteristic of Neoplatonism; confession and contrition are characteristic of the *Confessions,* which reflect directly the thought of St. Paul.[143]

From the study of the mediatorship of Christ, as found in St. Paul, the Saint had arrived at an understanding of the virtue of humility. Previously, the weakness of habitual sin had kept the Saint from union with God; but when he had studied the humility of Christ in the Incarnation, he found encouragement to practice the same virtue, and thus render himself receptive to the grace of the Mediator.[144]

It was the humility of Christ, willing to live among men and bear their weakness, that inspired the sinner Augustine to form the firm hope that He would heal all his infirmities. Hence, in the case of St. Augustine, the consideration of personal misery did not lead to sterile despair, but rather caused him to place all his

---

[142] See *ibid.*, 7, 18, 24: Quoniam Verbum caro factum est ut infantiae nostrae lactesceret sapientia tua per quam creasti omnia. Non enim tenebam Deum meum Jesum humilis humilem nec cujus rei magistra esset infirmitas noveram. . . . See also J. Mausbach, *Die Ethik des heiligen Augustinus,* 1.174: Das Brot der Starken ist in dem demütigen Jesus eine Milch geworden, die den kindlichen Geist zur Stärke heranwachsen lässt.

[143] See *Conf.,* 7, 21, 27: Inveni quidquid illac (in platonic writings) verum legeram hac cum connendatione gratiae tuae dici, ut qui videt, non sic *glorietur, quasi non acceperit,* non solum quod videt, sed etiam ut videat—quid enim habet *quod non accepit?* (I Cor. 4:7). . . . Non habent illae paginae vultum pietatis illius, lacrimas confessionis *sacrificium tuum, spiritum contribulatum, cor contritum et humiliatum* (Ps. 50:19).

[144] See *ibid.,* 7, 20, 26. See also Paul Henry, *Plotin et L'Occident,* Louvain, 1934, 111.

hope in the God-man and Mediator, whose Divine medicine can heal all the wounds of sin. Only in the humble Christ did the Saint find the beginning of salvation.[145]

Just as man has wandered away from God through pride, so must he return through the pathway of humility. Man must first descend into the depths of himself, recognize his sins, confess them before God, while beseeching His mercy, and then will he be able to ascend to God. Thus, he who has fallen from the grace of God by pride can regain it by humility.[146]

The virtue of humility, however, is also concerned with the question of man's merits. It realizes that whenever man enumerates his merits, he is counting Divine gifts.[147] This salutary perception that all the goodness of man comes from God leads the soul to accept at one and the same time the nothingness of man and the infinite power of God reaching into all his actions. To such truths St. Augustine gave a *real* assent. For example, the admission of his own moral illness is followed by the thought that Christ is his physician, and then he shows the perfect correspondence that exists between the misery of the sinner and the mercy of the Divine Physician.[148]

In the very writing of the *Confessions* the Saint practices an extraordinary humility. He reveals not only what he had been before he corresponded with Divine grace, but also the temptations of the flesh to which he was still subject as bishop. Even as he affirms that God's grace has healed him, he adds that he needs it still, inasmuch as concupiscence is not dead in him, but only weakened.[149]

---

[145] *Conf.*, 10, 43. 69.

[146] See *ibid.*, 3, 8, 16. See also *ibid.*, 4, 12, 19.

[147] See *ibid.*, 9, 13, 34: Quisquis autem tibi enumerat vera merita sua, quid tibi enumerat nisi munera tua? O si cognoscant se homines homines.

[148] See *ibid.*, 10, 28, 39: Ecce vulnera mea non abscondo: medicus es, aeger sum; misericors es, miser sum.

[149] See *infra*, ch. 3, 85-86, nn. 62-66; *Conf.*, 10, 29-31, 40-43 and 10, 43, 68, 70. See also Roland-Gosselin, *La morale de saint Augustin*, 242-243: Pour que personne ne l'estimât au-dessus de ce qu'il valait, il voulut faire connaître aux hommes non seulement ce qu'il avait été avant d'avoir reçu la grâce, mais encore ce qu'il était depuis. . . . Il répète que si la grâce de Dieu l'a guéri, il a encore besoin d'elle en abondance. La concupiscence n'est pas morte en lui, elle n'est qu'affaiblie.

Again, he exemplifies the same profound humility in several prayers found in the *Confessions.* In one of these the Saint attributes to God whatever progress he has made in his struggle against concupiscense and begs for the continuance of Divine grace; and in another he affirms that his strength is weakness if it is separated from Divine aid.[150]

St. Augustine, moreover, shows that the virtue of humility is founded upon the truth of man's limitations: "And what is any man but a man?"[151] In his thought humility is synonymous with intellectual probity. If humility conducts one to truth, truth also leads one to humility. Finally, the practice of this virtue opens the heart to the love of God. God chooses to dwell in the humble of heart.

Related to the virtue of humility like corollary virtues are love of truth and docility. The desire to know truth seems to have been in the soul of St. Augustine from his earliest years, and it may be considered the dominant trait in his character. In his description of his childhood the Saint says that he watched over the integrity of his senses, and, even though his childish thoughts may have dwelt upon unimportant matters, always he was aware of his love for truth.[152]

For him God is Truth, and he identifies his desire for truth with his desire for God. Even after he had fallen into the Manichean heresy, this passionate love of truth remained very much alive: "O truth, truth, how inwardly then did the very

---

[150] See *Conf.,* 10, 30, 42. See also *ibid.,* 4, 16, 31: Tu portabis; tu portabis et parvulos et *usque ad canos* (Is. 46:4) tu portabis, quoniam firmitas nostra quando tu es, tunc est firmitas, cum autem nostra est, infirmitas est.

[151] *Ibid.,* 4, 1, 1: Et quis homo est quilibet homo cum sit homo? (Translation is the writer's.) See also Roland-Gosselin, *La morale de saint Augustin,* 17-18: Pour lui l'humilité n'est que de la probité intellectuelle. Si l'humilité conduit à la vérité, la vérité conduit à l'humilité. . . . Surtout l'humilité ouvre le coeur tout grand à l'amour. See also *Conf.,* 11, 31, 41: O quam excelsus es, et humiles corde sunt domus tua. Tu enim *erigis elisos* (Ps. 144:14) et non cadunt quorum celsitudo tu es.

[152] See *Conf.,* 1, 20, 31: Custodiebam interiore sensu integritatem sensuum meorum inque ipsis parvis parvarumque rerum cogitationibus *veritate delectabar* (italics mine). See also Campbell and McGuire, *The Confessions of St. Augustine,* 91, n. 260.

quintessence of my soul sigh after thee, when they did often and in many ways cry out thy name to me, but with the voice alone, or in many ponderous books."[153] Eventually it was the pursuit of truth which caused him to abandon the teachings of Mani.

The Saint's desire for truth was not in vain. God rewarded it. Thus, while Augustine in his thirty-first year was striving for truth, God freed him from the fetters of astrology, and at the same time did not permit him to slip into any other heresy, thereby enabling him to cling to those truths of the Faith already embraced.[154] Hence the Saint affirms that God gives truth to all who sincerely seek it.

God speaks clearly, but many do not hear clearly because of the tumult of passions and the distractions of dissipation.[155] In condemning his own tardiness the Saint points out that it was dissipation that kept him from the knowledge and love of the God within his own conscience.[156] Thus it is the *will* that prevents many from hearing God. They consult Him concerning the things that they desire, but they do not always hear what they would like to hear. The man who is not eager to hear from God an approval of his desires is a happy exception. Such a one is truly *docile,* because he is ready to accept what he hears from God.[157]

The *docile* man is ready to transform truth into action. He is willing to seek advice to solve his doubts, as St. Augustine turned

---

[153] *Conf.,* 3, 6, 10: O veritas, veritas, quam intime etiam tum medullae animi mei suspirabant tibi, cum te illi sonarent mihi frequenter et multipliciter voce sola et libris multis et ingentibus. See also *ibid.,* 4, 11, 16. See also *De lib. arbit.,* 1, 2, 4 (ML 32.1224): Quo casu ita sum afflictus et tantis obrutus acervis inanium fabularum, ut nisi mihi *amor inveniendi veri* (italics mine) opem divinam impetravisset emergere inde, atque in ipsam primam quaerendi libertatem respirare non possem. "Fabularum" refers to Manicheanism.

[154] See *Conf.,* 7, 7, 11. See also A. Vega, *Obras de San Agustin,* 27.

[155] See *ibid.,* 10, 23, 33: Cur ergo non de illa (veritate) gaudent? Cur non beati sunt? Quia fortius occupantur in aliis, quae potius eos faciunt miseros quam illud beatos, quod tenuiter meminerunt. See also *ibid.,* 10, 26, 37: Veritas, ubique praesides omnibus consulentibus te simulque respondes omnibus diversa consulentibus. Liquide tu respondes, sed non liquide omnes audiunt. . . .

[156] See *supra,* ch. 1, 1, n. 3.

[157] See *Conf.,* 10, 26, 37.

to Simplicianus for counsel. He is ready to accept correction according to the example of Alypius and St. Monnica. He embraces truth readily, as Alypius readily joined St. Augustine in the decision to seek Baptism.[158]

Thus the virtue of humility not only results in a heartfelt acceptance of personal limitation, but it gives birth to docility in seeking and in accepting the advice and corrections of truth.

F. FAITH, HOPE AND THEIR COROLLARIES

Thus far the virtues of charity and humility, so closely associated in the *Confessions,* have been discussed. Now, two other theological virtues, faith and hope, with their corollaries, will be considered. While this arbitrary arrangement is followed, it must not be forgotten that the *Confessions* give neither formal definitions nor logical divisions of the various virtues. This was not the purpose of St. Augustine in writing his work.

In regard to the virtue of faith as found in the *Confessions,* it seems best to review basic points from the Saint's theory of knowledge. Since the *Confessions* do not make any formal distinctions between the light of reason and the light of Faith, this summary will be based upon students of the problem—Portalié and Boyer.[159] According to these scholars, knowledge is called *light* by St. Augustine. What the sun is to the eye, truth is to the intellect. To grasp a truth is to perceive a light. Just as man subsists in the eternity of God, and just as he is attracted by the goodness of God, so is he enlightened by the truth of God.

Thus, St. Augustine's theory of knowledge, according to Portalié, is not an isolated problem, but one aspect of a more universal mystery, our dependence upon God: The human intellect has need of the light of God as its sun to know the truth, just as the will has need of grace from God to practice virtue. This necessity extends to the supernatural sphere, in which God Himself mysteriously determines the first perceptions of man, and in which the Holy Ghost enlightens the soul with a knowledge to which it has no claim by nature.[160]

---

[158] See *ibid.,* 8, 1, 1. See also *ibid.,* 6, 7, 12; *ibid.,* 9, 8, 18; *ibid.,* 8, 12, 30.

[159] See *supra,* ch. 2, 27, n. 77, where the sources are noted.

[160] See *supra,* ch. 2, 26-27.

In several passages of the *Confessions,* moreover, the transcendent nature of truth is expounded. Everywhere truth has accompanied the Saint, teaching him what to avoid and what to desire, directing and commanding him. Truth is the unchangeable light, and he who knows the truth knows what that light is: It is Eternity, it is Love, it is God. In the possession of this Truth the happiness of man is found.[161]

It is significant that in the first chapter of the *Confessions* St. Augustine asks how one can call upon God if he does not know Him. Here, as the context shows, he is speaking of the knowledge of faith rather than merely natural knowledge. He quotes a passage from St. Paul (Rom. 10:14 ff.) in which the Apostle teaches both the necessity of belief in the Gospel and the necessity of a preacher to explain it. Faith, then, is necessary.[162]

Likewise it was necessary that Divine Providence intervene and establish an external agency through which man would find the doctrine of Christ and the means of salvation. In the Saint's doctrine the Divine authority of the Church is the rule of faith. Most especially is the authority of the Church to be invoked in the explanation of the Scriptures. Thus, speaking of the two-year period during which St. Augustine listened to the sermons of St. Ambrose on the Scriptures, Boyer points out that the Saint's acceptance of the explanation of the Scriptures by St. Ambrose was equivalent to belief in the authority of the Church teaching the Revealed Word.[163]

---

[161] See *Conf.,* 7, 10, 16: Nec ita erat supra mentem meam, sicut oleum supra aquam, nec sicut coelum super terram, sed superior, quia ipsa fecit me, et ego inferior, quia factus ab ea. Qui novit veritatem novit eam, et qui novit eam novit aeternitatem. Caritas novit eam. *O aeterna veritas et vera caritas et cara aeternitas* (italics mine). Tu es Deus meus, tibi suspiro *die et nocte* (Ps. 1:2). Et cum te primum cognovi, tu assumsisti me ut viderem esse quod viderem et nondum me esse qui viderem. See also *ibid.,* 10, 40, 65: . . . quia *lux es tu permanens* (italics mine), quam de omnibus consulebam, an essent, quid essent, quanti pendenda essent: et audiebam docentem et jubentem; *ibid.,* 7, 17, 23 and 7, 18, 24; *supra,* ch., 1, 1-2.

[162] See *Conf.,* 1, 1, 1: Sed quis te invocat nesciens te? . . . *Quomodo autem invocabunt, in quem non crediderunt? Aut quomodo credent sine praedicante* (Rom. 10:14)? See also *ibid.,* 13, 16, 19. See also Portalié, *op. cit.,* 1.2334; Mausbach, *op. cit.,* 1.173.

[163] See *Conf.,* 7, 7, 11: . . . credebam . . . *scripturis sanctis,* quas ecclesiae tuae catholicae conmendaret *auctoritas* (italics mine), viam te posuisse salutis

Even after he had listened to the sermons of St. Ambrose, however, Augustine kept his judgment in a suspended state, equivalent in some respects to that of the modern indifferentist. While this hesitation is understandable in view of the fear that possessed him of lapsing into some new error, nevertheless during this period he did not advance either in the acquisition of Divine truth or in the struggle against carnal habit. As he himself affirms, his soul could have been healed only by believing.[164]

Faith would have purified his judgment, and would have guided it towards the truth. At this period, however, it seems that worldliness and the desire for carnal pleasures beclouded the judgment of the sinner Augustine and made him reluctant to plumb the depths of truth, especially since he sensed that its full import would be an indictment of his manner of life. In short, the position of indifferentism was a moral escape enabling him to continue more or less undisturbed in the enjoyment of pleasures that would have to be sacrificed as soon as he admitted his obligation to embrace the Faith of his mother. This point will be developed more completely when the problem of *culpable ignorance* is out-

---

humanae ad eam vitam, quae post hanc mortem futura est. Citing this passage, Boyer concludes: Croire à l'Écriture que lui expliquait Ambrose et croire à l'Église, c'était pour lui une seule et même chose. (*Christianisme et Néo-Platonisme dans la formation de saint Augustin,* 65); *Conf.,* 6, 11, 19; P. Battifol, *Le Catholicisme de saint Augustin* (Paris: Gabalda, 1929), 5-6: Le Manichéisme l'a mis aux prises avec le problème de la vérité: douter de tout ne résout pas le problème et aggrave la langueur: Augustin résout le problème par le recours à une autorité divine de fait, le Catholicisme conçu et aimé comme règle de foi. On this point see also Tertullian, *De praescriptionibus,* 37 (ML 2.50-51): Si haec ita se habent ut veritas nobis adjudicetur, quicumque in ea regula incedimus quam Ecclesia ab Apostolis, Apostoli a Christo, Christus a Deo tradidit, constat ratio propositi nostri, definientis non esse admittendos haereticos ad ineundam de Scripturis provocationem, quos sine Scripturis probamus ad Scripturas non pertinere. Si enim haeretici sunt, Christiani esse non possunt non a Christo habendo quod de sua electione sectati haereticorum nomine admittunt. Ita non Christiani, nullum jus capiunt Christianarum litterarum. The same notion is developed in other parts of the same work: *De praescriptionibus,* 15-19 (ML 2.28-30); 38-40 (ML 2.51-55).

[164] See *Conf.,* 6, 4, 6.

lined.[165] Here it suffices to state that the Saint's flight to indifferentism was not without moral guilt. It raises the question, moreover, of moral obstacles to the possession of the Catholic Faith.

Certainly, worldliness and its customary associate, obsession with the flesh, hindered Augustine in his journey towards the Faith. No doubt, it hinders others also. But there is another *obex* that brings with it, not mere reluctance to embrace the Faith, but blindness to the very truth of the Faith. Such is pride of intellect.

Augustine exemplified pride of intellect when he turned his back to the light of God in his immoderate pursuit of pagan learning. He was so proud that he was willing to hold even that God was in error rather than admit that he had gone astray willingly. In punishment he lay in error. In short, spiritual blindness became the Divine punishment for his stiffnecked pride.[166]

Commenting on "dorsum enim habebam ad lumen," Wangnereck says that the back of the soul is *forgetfulness*. In sinners this forgetfulness is culpable, because it is voluntary, and because they do not really forget God, but rather do not *want* to remember Him. On the other hand, the face of the soul is the *mindfulness* of God. Consequently, just as he who turns his back to the light, cuts off the light from his own eyes, so also the sinner, unmindful of God, does not receive the rays of Divine light.[167]

In another beautiful paradox the Saint himself contrasts blind Tobias teaching his son the way of life by the light of faith with those who, having become enamored by the glittering light of earthly beauty and seduced by its pleasures, are blind to the things of God. In this paradox the Saint sees a moral, namely, the obligation to resist the seductions of the eyes, which can weaken faith and cause its victim to wander from the practice of virtue.[168]

In the Saint's journey towards the Church, however, he did

---

[165] See *infra*, ch. 2, 65-77. See also *Conf.*, 6, 10, 17; *ibid.*, 6, 11, 18-19.

[166] See *ibid.*, 4, 15, 26. See also *infra*, ch. 3, 132-135.

[167] See *ibid.*, 4, 15, 30: Dorsum enim habebam ad lumen et ad ea quae inluminantur, faciem: unde ipsa facies mea, qua inluminata cernebam, *non* inluminabatur. See also Wangnereck, *Confessionum*, 134, n. 2: Culpabilis haec in peccantibus est, quia voluntaria: potius enim *nolunt* meminisse Dei quam ut proprie ejus obliviscantur . . . (italics mine).

[168] See *ibid.*, 10, 34, 52.

reach a stage where moral deviations did not shake his belief in the teachings of the Church, which already he had accepted, but simply retarded him from the efficacious resolution to give up the slavery of the flesh and to embrace the practice of the Faith.[169]

Hope: The teaching of the *Confessions* on the virtue of hope is rooted in the mediatorship of Christ. The fact that He is both God and Man at one and the same time makes Him the perfect Mediator, capable of reconciling completely sinful men with their God. He has raised us from the level of servants to the dignity of sons of God. Hence, Augustine places complete confidence in Christ to heal all his infirmities, for the medicine of Christ is mightier than all of his sins. *Otherwise* Augustine would have *despaired.* Indeed, if God had not become Incarnate and dwelt among us, we might imagine that God was very far away from us and lose all hope for salvation.[170]

Augustine shows that the very notion of hope includes the idea of struggling against difficulties. For example, he realized the obstacles that would face him on the road back to virtue; he knew that rooting out the deeply entrenched habit of impurity would be an arduous and painful task; yet he trusted that he would be able to do all this with the aid of God's grace. Such was hope in actual practice. It is significant, moreover, that hope includes reliance upon Divine grace. The God who made Augustine would also remake him.[171]

God stirs the soul up from the sleep of despair by the sweetness of His grace, and by its power He makes the weak strong, provided the sinner remain conscious of his own weakness. Thus, all hope is founded, not upon one's own worth, but upon the infinite

---

[169] See *ibid.*, 7, 5, 7: *Stabiliter* tamen haerebat in corde meo in Catholica ecclesia *fides Christi tui* (italics mine). See also *ibid.*, 7, 7, 11.

[170] See *ibid.*, 10, 3, 4: Verum tamen tu, medice meus intime, quo fructu ista faciam, eliqua mihi. Nam confessiones praeteritorum malorum meorum, quae remisisti et texisti, ut beares me in te, mutans animam meam fide et sacramento tuo, cum leguntur et audiuntur, excitant cor, ne dormiat in desperatione et dicat: 'non possum,' sed evigilet in amore misericordiae tuae et dulcedine gratiae tuae, qua potens est omnis infirmus, qui sibi per ipsam fit conscius infirmitatis suae.

[171] See *Conf.*, 5, 2, 2. See also *ibid.*, 9, 4, 10.

mercy of God. Accordingly, towards the end of his *Confessions,* the Saint repeatedly encourages us to hope in the Lord.[172]

Hope and persevere, says the Saint, until the darkness of earth is changed into the sunlight of heaven. Thus it is hope that keeps before the mind the glory of heaven as an aid to perseverance. In line with this thought St. Augustine concludes his *Confessions* with a prayer to obtain the happiness of heaven, in which he offers God his good works, fully realizing that they are really gifts from God.[173]

Another important component in the virtue of hope is the fear of death and of judgment. In St. Augustine's case this fear acted as a most effective stimulus to repentance. Even in the whirlpool of vice this fear never left his mind. First, he feared death and judgment; then, he began to hope for Divine mercy; finally, he began to amend his past life. Thus fear led to hope, hope to repentance. This salutary fear restrained him from continued lust and goaded him onward to seek the truth. He was afraid that, were death to overtake him in his state of indecision, he would be held accountable by God for his ignorance.[174]

As the virtue of hope grew in St. Augustine, it became linked with an intense penitential love of God. The keenness of his grief for his past sins was matched only by the completeness of his trust in God's mercy. No longer did he want to live apart from God, because then he lived so badly; now he wanted God to be his life.[175]

Such is the doctrine of the *Confessions* on the virtue of hope. At this juncture then we shall study two virtues that are very

---

[172] See *ibid.,* 10, 3, 4. See also *ibid.,* 10, 29, 40: Et *tota spes mea* (italics mine) non nisi in magna valde misericordia tua.

[173] See *ibid.,* 13, 14, 15. See also *ibid.,* 11, 29, 39; *ibid.,* 13, 38, 53.

[174] See *Conf.,* 6, 16, 26: Nec me revocabat a profundiore voluptatum carnalium gurgite nisi *metus mortis et futuri judicii tui* (italics mine), qui per varias quidem opiniones numquam tamen recessit de pectore meo. See also *ibid.,* 6, 11, 18: Vita misera est; mors incerta est; subito obrepat: Quomodo hinc exibimus? Et ubi nobis discenda sunt quae hinc *neglеximus?* Ac non potius hujus *neglegentiae supplicia luenda* (italics mine)? Boyer, *Christianisme et Néo-Platonisme . . . ,* 74.

[175] See *Conf.,* 12, 10, 10: *Erravi et recordatus sum tui* (Ps. 118:176). . . . Non ego vita mea sim: male vixi ex me, mors mihi fui: in te revivesco.

closely related to the three theological virtues already discussed; these virtues are praise of God and gratitude towards Him.

The virtues of praise of God and of gratitude towards Him find repeated expression in the *Confessions.* The very word *confessio* connotes both praise and thanksgiving. The Saint gives expression to his gratefulness for all the gifts of God, especially for the grace of conversion. Even if only the material things of the universe were made for man, he would still have the duty to praise God. All inarticulate creation reminds man of his obligation to express the praises of the Creator of all. Even distractions made the Saint keenly aware of this duty.[176]

It is not God, however, but man, who benefits from the fulfillment of this duty; for God does not *need* the adoration of man.[177] Closely connected, moreover, with the obligation to praise God is the problem of human praise, a problem that beset the tender conscience of the Saint very sorely. Here the problem will be formulated and discussed briefly; later, in treating the temptation to *pride of life,* the subject will be studied more closely.

As one of the amenities of social life, man bestows upon, and receives from, his fellowman honor and praise, without which social life would be very uncongenial. This condition the Saint accepts as good, but at the same time he feels that it contains a danger, namely, that one should desire to be praised and to be loved, not on account of the gifts of God in him, but *in place of God.* One does this when he loves more the praises of men than the gift of God on account of which he is praised. To avoid this danger, while accepting praise from another, one should endeavor to love truth more than praise, and to refer whatever praises and affection he receives to the glory and love of God.[178]

Praise may be accepted with moderate pleasure. In fact, the acceptance of praise from another can benefit one's neighbor, who thereby takes pleasure in the gift of God in man. It is very difficult to possess an accurate knowledge of the motivation that causes

---

[176] See *supra,* ch. 2, 30. See also *ibid.,* 7, 13, 19; *ibid.,* 10, 34, 53; *ibid.,* 5, 1, 1 and 9, 1, 1.

[177] See *ibid.,* 13, 1, 1.

[178] See *Conf.,* 10, 36, 59. See also *ibid.,* 10, 37, 60; *ibid.,* 10, 37, 61.

one to accept praise, since usually we are not able to determine whether praise is agreeable to us because it pleases our self-love, or because it contributes to the reflected glory of God in his creatures. Indeed so elusive is the temptation to love praise of self that it escapes the searching scrutiny of the Saint's delicate conscience.[179] The practical solution of the problem lies in the love of truth more than the love of praise and in the intention that our neighbor profit even when we are praised.[180]

In regard to the exercise of the virtue of gratitude Augustine considers three different kinds of gifts. The first type belongs to the supernatural order. These include the graces that the Saint received, especially the graces of conversion, the Divine light by which he was able to believe the truths of faith, and the Divine impetus to the will by which he was able to travel towards the fatherland of heaven. The second class of gifts for which he is grateful belong to the natural order, and these include his talents even as a boy. The third category of Divine gifts are those of his son, Adeodatus, who, according to his father, possessed unusual gifts of mind. Like his own natural gifts, these came from the Creator. Indeed, Augustine confesses that there is nothing of himself in his son, except the sin in which he begot him.[181]

---

[179] See *Conf.*, 10, 37, 60.

[180] See *ibid.*, 10, 37, 61. See also *ibid.*, 10, 37, 62: Ecce in te, veritas, video non me laudibus meis propter me, sed propter proximi utilitatem moveri oportere.

[181] See *ibid.*, 9, 4, 7: Et quando mihi sufficiat tempus conmemorandi omnia magna erga nos beneficia tua in illo tempore praesertim ad alia majora properanti? Revocat enim me recordatio mea, et dulce mihi fit, Domine, confiteri tibi, quibus internis me stimulis perdomueris, et quemadmodum me conplanaveris humilitatis montibus et collibus cogitationum mearum. . . . See also *supra*, ch. 2, 32; *ibid.*, 8, 1, 1 and 9, 1, 1.

For natural gifts see *ibid.*, 1, 20, 31: At ista omnia Dei mei dona sunt, non mihi ego dedi haec et bona sunt et haec omnia ego. Bonus ergo est qui fecit me, et ipse est bonum meum et illi exulto bonis omnibus quibus etiam puer eram. See also *ibid.*, 9, 6, 14: Adeodatum ex me natum carnaliter de peccato meo. Tu bene feceras eum. Annorum erat fere quindecim et ingenio praeveniebat multos graves et doctos viros. Munera tua tibi, confiteor, Domine, Deus meus, . . . nam ego in illo puero praeter delictum non habebam. See also Mausbach, *op. cit.*, 1.8-9.

G. OTHER MORAL VIRTUES

Of the moral virtues the *Confessions* mention briefly continence, chastity, justice, and courage. The general notion of continence has five diverse applications in the *Confessions*: (1) In its widest sense continence is used to denote control over the three great temptations, namely, the concupiscence of the flesh, the concupiscence of the eyes, and the pride of life. According to Augustine, following St. John (I John 2:15-16), these are the sources of all sins.[182]

(2) In a more restricted sense continence denotes moderation in the use of food and drink. In the Saint's thought food and drink are medicines to promote health. One does not take an overdose of medicines; hence, one should not take an excess of food and drink. The mortification of the sense of taste demands a daily repression possible only to one who acts with the aid of Divine grace.[183] Success in this daily struggle is a sign that God has already given one such Divine help.[184]

---

[182] See *Conf.*, 10, 30, 41: Jubes certe ut contineam *a concupiscentia carnis et concupiscentia oculorum et ambitione saeculi.* See also *Enar. in Ps.* 8, sect. 13 (ML 36.115-116): Haec autem tria genera vitiorum, id est voluptas carnis, et superbia, et curiositas omnia peccata concludunt. Quae mihi videntur a Joanne apostolo enumerata, cum dicit: *Nolite diligere mundum, quoniam omnia quae in mundo sunt concupiscentia carnis est, et concupiscentia oculorum et ambitio saeculi* (I John 2:15-16). Per oculos enim maxima curiositas praevalet; et reliqua vero quo pertineant manifestum est; H. Merkelbach, *op. cit.,* 2.978, where he defines curiosity thus: Sed circa delectationem *cognitionis omnium sensuum* est curiositas et vocatur concupiscentia oculorum. Hinc delectatio mere sensibilis sine ratione quaesita pertinet ad curiositatem. The threefold division of the sources of sin, found first in St. John, is repeated by St. Augustine, and continues to appear in Theology down through the years.

[183] See *Conf.*, 10, 31, 43-45: Est alia *malitia diei* (Matt. 6:34), quae utinam sufficiat ei. Reficimus enim cotidianas ruinas corporis edendo et bibendo. . . . Nunc autem suavis est mihi necessitas, et adversus istam suavitatem pugno, ne capiar, et cotidianum bellum gero in jejuniis. . . . Hoc mihi docuisti, ut quemadmodum medicamenta sic alimenta sumpturus accedam. Sed dum ad quietem satietatis ex indigentiae molestia transeo, in ipso transitu mihi insidiatur laqueus concupiscentiae. . . . His temptationibus cotidie conor resistere et invoco dexteram tuam. . . . *Nemo enim potens esse continens nisi tu des* (Sap. 8:21). See also Wangnereck, *op. cit.*, 400-401.

[184] See *ibid.*, 10, 31, 45: *Aufer,* inquit, *a me concupiscentias ventris* (Ecclus. 23:6). Unde adparet, sancte Deus, te dare, cum fit quod imperas fieri.

(3) In another passage Augustine uses the term continence in the sense of restraint of *inordinate* tendencies to carnal indulgence. Referring to his fear that he could not do without this form of pleasure, he reveals how he possessed a false conception of continence, considering it a virtue within the natural powers of man, but beyond his *individual* reach.[185] Only later did he realize that Divine grace could cure this infirmity; and then he drew up the formula: "Da quod jubes et jube quod vis."[186] (Give me the power to do what you command, and command whatever you will.) God is besought to grant man the grace to carry out the Divine command of continence. Without Divine grace no one is able to practice this virtue; indeed it is a gift of Divine wisdom to know whose gift this is. Accordingly, the Saint counsels us to ask God for this virtue, assuring us that God will give us the grace to carry out His command.

(4) The term continence is used also in the sense of virginal or *perfect chastity,* that is, complete abstention from all venereal pleasure. This virtue is personified as a very beautiful lady, "casta dignitas continentiae" (*Conf.*, 8, 11, 27), surrounded by all her imitators, who are able to follow her counsel only by the grace of God.[187] This form of continence is a counsel rather than a command.

---

[185] See *Conf.*, 6, 11, 20: Putabam enim me miserum fore nimis, si feminae privarer amplexibus, et medicinam misericordiae tuae ad eandem infirmitatem sanandam non cogitabam, quia expertus non eram, et propriarum virium credebam esse continentiam, quarum mihi non eram conscius, cum tam stultus essem ut nescirem, sicut scriptum est, neminem posse esse continentem, nisi tu dederis.

[186] *Ibid.*, 10, 29, 40 (The English translation is my own). The Latin formula is repeated in *ibid.*, 10, 31, 45 and 10, 37, 60. Concerning this formula Gilson (*Introduction* . . . , 207) says: Voilà l'un des thèmes essentiels des *Confessions.*

[187] See *Serm.* 38 (ML 38.235): In frenandis libidinibus et coercendis voluptatibus, ne seducat quod male blanditur, et enervet quod prosperum dicitur continentia nobis opus est: non credere felicitati terrenae, ut usque ad finem quaerere felicitatem, quae non habet finem. See also Wangnereck, *op. cit.*, n. 392; H. Merkelbach, *Summa Theologiae Moralis* (Paris: Desclée, 1938), 2.960; *infra*, ch. 2, 59-60. A specific reference to chastity as a counsel is found in *Conf.*, 10, 30, 41: Jussisti a concubitu et de ipso conjugio melius aliquid, quam concessisti, monuisti. Et quoniam dedisti factum est, et antequam dispensator sacramenti tui fierem.

(5) Finally, the term continence is used to denote freedom from all inordinate attachments to creatures. This detachment of spirit gathers together our dissipated powers and reunites them with our Creator, from whom too many distractions separate us. Man is not able to love God perfectly when he crams his mind with other affections: "For he loves Thee too little, who loves anything together with Thee, which he loves not for Thy sake."[188]

As it has been pointed out already,[189] it seems that the above quotation refers, not to mortal, or even venial sin, but rather to an affection for a creature that does not transgress the law of God, but simply exists independently of one's love for God. Such an affection tends to diminish the love of God within the soul.

This opinion rests upon the notion of the *limited* capacity of human love, which necessarily becomes weaker by any sort of division. The intensity of the soul's love for God is diminished whenever it harbors, independently of its habit of charity, a crowd of affections toward many creatures. There is even an added danger that in the dissipation of our affections on many created things we may lose the love of God entirely. With good reason, then, the Saint discourages the wasting of affection on trifles and insists that one refer all his love to God. One should aim at the concentration of supernatural love on the One Infinite Goodness.[190] This holy unity seems to be the ideal implicit in the above quotation.

---

[188] *Ibid.*, 10, 29, 40: Minus enim te amat, qui tecum aliquid amat, quod non propter te amat. It is pertinent to consider the two sentences immediately preceding this quotation: *Et cum scirem,* ait quidam, *quia nemo potest esse continens, nisi Deus det, et hoc ipsum erat sapientiae, scire cujus esset hoc donum* (Sap. 8:21). Per continentiam quippe colligimur et redigimur *in unum* (italics mine) a quo in multa defluximus.

[189] See *supra,* ch. 2, 41. In his explanation of venial sin St. Thomas (S.T. I-II, 88, 1 ad 1) uses terminology that is as difficult to understand as the "minus amat te" of St. Augustine. He stated that venial sin fulfills the notion of sin imperfectly, but he does not state how venial sin fulfills the idea of sin: Non est contra legem, quia venialiter peccans non facit quod lex prohibet, nec praetemittit ad quod lex per praeceptum obligat; sed facit praeter legem, quia non servat modum rationis, quem lex intendit. The meaning of "praeter legem" and "modum rationis" is not clear.

[190] See *supra,* ch. 2, 35-37, where the question of friendship is treated; and 40-41, where the use of material things is considered.

In all these usages of the term continence, then, is found the idea of restraint from any form of earthly pleasure which may diminish or destroy the love of God in our hearts. One does not find in the *Confessions* any trace of the Aristotelian concept, adopted by St. Thomas, that continence is not a perfect virtue, but a certain beginning of virtue, subjecting the sensitive appetite to reason, and restraining the vehemence of concupiscence.[191]

If in the Saint's journey towards the Faith abstention from carnal pleasures seemed beyond his power, it is not surprising that he regarded the state of perfect chastity as even more impossible to him. This is apparent in his acquiescence in his mother's designs for his marriage. Already it was determined that, as soon as the maiden selected had come of age, Augustine would be married.[192]

It is curious to note that Augustine had prayed for chastity as a young man. It was, however, a *rationalized* prayer, since at that time he did not want this virtue, and he was afraid that God might answer his prayer immediately and extinguish the fires of concupiscence, which he wanted to indulge.[193] This rationalization continued into the years of maturity and precluded any *sincere* endeavor to practice chastity until Divine grace caught up with him in his thirty-second year.

---

[191] See *Summa Theologica,* 2-2, 155, 1 (Marietti, 1938): Hoc autem modo continentia habet aliquid de ratione virtutis, in quantum scilicet ratio firmata est contra passiones ne ab eis deducatur; non tamen attingit ad perfectam rationem virtutis moralis, secundum quam etiam appetitus sensitivus subditur rationi sic ut in eo non insurgant vehementes passiones rationi contrariae. See also *ibid.*, 1-2, 85, 3, ad 2.

[192] See *Conf.*, 6, 13, 23: Et instabatur inpigre, ut ducerem uxorem. Jam petebam, jam promittebatur maxime matre dante operam, quo me jam conjugatum Baptismus salutaris ablueret, quo me in dies gaudebat aptari et vota sua ac promissa tua in mea fide conpleri animadvertebat. . . . et puella petebatur, cujus aetas ferme biennio minus quam nubilis erat, et quia ea placebat, exspectabatur. See also *ibid.*, 6, 6, 9; 6, 11, 19; and 6, 12, 21.

[193] See *ibid.*, 8, 7, 17: At ego adulescens miser valde, miserior in exordio ipsius adulescentiae, etiam petieram a te castitatem et dixeram: 'Da mihi castitatem et continentiam, sed noli modo.' Timebam enim, ne me cito exaudires et cito sanares a morbo concupiscentiae, quem malebam expleri quam extingui.

Then the power of group good example attracted him to the virtue of perfect chastity and deeply stirred his conscience. A period of intense moral introspection ensued, and at the end of this conflict came both the grace of conversion and the resolution to practice perfect chastity. Although the subject of *good example* will be considered in a more complete fashion later,[194] at this point it seems best to indicate its influence over Augustine in his struggle for this virtue.

First, Simplicianus told him the story of the conversion of the famed Victorinus.[195] This made Augustine long to imitate Victorinus. Then, Pontitianus recounted the wonders of St. Antony and the extraordinary manner in which the two courtiers had renounced their worldly positions and had embraced immediately an ascetic life. This *repetition* of narratives, filled with many models of renunciation, weighed upon the already troubled conscience of the young man and created a salutary dissatisfaction with self, which, in turn, made him face himself and inquire of himself why he was hesitating so long to give up his life of sin and follow these holy men.[196]

Thus, the good example of others tore away from the soul of Augustine the facade of self-deceit. He knew now what he should do; but still he lacked the courage to attempt it, since he was not aware of the truth that one can exercise chastity only by Divine grace. While engrossed in the discouraging realization of his own helplessness, however, his imagination conjured up a vision of Lady Chastity. Very significantly, she was surrounded by a multitude of men and women of every age and condition, thereby making herself more attractive in the multitude of her followers.[197]

---

[194] See *infra*, ch. 4, 139-143.

[195] See *Conf.*, 8, chapters 2-5 inclusive.

[196] See *ibid.*, 8, chapters 6-7 inclusive. See also *supra*, ch. 2, 19, n. 38.

[197] See *ibid.*, 8, 7, 18; Consumpta erant et convicta argumenta omnia. Thus group good example uncovered rationalization. Then comes Lady Chastity. *Ibid.*, 8, 11, 27: Aperiebatur . . . casta dignitas continentiae, serena et non dissolute hilaris, honeste blandiens ut venirem, neque dubitarem et extendens ad me suscipiendum et amplectendum pias manus *plenas gregibus bonorum exemplorum* (italics mine). Ibi tot pueri et puellae, ibi juventus multa et omnis aetas et graves viduae et virgines anus et in omnibus ipsa continentia nequaquam sterilis, sed fecunda mater filiorum. . . .

When Lady Chastity smiled at Augustine, she seemed to inquire: Why cannot you do what all these are doing? Do you believe that they can do it by their natural powers alone? Is it not rather by the grace of God? Why then do you try to do it alone? Cast yourself fearlessly upon Him, and He will heal your weakness and will help you to practice chastity also.[198] Perfect chastity, then, is a special gift of God, which enables one to serve God without the care of family and with undivided attention.[199]

Two other moral virtues are treated by St. Augustine in his graphic description of the integrity of Alypius at Rome. During his period in public office as an assessor to the Count of the Italian Treasury, Alypius refused to accept bribes. This was greatly wondered at, not only because of the widespread political corruption, but also because he refused to cower before one of the most influential senators, who tried to persuade Alypius to allow him something forbidden by the laws. Alypius resisted bribes and scorned threats from this public official, and thus exemplified the moral virtues of *justice* and of *courage* in public life. Again, when he was offered the opportunity to buy books at a discount, as a sort of privilege in view of his position, he refused to take advantage of this, feeling that it was against the very spirit of justice, which St. Augustine terms "aequitas."[200]

---

[198] See *loc. cit.*: Et inridebat me inrisione hortatoria quasi diceret: 'Tu non poteris quod isti, quod istae? An vero isti et istae in se ipsis possunt, et non in Domino Deo suo? Dominus Deus eorum me dedit eis. Quid in te stas et non in te stas? Proice te in eum, noli metuere; non se subtrahet, ut cadas. . . . Excipiet et sanabit te.'

[199] See *Conf.*, 8, 12, 30: Convertisti enim me ad te, ut nec uxorem quaererem nec aliquam spem saeculi hujus stans in ea regula fidei, in qua me ante tot annos ei revelaveras. . . . See also *ibid.*, 10, 29, 40 and 10, 30, 41.

[200] See *Conf.*, 6, 10, 16: Hoc solo autem paene iam inlectus erat studio litterario, ut pretiis praetorianis codices sibi conficiendos curaret, sed consulta *justitia* deliberationem in melius vertit utiliorem judicans *aequitatem* (italics mine), qua prohibebatur quam potestatem, qua sinebatur. Praetorian prices were also known as fixed prices. It was the privilege of the praetor to purchase things at a certain fixed price. See E. Pusey, *Confessions of St. Augustine,* 109, n. 3.

One may draw a fine distinction between *aequitas* and *justitia,* as Aristotle does: See *Nichomachean Ethics,* bk. 5, ch. 10, 144-146 (trans. Browne), Lon-

Herein, then, not only does St. Augustine give us a concrete model in the practice of virtue, but he also shows that virtue is a positive quality, not merely the absence of the opposite vice. The justice of Alypius was tried by the bait of greed; his courage, by the goad of fear.[201]

---

don: Henry G. Bohn, 1914. Here Aristotle says that equity and justice are not absolutely the same, yet not generally different. Equity is higher than justice, inasmuch as it is the correction of law, whenever law is defective owing to its universality. Accordingly, the equitable man is not ready to "push the letter of the law to the furthest on the worst side, but is disposed to make allowances, even though he has the law in his favor."

This is exactly what Alypius did. In strict justice he could have taken advantage of the praetorian prices, since these were a privilege of his office. But he thought that it was more in accord with the spirit of justice to forego the use of his privilege. In the above passage of the *Confessions,* therefore, St. Augustine uses the word aequitas to denote the fullness of justice, or the spirit behind the letter of the law.

[201] See *Conf.*, 6, 10, 16.

CHAPTER III

Obstacles Along the Way to God

Not only do the *Confessions* suggest the way to God, but they also describe many and diverse obstacles met along the pathway. In this chapter the writer shall delineate the various enemies of happiness, and the havoc that they produced in Augustine's soul; and in the following chapter we shall consider some concrete remedies he used against them. Since ignorance and its associates blurred his view of the road, it should be discussed first. Another subject that has to be reflected upon before considering one of the deepest problems of man, division of will, is concupiscence; for one need have an accurate knowledge of the vehemence of passion to handle the other competently. Although this problem is sometimes referred to as "weakness" of will, or "conflict" of will, the Saint shows that it is essentially division of will.

Closely connected with this problem of will, is the question of bad habit, viewed both in its origin and in its effects, and also the topic of defective education, which to some degree involves both ignorance and the formation of vain motives. Going beyond the mere obstacles to the practice of virtue, one finally comes to the consideration of that which is the very negation of virtue, and the most effective obstacle on the road to happiness: sin. Analyzing sin from a rich variety of viewpoints, the Saint investigates its nature, its internal and external sources, and its effects.

We shall restrict our study of ignorance to those passages of the *Confessions* wherein one finds concrete examples of *culpable* ignorance. Such an investigation will contribute to our knowledge of the morality of ignorance, and at the same time will avoid any endeavor to judge authoritatively a question properly left in the hands of the God of St. Augustine's conscience, namely, the degree to which he was guilty of his Manichean errors. Well aware, then, that the question of ignorance may be handled in other ways, we find it best to begin with the background of Manicheanism—the fundamental source of his errors.

One may summarize the principal Manichean errors of Augustine under three headings: (1) There were two primary principles, or causes of all things. The principle of Light (Ormazd) was good, and the principle of Darkness (Ahriman) was evil. Light and Darkness were both eternal principles, engaged with one another in unceasing strife. (2) Both principles were matter, and hence all things were composed of matter. Evil, therefore, was conceived as a material substance. (3) Completely misunderstanding the actions of the patriarchs and prophets, he rejected the Old Testament.[1]

As a Manichean, moreover, Augustine believed that Christ was a phantasm, not born in the flesh, but drawn, as it were, out of the great lucid mass of substance, which he conceived as God.[2]

---

[1] See F. Burkitt, *The Religion of the Manichees* (Cambridge U. Press, 1925), 17-33, 38-40, 78-82. The author points out that for Mani the ultimate antithesis was not between God and man, but between Light and Darkness (39). See also Pr. Alfaric, *L'évolution intellectuelle de saint Augustin,* 75-158: Ils concluaient donc que le monde résulte de deux principes contraires et éternels. Puis, de cette affirmation très générale ils déduisaient un système très vaste (75). . . . La dogmatique manichéenne part de l'opposition du bien et du mal. Elle enseigne comment l'un et l'autre ont existé de touté eternité, comment de leur mélange est résulté le monde (95). . . .

Burkitt (*op. cit.,* 82) points out that Mani followed Marcion in his rejection of the Old Testament, and Alfaric (*op. cit.,* 76) adds: Pour eux tout l'Ancien Testament était l'oeuvre du diable. Ils reprochaient surtout à la Genèse d'avoir fait Dieu à l'image de l'homme et glorifié des patriarches fort peu recommandables. Aux Catholiques qui voulaient associer la Loi et l'Évangile, ils objectaient qu'on ne doit pas coudre une pièce neuve sur un vieil habit (Matt. 9:16). . . . Alfaric points out, moreover, that along with the law of Moses, the Manicheans rejected also the writings of the prophets (189).

While many texts may be drawn from the *Confessions* to show the chief Manichean errors of the Saint, we shall confine ourselves to the most pertinent: See *Conf.,* 5, 10, 19-20. See also *ibid.,* 7, 1, 2; *ibid.,* 3, 7, 12; *ibid.,* 3, 7, 14.

[2] See F. Burkitt, *op. cit.,* 38, where it is pointed out that Mani considered himself as the last and final mouthpiece of Revelation and as the prophet of Jesus. "To Mani Jesus was a Divine Being, who appeared on earth, but was never born of woman." See also *Conf.,* 5, 10, 20: Ipsum quoque salvatorem nostrum, unigenitum tuum, tamquam de massa lucidissimae molis tuae porrectum ad nostram salutem ita putabam, ut aliud de illo non crederem

During this period, therefore, he held that whatever existed had only a corporeal being; and this led him to believe that evil also was an unbounded material substance, similar to earth or to vapor, and foul and hideous.

These notions tended to discourage him in his effort to practice virtue, disposing him to carnal indulgence;[3] but it is not surprising that errors of this sort should have their repercussions in the practical moral order. As the Saint himself points out in the *Confessions,* just as depraved emotions lead to deeds of violence and of lust, so also do errors contaminate the moral life of man. In acts of violence and lust the source is a disordered emotion, which has never been subordinated properly to the rule of reason, and which bursts forth rebelliously; likewise, the intellect produces evil actions whenever it is corrupted by false opinions.[4]

In the same passage Augustine concludes that in this Manichean period he was ignorant of his need for the supernatural light of faith. God is the lamp which enlightens the soul in darkness.[5]

Earlier in the fourth book Augustine had recounted how his false notion of God had hindered him from invoking his Creator during his most bitter grief consequent upon the death of his dear friend. In this trial he did not turn to his God for solace, because he was not disposed to seek consolation from a Divinity, who was a vague shadow and hence incapable of lending him firm support. In short, his error was his God.[6]

---

nisi quod possem vanitate imaginari. Talem itaque naturam ejus nasci non posse de Maria virgine arbitrabar, nisi carni concerneretur. Concerni autem et non coinquinari non videbam, quod mihi tale figurabam.

[3] See C. Boyer, *Christianisme et Néo-Platonisme dans la formation de saint Augustin,* 49: Le manichéisme favorisait l'immoralité, en fait; et par ces principes, il désespérait l'effort vertueux, puisqu'il concevait le mal comme une substance immuable.

[4] See *Conf.*, 4, 15, 25: Sicut enim facinora sunt, si vitiosus est ille animi motus, in quo est impetus, et se jactat insolenter ac turbide, et flagitia, si est inmoderata illa animae affectio, qua carnales hauriuntur voluptates, ita errores et falsae opiniones vitam contaminant si *rationalis mens* (italics mine) ipsa vitiosa est.

[5] See *loc. cit.*

[6] *Conf.*, 4, 7, 12: Ad te, Domine, levanda erat et curanda, sciebam, sed nec volebam nec valebam, eo magis quod mihi non eras aliquid solidum et firmum, cum de te cogitabam. Non enim tu eras, sed vanum phantasma, et error meus erat Deus meus.

The consequences of this error point indirectly to the necessity of a correct concept of God as the prerequisite for loving Him. At the very beginning of his *Confessions* the Saint inquires how can he praise Him unless he know Him?[7] And in the fourth book he develops the same notion: How can he love Him, who knows not how to conceive of anything except a completely corporeal splendor? It is not that Augustine is trying to excuse himself for his failure to know and to love God. He judges his own pursuit of false ideas as a form of spiritual fornication, implying thereby that he did incur some moral guilt in his pursuit of unrealities.[8]

From the viewpoint of culpability the ignorance of Augustine can be traced to two fertile sources: pride and worldliness. Pride had been very powerful in leading him into the Manichean error.[9] Even later, at Milan, when he had cast Manicheanism aside, he was still the child of pride. He sought the truth without recourse to prayer; he was too eager for disputes. This is his own testimony,

---

[7] See *ibid.*, 1, 1, 1.

[8] See *ibid.*, 4, 2, 3.

[9] See *ibid.*, 4, 14, 23: Et errabam tyfo et circumferebar *omni vento* (Eph. 4:14). See also E. Gilson, *Introduction à l'étude de saint Augustin*, 302, where the author holds that the origin of the Saint's incapacity to conceive a spiritual substance was "confiance coupable dans une raison viciée par un coeur corrumpu." Later the author develops the same thought (310): La racine du mal dont souffrent les hommes, c'est celle du mal dont il a tant souffert lui-même: l'orgueil. La volonté de trouver la vérité philosophique par la raison seule c'est, appliquée à l'ordre de la connaissance, cette volonté de se passer de Dieu qui mène en tout l'activité de l'homme. L'échec douloureux d'une raison qui capitule devant la foi, et d'une volonté qui s'offre à la grâce, c'est la leçon même par laquelle Dieu nous rappelle au sentiment de notre dépendance.

It is interesting to note that Pr. Alfaric (*L'évolution intellectuelle de saint Augustin*, 73), in seeking the motivation behind the Saint's acceptance of Manicheanism, finds this same independence of judgment: Seulement, il sentait désormais le besoin de rencontrer une doctrine qui lui permît d'être chrétien tout en faisant un libre usage de sa raison. En ce moment-làméme, le Manichéisme vint fort opportunément lui en offrir le moyen. See also J. Capello, *Confessionum libri tredecim* (Rome: Marietti, 1948), xix: Quaerenti causam mali sui nec invenienti, quia ipse non gerebat mentem purgatam, facilis ratio Manichaei occurrit et falsissimam persuasionem induxit se non libera voluntate peccare, sed necessitate pulsum a quodam principio malo.

as he reviews the entire period of his errors. For a long time he had condemned the Church for doctrine that he had *imagined* her to teach. In short, temerariously he had condemned what by inquiry he should have learnt.[10]

He observes the same sort of pride in many of the learned who knew not the way of Christ, considering themselves to be as exalted as the stars, only to be cast down like Lucifer into the blindness of the foolish. For, although they enunciate many true things about the creature, they do not seek the Maker of the creature in a religious spirit, and hence they do not find him. One cannot fail to notice in this passage the thoughts of St. Paul.[11]

Developing the relationship of pride and ignorance still further, the Saint points out that no moral injury can come to the man who may be ignorant of some aspect of corporeal creation, but who, nevertheless, possesses a correct concept of God. Such ignorance, however, can be a moral detriment to him who stubbornly insists upon joining questions about the material universe with the doctrines of religion, while at the same time refusing to admit that he is ignorant. Such was the serious fault of Faustus, who, at first, pretended to know what he did not know, arrogating to himself the Holy Ghost, and obstinately teaching error.[12] In the positive ignorance of Faustus, moreover, one detects the earmark of heresy, namely, obstinacy, or the stubborn adherence to false doctrine. This brings moral injury upon its possessor: "But it doth hurt him if he esteem the matter to belong to the very essence of true doctrine, and will yet needs affirm with pertinacity that whereof he is ignorant."[13]

---

[10] See *ibid.*, 6, 3, 3. See also *ibid.*, 6, 3, 4: Eo quippe temerarius et inpius fueram, quod ea quae debebam quaerendo discere accusando dixeram.

[11] See *ibid.*, 5, 3, 5.

[12] See *ibid.*, 5, 5, 9. See also *ibid.*, 5, 5, 8: Ista vero quia non noverat, inpudentissime audens docere, prorsus illam nosse non posset. Vanitas est enim mundana ista etiam nota profiteri, pietas autem tibi confiteri. Non enim parvi se aestimari voluit, sed Spiritum Sanctum, consolatorem et ditatorem fidelium tuorum, auctoritate plenaria personaliter in se esse persuadere conatus est.

[13] *Ibid.*, 5, 5, 9: Obest autem, si hoc ad ipsam doctrinae pietatis formam pertinere arbitretur et pertinacius affirmare audeat quod ignorat.

In addition to pride, another potent factor in culpable ignorance is worldliness, or the inordinate love of creatures and of created pleasures. Already it has been stated that dissipation in a multiplicity of pleasures beclouds the mind and prevents it from learning the truth, and that indifferentism in religion is really an escape from the acknowledgment of certain moral truths that would force one to change his way of living, if he were to give a real assent to them.[14] This position of indifferentism is contrary to the very purpose of the natural gift of intellect.

Man can and should discover God through the visible works of His creation by the use of his intelligence. Oftentimes, however, man becomes infatuated with the love of created objects, becomes the slave of the things he loves; and slaves are not capable of judgment.[15] When, therefore, such men do not arrive at the knowledge of God, they are certainly guilty of culpable ignorance.

Probing further the related questions of worldliness and of indifferentism, the Saint shows that no true progress towards the possession of truth is made, so long as one continues to gratify his desires for worldly enjoyments. In this state of sweet ignorance an individual finds it easy to repeat the words that St. Augustine used during his period of indifferentism: "Tomorrow I shall find it out, behold it will appear plainly, and I will embrace it."[16]

In the time preceding his conversion the soul of the Saint was caught in a vicious circle. Immersion in worldly pursuits meant lack of time for an earnest investigation of truth; and without the possession of truth there would be no reason for changing his manner of life. On the contrary, the strong pull of pleasure would foster a philosophy of life justifying worldliness and indulgence. Only the hope of an eternal reward would lead him to sacrifice temporal pleasures, but Augustine nourished no such hope. Consequently, he remained in a moral rut.

Hence, it seems that more than intellectual effort is required to come to the possession of the truth. First one must reform his

---

[14] See *supra,* ch. 2, 49-50.

[15] See *Conf.,* 10, 6, 10.

[16] *Ibid.,* 6, 11, 18: Cras inveniam; ecce manifestum apparebit et tenebo. See also *ibid.,* 6, 4, 6.

manner of life by *volitional* acts of penance and detachment; then God will give him the light to see the truth. For a long time this is exactly what Augustine did *not* do. In short, his love of the world, and his delay in sacrificing its pleasures prolonged the period of ignorance; and for this Augustine pleads guilty: "Shall I not rather undergo the torments due to such negligence?"[17]

The use of the term "negligentia" implies moral guilt, and in the above passage it derives special cogency from the context. Augustine is afraid that death will overtake him before he arrives at the possession of truth; and then God will punish him for his *negligence.* It is pertinent, moreover, to note that in the same chapter he denies the fundamental principle of the Academy, namely, that one cannot possess certitude for the ordering of life, while at the same time he implies the source of their weakness. They have not sought the truth with *sufficient diligence.*[18]

Implied in his criticism of the Academy, therefore, is the duty of applying moral diligence in the pursuit of truth. He realized that seemingly pressing demands upon his time were trifles when compared with the needs of his soul for eternal values. So in the year before his conversion putting aside all distractions, he concentrated on the pursuit of truth. Already he had discovered that the Catholic Church did not teach those things concerning which he had accused her so falsely. With new hope, then, he kept knocking at the door of truth, giving us in his own actions a clear example of the use of moral diligence in the quest for truth.[19]

The final victory over ignorance and the achievement of truth were impeded, however, in the case of Augustine by a process of wishful thinking known as rationalization, which we shall analyze briefly from the psychological and moral points of view. Basically

---

[17] *Ibid.*, 6, 11, 19: An non potius hujus negligentiae supplicia luenda sunt?

[18] See *loc. cit.* See also *ibid.*, 6, 11, 18: O magni viri Academici! Nihil ad agendam vitam certi conprehendi potest. Immo quaeramus *diligentius* (italics mine) et non desperemus.

[19] See *ibid.*, 6, 11, 18. See also *ibid.*, 7, 5, 7: Talia volvebam pectore misero, ingravidato curis mordacissimis de timore mortis et non inventa veritate: stabiliter tamen haerebat in corde meo in Catholica ecclesia fides Christi tui, . . . in multis quidem adhuc informis et praeter doctrinae normam fluitans, sed tamen non eam relinquebat animus, immo in dies magis magisque inbibebat.

rationalization is the common habit of making excuses for our defects. Spontaneously we use our reasoning power "to justify and ennoble what is really unjustifiable and base in one's own conduct."[20] The will and the emotions desire that their objects find acceptance in the court of conscience; hence, rationalization is *wishful* thinking, reasoning logically from false premises to a plausible conclusion under the influence of the emotions. Far from being a purely intellectual process, then, it involves the will and many emotional elements, such as concupiscence, fear, and pride.

As we shall see, rationalization is often the weapon of concupiscence to justify a forbidden pleasure or to delay the fulfillment of a counsel; again, it is the mask of fear, inasmuch as the full realization of truth would demand the renunciation of illicit pleasure; and, finally, it provides pride with respectability, enabling the individual to maintain an exalted opinion of himself, while avoiding the humiliation of guilt. It leads to spiritual blindness and to hatred of the truth, both of which we shall discuss later.[21]

From this brief analysis it is clear that this process does involve a form of *affected* ignorance, which, however, is not always admitted by its possessor. He pretends that he does not see the evil in an action, substituting for the major premise:—Evil must be avoided—another major:—Pleasure must be sought. From some form of this premise the conclusion is established (at least to the satisfaction of the reasoner) that the desired pleasure is good and justifiable.[22] Such pretense is sinful without doubt.

---

[20] T. V. Moore, *Personal Mental Hygiene* (Grune and Stratton, N. Y., 1944), 280. See also M. Adler, *What Man Has Made of Man* (Longmans, Green and Co., N. Y., 1937), 62-63: If you desire to prove that conclusion, and invent the premises to that end, without any honest regard for their intrinsic truth or falsity, your thinking is only formally logical, but essentially wishful. It is rationalization.

[21] See *infra,* ch. 3, 132-135 for spiritual blindness; see *infra,* ch. 3, 75-77 for hatred of truth.

[22] See S.T., 1-2, 77, 2, ad 4: Ille qui habet scientiam in universali propter passionem impeditur ne possit sub illa universali sumere, et ad conclusionem pervenire: sed assumit sub alia universali quam suggerit inclinatio passionis et sub ea concludit. Unde Philosophus dicit in VII *Ethic.* quod syllogismus incontinentis habet quattuor propositiones, duas universales;

With this concept of rationalization in mind, it remains for us now to select a few examples of this dynamic process from the *Confessions.* The first example is taken from the period of internal struggle that immediately preceded Augustine's renunciation of worldly ambitions to dedicate himself to the study of Divine truth. Here it must be noted, however, that it was not a question of sin, but rather a question of counsel. Should he embrace an ascetic life of celibacy and renounce even the legitimate pleasures of marriage? He felt drawn towards the former, but he feared that it would be very difficult to renounce the pleasures of the latter; so he avoids a decision for a while by rationalization.[23]

Thus he reasons with himself: It would be disgraceful to relapse into the pleasures of the flesh after he had renounced them. But such a renunciation is very difficult. So why not seek a wife, some friends, and a modest position of honor? This will be sufficient to satisfy him. After all, many great men have possessed a wife, and yet were able to devote themselves to the pursuit of wisdom. So why may he not follow their example?

Here one may detect the two conflicting poles of desire in Augustine. He is drawn towards a life of celibacy and of complete dedication to God; and, on the other hand, he is drawn towards the pleasures of the world, and of marriage. The resultant conflict causes him to rationalize in favor of the lower goal without, however, making any decision. Thus, this passage shows how rational-

---

quarum una est rationis, puta, nullam fornicationem esse committendam; alia est passionis, puta, delectationem esse sectandam. Passio igitur ligat rationem ne assumat et concludat sub prima, unde ea durante—assumit et concludit sub secunda. The immediacy of passion produces a sort of emotionalized thought; hence concupiscence is a source of rationalization. See also *ibid.*, 1-2, 48, 3, ad 2: Concupiscentia autem dicitur esse latens et insidiosa, quia ut plurimum delectabilia quae concupiscuntur habent turpitudinem quandam et mollitiem in quibus homo vult latere. Thus concupiscence seeks a mask.

[23] See *Conf.*, 6, 11, 19: Jucunda sunt etiam ista, habent non parvam dulcedinem suam; non facile ab eis praecidenda est intentio, quia turpe est ad ea rursum redire. (So he figures this way out) . . . Ecce jam quantum est, ut inpetretur aliquis honor. Et quid amplius in his desiderandum? . . . Et ducenda uxor cum aliqua pecunia . . . et ille erit modus cupiditatis. Multi magni viri et imitatione dignissimi sapientiae studio cum conjugibus dediti fuerunt.

ization was utilized by concupiscence to delay Augustine from the decision—not merely to embrace Christianity, but also to practice celibacy.

It is meaningful, moreover, that even though sin was not necessarily involved in his procrastination, he censures himself for it at the time that he wrote his *Confessions*: "Time still slipped away, and I was slow in being converted to my Lord; from day to day I deferred to live in thee, but I deferred not to die daily in myself. While I thus desired a happy life, I yet feared to seek it in its true abode, and I fled from it while yet I sought it."[24] (Notice the paradox of fear and love.) As a result of this rationalized ignorance, he failed to understand that continence is a gift of Divine grace.[25]

In this first example of rationalization concupiscence was seen to be an important factor, but in the second example, which we are now going to discuss, the motivation of pride is apparent. While at Rome with the Manicheans, Augustine had believed that it was not man who sinned, but some other unknown nature within him, but not of him. This belief delighted his pride, inasmuch as it freed him from the humiliation of guilt. Whenever he had done any evil, therefore, instead of confessing it to God, and seeking forgiveness, he loved to excuse himself, and to accuse the "foreign" nature within him, about which he knew nothing, except that he disowned it.

Here pride rationalizes itself into spiritual blindness; and, hence, his sin became incurable in the measure that he refused to judge himself a sinner. Indeed he preferred to consider God as overcome by the evil power within himself rather than to regard himself as conquered by God for his sanctification. Appropriately, the Saint concludes this retrospective passage with a few lines from Psalm 140, in which the inspired author prays that his heart may not be turned aside into malicious speech to make excuses for sin.[26]

---

[24] *Ibid.*, 6, 11, 20: Transibant tempora, et tardabam *converti ad Dominum* et differebam *de die in diem* (Ecclus. 5:8) vivere in te et non differebam cotidie in memet ipso mori: amans beatam vitam timebam illam in sede sua et ab ea fugiens quaerebam eam.

[25] See *loc. cit.*

[26] See *Conf.*, 5, 10, 18: Adhuc enim mihi videbatur non esse nos, qui peccamus, sed nescio quam aliam in nobis peccare naturam et *delectabat superbiam*

After Augustine had repudiated Manicheanism, but before his conversion, he found this doctrine of projecting one's guilt upon God to be repulsive. He says, consequently, that the Manicheans were *filled with malice,* because they were willing to believe that the Divine Substance dwelling within them had suffered evil rather than that their own persons had committed it.[27] In this fashion the Manicheans rationalized themselves into a position in which they were free from the responsibility for their own evil actions.

The third example of rationalization is taken from the Saint's description of his early education, wherein he was forced by teachers, drunk with the wine of error, to learn seductive passages from the classics. For an example he cites a passage from Terence's *Eunuch,* in which a lewd youth is brought upon the stage. This youth sets up Jupiter as his model of seduction; and then he proceeds to excite himself to lust as if by heavenly authority, arguing in this fashion: If great Jupiter descends from heaven to commit adultery, then why may not he, a mortal man, do the same? So, he concludes, he committed adultery, and he sees no reason to be ashamed of it.[28]

Thus a classical poet rationalizes the sin of adultery. This was merely one instance within a general tendency that may be termed *social rationalization.* The Saint himself calls it the hellish torrent

---

meam (italics mine) extra culpam esse, et cum aliquid mali fecissem, non confiteri me fecisse ut sanares animam meam, quoniam peccabat tibi sed excusare me amabam et accusare nescio quid aliud, quod mecum esset et ego non essem . . . . et id erat peccatum insanabilius, quo me peccatorem non esse arbitrabar, et execrabilis iniquitas, te, Deus omnipotens, te in me ad perniciem meam, quam me a te ad salutem malle superari. Nondum ergo posueras *custodiam ori meo et ostium continentiae circum labia mea,* ut non declinaret *cor meum in verba mala ad excusandas excusationes in peccatis* . . . (Ps. 140:3 ff.). Although St. Augustine understands Psalm 140:3 ff. as a reference to excuse-making, the new translation of the Hebrew text expresses a different meaning. See *Liber Psalmorum,* Pontifical Institute Edition, Rome, 1945, p. 295, where Ps. 140:3-4, reads as follows: Pone, Domine, custodiam ad os meum, excubias ad ostium labiorum meorum. Ne inclinaveris cor meum ad rem malam, ad impie patranda facinora.

[27] See *ibid,* 7, 3, 4.

[28] See *ibid.,* 1, 16, 26.

of human *custom,* into which the Sons of Eve are sucked and swept away:

> But woe be unto thee, O thou torrent of human custom, who shall be able to resist thee? How long wilt thou toss and roll those sons of Eve into that spacious and hideous sea, over which even they who are best shipped can hardly pass? Have I not read in thee of Jupiter, the thunderer and adulterer? These two things cannot both be true, but this was said that it might carry an authority to make men imitate that true adultery, to which that false thunder might play the broker. Yet which of our grave Masters would be able, with patient ear, to hear a man cry out in that same school and say, 'This was but a fiction of Homer's. He hath ascribed the faults of men unto the gods: would rather he had drawn their virtues down to us?' But rather is it true to say that he feigned them that, by attributing divine things to wicked men, they might not be thought sins; and to the end that whosoever should commit them might rather be esteemed to have imitated heavenly gods than wretched men.[29]

In this manner do humans project the guilt of adultery, and of other sins, upon the gods in order to find justification for their own foul deeds. Depraved custom transfers its own crimes to the gods; and, as Augustine adds, it attributes a divine nature to wicked men, so that crimes may be no longer considered crimes. The young also learn how to reason away their misdeeds, as they are forced to learn classical lines replete with depraved reasonings.

A fourth example of rationalization seems to lurk in the prayer

---

[29] *Conf.*, 1, 16, 25: Sed vae tibi, flumen moris humani! Quis resistit tibi? . . . Quousque volves Evae filios in mare magnum et formidulosum, quod vix transeunt, qui lignum conscenderint? Nonne ego in te legi et tonantem Jovem et adulterantem? Et utique non posset haec duo, sed actum est ut haberet *auctoritatem imitandum verum adulterium* (italics mine) lenocinante falso tonitru. Quis autem paenulatorum magistrorum audit aure sobria ex eodem pulvere hominem clamantem et dicentem: '*Fingebat haec Homerus et humana ad deos transferebat; divina mallem ad nos?*' (Cicero, *Tuscul.*, 1, c. 26.) Sed verius dicitur, quod fingebat haec quidem ille, sed hominibus flagitiosis divina tribuendo, ne *flagitia flagitia putarentur, et ut quisquis ea fecisset, non homines perditos, sed caelestes deos videretur imitatus* (italics mine). The reference is to Cicero in *Tusculan Disputations,* book 1, c. 26.

of the youthful Augustine: "Give me chastity and continence, but do not give it yet."[30] From the retrospective tenor of this passage it is clear that these were not the exact words of the youth, but rather a literary device to convey forcibly the inconsistency between prayer and conduct that characterized the early youth of Augustine. The prayer seems to express the conflict between flesh and spirit already raging within the soul of the youth. His spirit begs God for chastity, while the tendencies of the flesh were afraid that God would hear his prayer immediately, and promptly heal the wounds of concupiscence, which would be just what they did not want.[31]

It is evident that the prayer is not a full-hearted utterance, but the expression of a divided will, which at that time was drawn more to concupiscence than to the higher ideals of the soul. The youth did not want to admit this, even to himself; rather he wanted to feel that at least he had prayed for chastity; and so he prays weakly, as if he were saying: "Yes, I want chastity, but I want carnal pleasures too; so hold it off for a while."

As one reflects upon these rationalizing tendencies in Augustine, and as he recalls his passionate love of truth, which permeates the narrative of the *Confessions,* one begins to wonder how he can reconcile these contrary tendencies within the same person. Basically, it seems but another facet of the general conflict between the call of Divine grace and the call of the flesh. His desire for truth was wholly consonant with his longing for a higher kind of life. The pursuit of these higher ideals is very difficult, and so it is not surprising that for a while the strong allure of carnal delights rendered them largely inefficacious. The same concupiscence which detoured him during this period from the pathway of happiness, succeeded also in masking itself in plausible arguments. This was rationalization.

Meanwhile Augustine's strong love of truth was never completely inactive. He left the Manicheans as soon as he realized

---

[30] *Conf.,* 8, 7, 17: Da mihi castitatem et continentiam, sed noli modo. See also E. Portalié, "Augustin," DTC, 2269: Au début de cette crisis, il pria, mais sans désir sincère d'être exaucé: *Da mihi castitatem, sed noli modo* (*Conf.,* 8, 7, 17).

[31] See *loc. cit.*

that their religion could not be true; he lingered only briefly with the indifferentists of the Academy; and during the period immediately preceding his conversion, he was tortured with doubts and stings of conscience that would not have found entrance into a soul that was indifferent to the truth.[32] Thus, it seems that the two opposite tendencies—to seek truth, and to look for excuses for faults and sins—dwelt in the Saint, as they dwell in almost every human being, but in Augustine the ardor for truth was much stronger than its opposite.

From the recognition of these opposite tendencies within man, therefore, one may garner a salutary truth for the practical moral order: There is need for rigorous honesty in examining the motives of our conduct. Behind delay in making a decision may lurk the pleasure of concupiscence or the fear of losing it; hence, there is wisdom in the daily examination of conscience for the uncovering of motives that can falsify conscience itself. Thus, we arrive in our chain of thought at the mature form of rationalization known as *hatred of truth.*

The Saint discusses the hatred of truth in Book 10, which is very different from the first nine books of the *Confessions,* inasmuch as he writes herein with the objectivity of a philosopher, standing apart from life, rather than as a narrator, describing warfare within his own soul. First of all, he answers his own query, namely, whether men would rather joy in truth or in falsehood, by a comparison. Just as all men desire to be happy, so all desire to rejoice in the truth. Besides, many may wish to deceive others; but no one wants to *be* deceived.[33]

If these be the desires of men, why are they not happy, and why do they not rejoice in the truth? The reason is, Augustine continues, that they are too absorbed in other things which have more power to make them miserable than to make them happy. For the same reason they come even to hate the truth and the preachers of truth. They desire that the thing which they love be truth;

---

[32] See *Conf.,* 7, chap. 1-3 inclusive. See also *ibid.,* 6, 4, 6: Tenebam cor meum ab omni adsensione timens praecipitium et suspendio magis necabar. . . . See also *ibid.,* 6, 4, 5; Portalié, *op. cit.,* 2270-2271.

[33] See *Conf.,* 10, 22-23, 32-34.

thence, they love a false good as if it were true, and hate truth. Since, moreover, they do not want to admit that they are in error, they endeavor to consider their object as in agreement with truth.[34] "Therefore do they hate truth for the sake of the thing which they love instead of truth."[35]

There is another reason, too, why men hate truth: It exposes their faults. They love it when it merely enlightens, but does not touch their manner of life; but they hate it when it becomes *personal.* "They love truth when it shineth fair upon them, but they hate it when it reproveth them. And because they themselves would not be deceived, who yet desire to deceive others, they love truth when it discovers itself, but they hate it when it discovers them."[36]

For this perversity truth punishes them. She exposes the wickedness of those who seek to remain hidden, while she hides herself from them, allowing them to become spiritually blind. Such, however, is characteristic of human depravity.[37] For example, the impure wish the pleasure of the flesh to be their true joy; and drunkards are provoked by their love of wine to hate the truth. In both cases the victims reason according to their inordinate passions, and become established in their evil habits.[38]

---

[34] See *Conf.,* 10, 23, 34.

[35] *Loc. cit.*: Itaque propter eam rem oderunt veritatem, quam pro veritate amant.

[36] *Conf.,* 10, 23, 34: Amant eam lucentem, oderunt eam rearguentem. Quia enim falli nolunt et fallere volunt, amant eam, cum se ipsa indicat, et oderunt eam, cum eos ipsos indicat.

[37] See *loc. cit.*: Sic, sic, etiam sic animus humanus, etiam sic caecus et languidus, turpis atque indecens latere vult se autem ut lateat aliquid non vult. Contra illi redditur ut ipse non lateat veritatem, ipsum autem veritas lateat.

[38] See *Conf.,* 6, 2, 2: Non enim obsidebat spiritum ejus vinulentia eamque stimulabat in *odium veri amor vini* (italics mine), sicut plerosque mares et feminas, qui ad canticum sobrietatis sicut ad potionem aquatam madidi nausiant. See also S.T., 1-2, 29, 5: Contingit autem verum aliquod particulare tripliciter repugnare vel contrariari *bono amato* (italics mine). Uno modo, secundum quod veritas est causaliter et originaliter in ipsis rebus, et sic homo quandoque odit aliquam veritatem dum vellet non esse verum quod est verum; alio modo, secundum quod veritas est in cognitione ipsius hominis, quae impedit ipsum a prosecutione amati, sicut si aliqui vellent

From the study, then, of rationalization and hatred of truth one may discern the development of that *pervert sense* that St. Paul describes in the first chapter of his epistle to the Romans. It may be called the process of becoming proud. First, one gives free rein to a passion, whether it be for carnal pleasure, or for drink; then, one fashions an argument to justify his indulgence (rationalization); and, finally, one becomes both blind in his reasoning and helpless in resisting a deeply entrenched passion. Proud blindness characterizes his actions. This question of spiritual blindness we shall discuss later.[39] Suffice it now to conclude this study of ignorance in the *Confessions* with the observation that rationalization, as a form of affected ignorance, can do immeasurable harm both to the conscience and to the moral life of the individual.

B. CONCUPISCENCE IN ITS VARIED FORMS

The next obstacle on the road to happiness is *concupiscence.* The word is used in the *Confessions* in several different senses.[40]

---

non cognoscere veritatem ut libere peccarent, ex quorum persona dicitur Job (21:14) *Scientiam viarum tuarum nolumus;* tertio modo, habetur odio veritas particularis tamquam repugnans, prout est in intellectu alterius; puta, cum aliquis vult jacere in peccato, odit quod aliquis veritatem circa peccatum suum cognoscat, et secundum hoc dicit Augustinus, quod 'homines amant veritatem lucentem; oderunt eam redarguentem.' (*Conf.*, 10, 23, 34.)

One may then develop an interesting parallel between St. Thomas and St. Augustine in regard to hatred of truth. The above quotation from the *Summa* seems to be the Angelic Doctor's paraphrase of *Conf.*, 10, 23, 33-34. Another interesting commentary on this section of the *Confessions* is found in Wangnereck, *op. cit.*, 383, nn. 2 and 4, where he says that the Saint teaches here that truth and happiness are to be found, not in any creature, but only in God, and that one cannot possess God except by the love of truth in all its forms.

[39] See *infra,* ch. 3, 132-135.

[40] References for the various types of concupiscence discussed in the *Confessions* will be found below. The division, as such, is not found in the book, although it is suggested in *Conf.*, 10, 30, 41: Jubes certe, ut contineam, *a concupiscentia carnis et concupiscentia oculorum et ambitione saeculi* (I John 2:16). Thus the Saint based his triple division of temptation and his twofold division of concupiscence on Scripture. It is interesting also to note how St. Thomas divides concupiscence (S.T., 1-2, 77, 5): Est autem duplex concupiscentia, sicut supra habitum est (1-2, 30, 3). Una quidem

Most frequently the term refers to inordinate carnal desires, but it is used also to denote the pleasant sensations of tasty food, nice smells, and beautiful music, not to mention beautiful colors. In general, all these sensations connote something pleasurable to the senses, so that the desire for all pleasant sensations may be termed *concupiscence of the senses.*

In contradistinction to this group of sensory pleasures one finds in the *Confessions* the term concupiscence used to denote not merely an inordinate desire for knowledge and news (inordinate curiosity), but also an inclination to know through bodily pain, coupled with a sort of morbid curiosity in regard to things of horror. The term *concupiscence of the eyes,* therefore, may be subdivided into inordinate, but normal, curiosity, and what we shall call *morbid curiosity.*

The question of sexual dreams will be considered after that of carnal desires. Since, moreover, the phenomenon of excessive grief bears a relationship to concupiscence of the senses, it will be discussed as one of its effects.

From the analysis of concupiscence in itself the mind naturally passes to the study of its relationships; and in the *Confessions* two pertinent interactions are discernible: the habit of concupiscence, as the source of moral proscrastination, and the effect of concupiscence upon the will. This leads us to the next topic: division of will.

The form of concupiscence most frequently mentioned in the *Confessions* is the inordinate desire for venereal pleasure. Since

---

naturalis, quae est eorum quibus natura corporis sustentatur: sive quantum ad conservationem individui, sicut cibus et potus, et alia hujusmodi; sive quantum ad conservationem speciei, sicut in venereis. Et horum inordinatus appetitus dicitur concupiscentia carnis. Alia est concupiscentia animalis, eorum scilicet, quae per sensum carnis sustentationem aut delectationem non afferunt, sed sunt delectabilia secundum apprehensionem imaginationis, aut alicujus hujusmodi acceptionis: sicut sunt pecunia, ornatus vestium, et alia hujusmodi. Et haec quidem animalis concupiscentia vocatur *concupiscentia oculorum,* sive intelligatur concupiscentia oculorum, id est, ipsius visionis, quae fit per oculos, ut referatur ad curiositatem . . . (*Conf.*, 10, 35); sive referatur ad concupiscentiam rerum, quae exterius oculis proponuntur, ut referatur ad cupiditatum, secundum quod ab aliis exponitur.

the first eight books of his autobiography are replete with references to its development and effects, it seems best to select passages representative of its various aspects. Naturally, we consider first the early milieu of Augustine, as described in the *Confessions.* To be sure, we are aware that some hold that the Saint's narrative of his early years is *pure* exaggeration, but this extreme view is tantamount to a denial of the validity of this book as personal history. If the *Confessions* are accepted as valid, then the facts of impurity committed by the future Saint must also be accepted as history.[41] The question of whether he *did* these things is distinct from the question of whether he is too severe in his judgment of his adolescent interlude.

During St. Augustine's early period of study in Madaura, approximately from his twelfth to his sixteenth year, he formed a loose code of moral conduct. This is not surprising if we consider that he was away from home and from the ethical ideals of Monnica, and if we remember that during this impressionable age he saw the pagan orgies and drank in the loves of Dido and Aeneas and learned Terence's eloquent defense of adultery.[42] Such an education hardly could form a Christian attitude towards the pleasures of the flesh. Consider then what happened when he came home to Tagaste in his sixteenth year. A period of enforced idleness ensued that provided an occasion for carnal sins. Soon the youth found loose companions in Tagaste to amuse him. He became one of the young men about town, haunting the squares and public places, seeking excitement and pleasure. Augustine

[41] See Boyer, *Christianisme et Néo-Platonisme dans la formation de saint Augustin,* 11, 12, 15, 27, 192, where the author insists that the moral disorders of which St. Augustine accuses himself in his sixteenth year are real. Boyer directs his argument especially against Gourdon and Alfaric, both of whom held that the Saint exaggerated his sins in order to bring out the healing power of grace. Thus Boyer says (27): Il reste des déclarations précises dont rien ne justifierait ni n'expliquerait l'inexactitude. Les termes sont trop vifs pour ne se rapporter qu'à des étourderies insignifiantes. Augustin parle de la sombre végétation de ses amours variées; il ne distinguait plus l'amitié de la concupiscence; il était englouti dans le gouffre des actes criminels. For additional arguments concerning the validity of the Confessions, see *supra, Intro.,* xviii-xx.

[42] See *supra,* ch. 3, 72-74 (rationalization).

himself states that he was dissipated and immersed in his fornications.[43]

Looking back over this turbulent age, the Saint regrets that no one tried to temper his disorder, so that the tides of his youth might have cast themselves upon the marriage shore, if they could not be calmed. Augustine felt that marriage would have been better than the concubinage in which he had lived. Concupiscence, then, would have found a remedy in marriage, but, as we know, no one counseled marriage for him. On the contrary, his father rejoiced in his son's puberty and looked forward to progeny, allowing him too much freedom; and even though Monnica warned her son against fornication and adultery, her advice was regarded as mere feminine concern.[44]

No doubt, her advice would have made a much deeper impression had it been supported, and not compromised, by the lax attitude of her husband towards his son's escapades. Monnica herself was not without fault. Even when she saw that she could not dissuade her son from his carnal indulgences, she did not counsel marriage, fearing that it would interfere with his pursuit of higher studies. For this her son gently censures her in his *Confessions*.[45] Hence, the early pagan education and environment of Augustine at Madaura, his father's ribald attitude, his too great liberty at a critical period of his adolescence—all these are extenuating circumstances in determining the guilt of the youth plunged in carnal indulgence.

But these factors did not excuse his guilt. He affirms that his invisible enemy, the devil, seduced him, because he was willing to be seduced.[46] When, moreover, he went to Carthage to continue his education, he became infatuated with love itself:

> I was not yet immersed in love, but I desired to be so. . . . I sought some object to love, loving the mere thought of love, and I despised the way of safety, wherein there were

[43] See *Conf.*, 2, 2, 2. See also Vernon Bourke, *Augustine's Quest of Wisdom*, 8-10.

[44] See *Conf.*, 2, 2, 3-4. See also *ibid.*, 2, 3, 6-7.

[45] See *ibid.*, 2, 3, 8.

[46] See *loc. cit.*: Calcabat me inimicus invisibilis et seducebat me, quia *ego seductilis eram* (italics mine).

> no pitfalls. . . . It was a dear thing to me to love and to be loved, and the more sweet if I arrived at carnal enjoyment of the person whom I loved. . . . I troubled therefore the water of friendship with the diet of unclean appetite, and I obscured the brightness thereof with hellish lust.[47]

Even though he was leading an immoral life, he tried to appear respectable and urbane. Thus, vanity—joined to impurity—accelerated his downward plunge; and he cast himself into inordinate indulgence in sexual love in a vain effort to salve, as it were, the sores of his soul, which was deprived of the internal delights of the grace of God. To this emptiness of soul the Saint ascribes the violence of his sexual urges.[48]

It was not long before the young student of rhetoric acquired a permanent mistress. As he himself says, he joyfully allowed himself to be tied by the bonds of sorrow, so that he might be scourged by the burning irons of jealousy, suspicion, fear, anger, and quarrels.[49] Here there is no hint that Augustine meant this as any kind of marriage; and, while it is true that he lived with this woman for approximately fifteen years, the passing of time did not change his own attitude towards the union.

At best it was a concubinage, for which he felt guilty;[50] and, although he was not baptized, he did not try to have his union re-

[47] *Conf.*, 3, 1, 1: Nondum amabam et amare amabam. . . . Quaerebam quid amarem, amans amare et oderam securitatem et viam sine muscipulis. . . . Amare et amari dulce mihi erat magis si et amantis corpore fruerer. Venam igitur amicitiae coinquinabam sordibus concupiscentiae candoremque ejus obnubilabam de tartaro libidinis.

[48] See *loc. cit.*

[49] See *loc. cit.*

[50] See *Conf.*, 9, 6, 14, where the Saint says that the only part which he had in Adeodatus was the *sin*: Adjunximus . . . puerum Adeodatum ex me natum carnaliter de peccato meo. He would not have spoken thus of lawful intercourse between husband and wife. Besides, the tone of all the passages dealing with his struggle against lust gives not the least hint that at any time he regarded his companion as his wife. To the objection, moreover, that the *Confessions* is a retrospective examination of conscience the reply may be made: Yes, that is true, but still an accurate one, taking great pains to describe the Saint's internal reflections on every occasion. If he had considered his concubinage as lawful in a previous period, he would have mentioned his ignorance in the account of his life. See also E. Portalié, "Augustin," DTC, 1.2269.

garded as a common-law marriage—as far as we know. Furthermore, in a later reference to his concubinage, he stresses the difference between an unlawful association and a lawful marriage covenant. He says that he had a mistress, whom he had taken in a wayward passion, devoid of understanding, and hence not through a reasonable choice sealed by matrimony. From living in this concubinage he had discovered how much it lacked of the true marriage state. In the latter self-restraint is exercised; whereas, in the bargain of lust, which is concubinage, children are born against their parents' will, although once born, they do constrain love.[51] This comparison becomes sharper when one recalls what Augustine had said already about concubinage as a state of vexation, replete with the characteristics of an *unstable* union, namely, jealousy, suspicion, fear, and the like.[52]

He, nevertheless, continued to live in concubinage even after he had decided—tentatively—to enter the catechumenate at Milan. Meanwhile, Monnica was very active in arranging a marriage for her son, which implies that she did not regard her son's present union as even a pagan marriage. It was not, however, until the young rhetorician had agreed to marry another that he dismissed the mother of Adeodatus; for the new engagement forced him to send her back to Africa.[53] Needless to say, this was a difficult separation. The woman, who had intimately shared his life for fifteen years, returned to Africa, vowing that she would never love another man, and Augustine himself portrays his feelings thus: "That mistress of mine, who was wont to be my bed-fellow, being torn from my side as an impediment to my marriage, my heart that cleaved to her was broken and wounded until it bled."[54]

---

[51] See *ibid.*, 4, 2, 2: In illis annis unam habebam, non eo quod legitimum vocatur conjugio cognitam sed quam indagaverat vagus ardor inops prudentiae, sed unam tamen—ei quoque servans tori fidem; in qua sane experirer exemplo meo, quid distaret inter conjugalis placiti modum, quod foederatum esset generandi gratia, et pactum libidinosi amoris, ubi proles etiam contra votum nascitur, quamvis jam nata, cogat se diligi. See also Bourke, *op. cit.,* 15-16.

[52] See *Conf.*, 3, 1, 1.

[53] See *Conf.,* 6, 13, 23. See also following notes.

[54] *Conf.*, 6, 15, 25: . . . avulsa a latere meo tamquam inpedimento conjugii cum qua cubare solitus eram, cor, ubi adhaerebat concisum et vulneratum mihi erat te trahebat sanguinem.

This sudden and violent suppression of a deeply rooted affection, which did include elements of true human love, left him more vulnerable to temptations of the flesh. He had detached himself from the long accustomed pleasure of concubinage with a woman to whom his heart still clung, but he had found no value to counterbalance the loss that he felt so keenly on the human level. It is not surprising, therefore, that he did *not* wait the two years before his future bride would come of age, and that he procured another mistress. For at this time he was still the slave of the *habit* of concupiscence, and he considered the vice his master.

Then it was that he realized that he was not so much attracted by the ideals of marriage as by lust. With a new mistress—the habit of lust grew stronger in him; yet the carnal pleasure found in her did not heal the wounds made by the cutting off of the former one. True, Augustine adds, the new mistress assuaged the desire for sexual satisfaction, but, at the same time increased the vigor and power of lust in him. His pains became less acute, but more desperate, that is, even as he gained the temporary release of carnal desires, he became *less hopeful* of overcoming the *habitual desire* for this kind of pleasure.[55]

As the habit of lust grew stronger in him, a certain form of fear appeared. It was not the salutary fear associated with the virtue of hope and penitence, but a rationalized fear that sought arguments to justify its manner of life.[56] For example, when Alypius had tried to dissuade Augustine from the intention of marrying, the latter had replied that many married men had cherished wisdom and served God faithfully. Immediately he adds that he resisted the arguments of Alypius, because he was *afraid* to be freed from the habit of concupiscence. How could he do without carnal delights? In the same discussion, moreover, he admits to Alypius that his main motive in seeking marriage was not the procreation of a family, but lust.[57]

Already it has been pointed out that rationalization is a product of fear and concupiscence; it may be more accurately described

[55] See *loc. cit.* See also *Conf.*, 6, 12, 21-22.

[56] See *supra*, ch. 2, 51-52 (hope); ch. 3, 68 ff. (rationalization).

[57] See *Conf.*, 6, 12, 21-22.

as a process of thought motivated largely by the fear of losing the pleasure of concupiscence. Augustine's half-hearted adolescent prayer for chastity, for example, hides such a fear.[58]

It is pertinent to note that, as he cleared away intellectual difficulties and moved closer to the Faith, both the habit of concupiscence, and its concomitant fear persisted. Thus, after he had gained the concept of the spirituality of God, he did not advance to the enjoyment of God, because he was enchained still by lust. He desired to cleave to God, but he was not yet purified. By this time, moreover, ignorance had ceased to be an excuse; but still he feared as much to be freed from the pleasures of the flesh, as one who is not their slave, dreads to be enmeshed in them.[59]

There remained nothing but mute fear, for all arguments and excuses had lost their force. Yet he *feared* to be restrained from carnal indulgence as he feared death itself. Indeed, even at the threshold of decision and conversion, the fear that he could not live without this source of venereal pleasure held him back.[60]

Since, then, such fear delayed the eradication of the habit of lust, it is profitable to study the implications of this aspect of concupiscence. In planning spiritual guidance for an individual who is addicted to some form of concupiscence, one should strike at fear, convincing the individual that he can do without the pleasure of the vice, if he is willing to cooperate with Divine grace. In addition, one should insist that the penitent begin *immediately* to battle against his vice, for procrastination will serve no purpose, except to increase the fear that one cannot practice continence.

---

[58] *Conf.*, 8, 7, 17.

[59] See *Conf.*, 7, 17, 23: Sed rapiebar ad te decore tuo moxque diripiebar abs te pondere meo et ruebam in ista cum gemitu et pondus hoc *consuetudo carnalis* (italics mine). See also *ibid.*, 8, 5, 11: Ego autem adhuc terra obligatus militare tibi recusabam et inpedimentis omnibus sic timebam expediri, quemadmodum inpediri timendum est. See also *ibid.*, 8, 5, 12.

[60] See *Conf.*, 8, 7, 18. See also *ibid.*, 8, 11, 26: Et audiebam eas jam longe minus quam dimidius, non tamquam libere contradicentes eundo in obviam, sed velut a dorso mussitantes et discedentem quasi furtim vellicantes, ut respicerem. Retardabant tamen cunctantem me abripere atque excutere ab eis et transilire quo vocabar, cum diceret mihi consuetudo violenta: 'Putasne sine istis poteris?' Thus poetically the Saint depicts the stubborn struggle of concupiscence against the gains of virtue.

Thus the Saint insists that we subject the flesh instead of allowing it to enslave us.[61]

More will be said about the *habit of lust* later; for the present, we will treat another aspect of carnal concupiscence, namely, its presence in erotic dreams, which, in the case of Augustine, were relics of his former vice. It should be remembered that it is the bishop of Hippo describing—not the actions of past life, but the temptations of the present. First, he points out that reawakened imaginations from his past life are the fertile source of such temptations: "Yet still there live in my memory . . . the images of those frailties which long custom hath fixed there."[62]

These images have no power over him while awake, but only while he is asleep; and then they gain an assent from the imagination of the dreamer, but not from reason and will. He is not responsible, therefore, for these dreams, because his conscious self resists these same images during waking hours, and because he does not give consent during sleep. Thus, after one awakens from an erotic dream, he understands that his conscious will has not given consent, and so he does not disturb himself, but returns to peace of conscience, regretting, however, that something impure has taken place in him, even though without his consent.[63]

Augustine implies that one is innocent of such dreams, provided that one resists these imaginations during waking hours. Then he asks a very provocative question—one to which it seems—there is no answer: "And whence cometh it to pass that oftentimes in my sleep also I make resistance; and being mindful of my purpose, do remain most chastely therein, without giving any assent to such illusions?"[64] He himself does not answer this question. Still the basic morality remains the same; namely, one is responsible for those thoughts *only* to which he *deliberately* gives consent.

---

[61] See *ibid.*, 4, 11, 17.

[62] *Ibid.*, 10, 30, 41: Sed adhuc vivunt in memoria mea . . . talium rerum imagines, quas ibi consuetudo mea fixit.

[63] See *loc. cit.*

[64] *Loc. cit.*: Et unde saepe etiam in somnis resistimus nostrique propositi memores atque in eo castissime permanentes nullum talibus inlecebris adhibemus adsensum?

Finally, Augustine asks another question: Whether God could quench even the impure motions of his sleep? He answers in the affirmative, and he adds the prayer that Divine grace may heal even these non-voluntary tendencies of his soul.[65]

This chapter thirty of book ten is remarkable in that the author, who is also a bishop, discusses temptations and sins of a most personal and delicate nature. He is very honest and humble in what may be called a *public* examination of conscience. Even as he shows that sexual dreams and nocturnal pollutions are not sinful in themselves, he prays with a wonderful confidence in God that he be purified from the least traces of concupiscence. For the omnipotent power of God can do more than man can conceive![66] Such confidence in God and such warfare against concupiscence is a far cry from the earlier Augustine, who was afraid to throw off the yoke of lust.

From the dynamics of concupiscence in the life of Augustine—his early addiction, his long years of slavery to it—his struggle and his triumph—one may discern that the most powerful remedy against it is the *healing* grace of God. We will discuss this again in the next chapter.[67] Now we will consider the various other forms of concupiscence of the senses.

The Saint shows how concupiscence steals into eating and drinking. The very sweetness of the necessity of taking sustenance easily becomes a snare of concupiscence. Inasmuch as one must eat and drink for health's sake, a perilous pleasure takes advantage of this necessity to tag along, and very often it attempts to assume the mastery in such a way as to make one do for pleasure what one wills to do only in view of his health.[68]

What is sufficient for health is too little for pleasure. Often then it happens that one does not know his true motive in asking for food—whether it be from alleged necessity, or from a desire for gratification. In this uncertainty the soul rejoices and finds therein an excuse to shield itself; for, under the cloak of health,

---

[65] See *ibid.*, 10, 30, 42.

[66] See *loc. cit.* See also Wangnereck, *Confessionum,* 395.

[67] See *infra,* ch. 4, 147-154.

[68] See *Conf.*, 10, 31, 43-44.

it may disguise the matter of gratification.[69] The Saint, moreover, accuses himself of eating too much occasionally. So he asks God for the grace of continence in eating and drinking. As we have already seen in our discussion of the virtue of continence, the practice of self-restraint is a *gift* of Divine grace: "Da quod jubes et jube quod vis."[70]

Concupiscence, however, does not have its root in the food or drink desired, but in the *inordinate* nature of the desire. Very probably directing his remarks to the Manicheans, who were forbidden to eat meat, he declares that he fears not the uncleanness of meat, but the uncleanness of *desire*. The people in the desert, for example, may be justly censured, not because they desired meat, but because this desire caused them to murmur against the Lord.[71] Thus, only when the desire for food or drink causes one to break the law of God, does it become inordinate, and, hence, sinful. Comparing the desire for food and drink with the desire for carnal pleasure, Augustine holds that the desire for food and drink demands more vigilant, even daily, suppression, while the desire for carnal delights is not as continual, and, often, after it is suppressed, does not become active for days.[72]

It seems that the Saint is too severe in judging himself in regard to food and drink. Suppose one does take a little more food than what seems sufficient for health simply because he enjoys the food, is this a fault? Hardly. Despite the satisfaction of concupiscence in this case, there is no transgression of the moral law. Still, as it has been pointed out already, his apparent rigorism springs from his ardent desire to combat concupiscence in all its diverse forms.[73]

---

[69] See *loc. cit.*: Nec idem modum utriusque est: nam quod saluti satis est delectationi parum est, et saepe incertum fit, utrum adhuc necessaria corporis cura subsidium petat an voluptaria cupiditatis fallacia ministerium suppetat. Ad hoc incertum hilarescit infelix anima et in eo praeparat *excusationis* (italics mine) patrocinium gaudens non adparere, quod satis sit moderationi valetudinis ut obtentu salutis obumbret negotium voluptatis. Notice in this passage another example of rationalization.

[70] *Conf.*, 10, 31, 45. In this section the reader may note the Pauline influence over Augustine.

[71] See *Conf.*, 10, 31, 46. See also E. Pusey, *Confessions,* 233, nn. 1-2.

[72] See *ibid.*, 10, 31, 47. See also *ibid.*, 10, 31, 44.

[73] See *ibid.*, 10, 34, 51.

The same alertness is shown in the question of music, but here it seems that he gave the problem more consideration than its importance demanded. In one passage he accuses himself of taking more pleasure in the music of the chanted psalms than in their meaning; but in the following section he admits too great severity in this matter, pointing out that one who is overanxious about this trivial form of deception becomes too strict with himself. Then he recalls the joyful tears that he shed during the first days of his conversion whenever he heard church music.[74] Indeed in a previous passage of book nine he had described how powerfully the hymns and canticles of the church had moved his soul to devotion: While the sounds were entering his ears, truth was filling his heart, kindling his affections and causing him to shed tears of sorrow for sin.[75] Significantly, he concludes this passage with the unqualified sentiment: "And happy did I find myself therein."[76] When, moreover, he considers that by the delight of the ears weak minds may rise to a feeling of devotion, he is inclined to favor singing in the church; but this favorable opinion is full of vacillation.[77]

Next, Augustine considers concupiscence of the eyes of the flesh, which is a subdivision of concupiscence of the senses, and hence distinct from concupiscence of the eyes, which will be treated in the following paragraphs. Although it is natural for the eye to love fair and varied forms, the soul must not become immersed in corporeal beauty, but rather should turn to the God who

[74] See *Conf.*, 10, 33, 49. See also *ibid.*, 10, 33, 50: Aliquando autem hanc ipsam fallaciam inmoderatius cavens erro *nimia severitate* (italics mine), sed valde interdum ut melos omnes cantilenarum suavium, quibus Davidicum psalterium frequentatur ab auribus meis removeri velim, atque ipsius ecclesiae. Thus he admits his excessive severity, and then recalls the days of his first conversion: Verum tamen cum reminiscor lacrimas meas, quas fudi ad cantus ecclesiae in primordiis recuperatae fidei meae, et nunc ipsum quod moveor non cantu, sed rebus quae cantantur, cum liquida voce et convenientissima modulatione cantantur, magnam instituti hujus utilitatem rursus agnosco.

[75] See *ibid.*, 9, 6, 14.

[76] *Loc. cit.*: Et bene mihi erat cum eis.

[77] See *Conf.*, 10, 33, 50.

fashioned both eye and color.[78] As we have indicated already, the eyes can be a source of temptation, inasmuch as many things entice man to sin.[79] So much for the concupiscence of the eyes of the flesh.

Far more dangerous in the opinion of the Saint is concupiscence of the eyes in the Scriptural sense. The term must be carefully distinguished from the other forms of concupiscence. In the *Confessions* concupiscence of the flesh is concerned with the *pleasure* that one derives from diverse sense objects, whereas concupiscence of the eyes delights not in the pleasures of the flesh, but in making experiments through the flesh. The soul utilizes the senses of the body to exercise a certain vain and curious desire, which springs from the desire to know; and, since sight is the principal sense used in the attainment of such knowledge, this inordinate tendency is called by Scripture *concupiscentia oculorum* (I John 2:16).

Pleasure seeks objects that are beautiful, melodious, fragrant, and the like; but curiosity seeks the opposites, not for the sake of suffering annoyance, but out of the desire of undergoing "experiences." For this reason concupiscence of the eyes seeks to know even the *bitter* and the *deformed,* while concupiscence of the flesh seeks only the *pleasant.*[80]

The Saint gives several examples of this form of concupiscence.

---

[78] See *Conf.,* 10, 34, 51: Pulchras formas et varias, nitidos et amoenos colores amant oculi. Non teneant haec animam meam; teneat eam Deus, qui fecit haec bona quidem valde. See also *ibid.,* 4, 12, 18.

[79] See *supra,* ch. 2, 40-41. See also *Conf.,* 10, 34, 52.

[80] See *ibid.,* 10, 35, 54: Huc accedit alia forma temptationis multiplicius periculosa. Praeter enim concupiscentiam carnis, quae inest in delectatione omnium sensuum et voluptatum, . . . inest animae per eosdem sensus corporis quaedam non se oblectandi in carne, sed experiendi per carnem vana et curiosa cupiditas nomine cognitionis et scientiae palliata. Quae quoniam in appetitu noscendi est, oculi autem sunt ad noscendum in sensibus principes, *concupiscentia oculorum* (I John 2:16) eloquio divino adpellata est. . . . (55) Ex hoc autem evidentius discernitur, quid voluptatis, quid curiositatis agatur per sensus, quod voluptas pulchra, canora, suavia, sapida, lenia sectatur, curiositas autem etiam his contraria temptandi causa non ad subeundam molestiam, sed experiendi noscendique libidine. See also Wangnereck, *Confessionum,* 407.

He notes how a group of people will flock around a mangled carcass to fill their mind with the morbid sight. From this same disease of curiosity arises the interest of crowds at the exhibition of monstrosities in theatres; and for the same reason the magical arts are cultivated. In religion also signs and wonders are requested of God Himself, not by way of confirmation of a religious truth or mission, but simply from idle curiosity. This is *tentatio Dei,* the malice of which consists in demanding from God proofs for the Divine attributes of goodness and of wisdom and of others. It is always sinful to doubt about matters pertaining to the Divine perfections.[81]

In addition to these there are other petty and contemptible curiosities, from which the soul finds it difficult to escape. Such are more fittingly called *distractions.* Frequently and even daily we both are tempted and succumb to these trivialities. Among these minor distractions Augustine describes several, one of which is tinged with humor. Sometimes while sitting at home, his attention is drawn away by a spider entangling flies in her web. Then he complains that his life is full of similar meanderings from prayer.[82] Certainly these spontaneous flights of attention are not sinful, because they are not wilful.

Since the passion of grief bears a relationship to concupiscence, it will be worthwhile to analyze the various types of sorrow that are described in the *Confessions.* The first kind is related to stage plays and is really a form of pleasure. For while man does not wish to suffer himself, he takes pleasure in feeling sorry for others.[83] This in itself is not wrong, but it can be dangerous, because the spectator of such dramas may become so affected with the desire for the same sort of pleasure as the actors seek that he exposes his soul to the danger of sin.

This reflection of Saint Augustine is deduced from his own experience during his adolescent days in Carthage. There he became infatuated with stage plays. He allowed himself to rejoice

---

[81] See *Conf.*, 10, 35, 55. See also S.T., 2-2, 97, 2: Ignorare autem vel dubitare de his quae pertinent ad Dei perfectionem est peccatum.

[82] See *ibid.*, 10, 35, 57.

[83] See *ibid.*, 3, 2, 2.

with illicit lovers in their sinful enjoyment of one another, and to sorrow with them when they were separated from each other. He fell into evil friendships, and this led him to conclude that the love of vain griefs in the theatre may lead to evil friendships. Even a good friendship may be contaminated by the lust approved on the stage.[84] Indeed it may be said that "they are the most affected by those things, who are the least free from such passions as are there expressed."[85]

Augustine, moreover, affirms that the sort of sympathy aroused in the audience by tragic dramas is not true mercy, but a sort of sterile and vicious pity. He argues that when a man suffers in his own person, it is called misery; but when he compassionates others, then it is called mercy. Now, in the theatre the spectator is not called upon to relieve the sorrow of another, but merely to grieve; and the greater the grief aroused, the greater the play is considered.[86] Thus, such vicarious emotions bring pleasure to the spectator rather than an attitude of mercy towards his neighbor; and in this respect the feeling is sterile of good works.

In opposition to such pity the Saint counsels that one should commiserate him who rejoices in his wickedness rather than sympathize with him who *is thought* to suffer a hardship in the loss of some pernicious pleasure. Such is true mercy, but in it grief finds no delight. One finds the attribute of mercy in its purity when he turns to God; for, while God loves souls far more purely than we, He takes pity upon them without the passion of sorrow. From this Augustine concludes that some sorrow may be allowed, but none sought purely for its own sake, inasmuch as true pity or mercy is caused by our neighbor's misfortune; and, were it possible, it would prefer that there were no misfortune over which to grieve.[87]

---

[84] See *ibid.,* 3, 2, 3. See also Campbell and McGuire, *The Confessions of St. Augustine,* 101, n. 13, where the authors point out that the stage plays seen by the youthful Augustine dealt almost exclusively with immoral love themes.

[85] *Ibid.,* 3, 2, 2: Nam eo magis eis movetur quisque, quo minus a talibus affectibus sanus est.

[86] See *loc. cit.*

[87] See *ibid.,* 3, 2, 3. See also *ibid.,* 10, 1, 1.

Finally, he points out that the love of griefs was a foul disease out of which came all manner of moral infection.[88] In his experience this tendency was a source of pleasure, closely associated with carnal concupiscence. In the light of his own experience his observations on the morality of vicarious grief should be evaluated. First, he points out how the wrong kind of sorrow can lead to dangerous and evil friendships; then, he draws a sharp distinction between vicious pity and true mercy; and, finally, he states that sorrow and grief may be allowed, provided one is interested in the true welfare of his neighbor.

Besides vicarious grief the *Confessions* consider also personal sorrow. Already we have noted the morbid grief that overwhelmed the adolescent Augustine upon the death of his intimate friend. It was morbid and immoderate, because it sprang from an inordinate friendship, and it possessed the quality of despair.[89] Now we shall consider the reaction of St. Augustine to the death of his mother. It seems that his attitude bordered on the rigorous; and in his retrospective analysis of his feelings on that occasion he insinuates that he placed too great a strain upon the weakness of human nature.

As soon as his mother died, a torrent of emotion surged within him, but he suppressed it, because he believed that his mother was now happy in heaven, and hence tears would be out of place. He even bade his son cease weeping. And so everyone went to and from the grave without tears. All this was too much for Augustine; and the day after the burial he broke down and wept freely. He realized then that it was asking too much of human nature to suppress tears at a mother's passing. Thus, as he looks back at himself, he makes several profitable observations.

He points out that he allowed himself to be annoyed by the realization that grief had such power over him on this loss. He was vexed at himself, because he had given in to the weakness of tears.[90] It seems as if he had expected God to give him complete

---

[88] See *ibid.*, 3, 2, 4.

[89] See *supra*, ch. 2, 35-37.

[90] See *Conf.*, 9, 12, 31-32. See also *ibid.*, 9, 12, 33: Et libuit flere in conspectu tuo de illa et pro illa, de me et pro me. Et dimisi lacrimas, quas continebam, ut effluerent quantum vellent, substernens eas cordi meo et requievit in eis, quoniam ibi erant aures tuae.

control over his feelings, and God, in turn, had allowed him to be disturbed by a double sorrow to teach him a lesson in the acceptance of human weakness—if what is perfectly lawful may be termed a "weakness." Thus he underwent the natural sorrow of a son, and the needless grief of one who is unwilling to admit the goodness of tears upon the death of one dearly beloved.

Even as bishop, moreover, he is doubtful whether it was right or wrong for him to weep over his mother. He feels that some of his readers may consider his grief sinful, but he disposes of this moral nuance (at least for *him* it was a problem) by recommending himself to the Divine Indulgence. It is better to seek the mercy of God in such trivial human frailties than to become scrupulous about them. In conclusion, man should accept his need to express grief as one of the limitations of his nature, practicing the virtue of humility, which acquiesces in its own weakness.[91]

---

[91] See *ibid.*, 9, 13, 34. In contrast to St. Augustine, who shed no tears on the day of his mother's funeral, St. Francis de Sales gave free course to his tears, as soon as he had closed his mother's eyes. Yet his grief contained no element of bitterness, but was resigned to the will of God. Thus, in a letter written to St. Jane de Chantal shortly after the death of his mother (*Oeuvres de saint François de Sales,* Annecy: Abry, 1906: 14.261-4) the Saint wrote: Confessons . . . que Dieu est bon et que sa miséricorde est à l'éternité. . . . Et pour moy, je confesse, ma Fille, que j'ay eü un grand ressentiment de cette séparation (car c'est la confession que je doy faire de ma foiblesse, apres que j'ay fait celle de la bonté divine); mais neanmoins, ma Fille, ça esté un ressentiment tranquille, quoy que vif. . . . Le coeur m'enfla fort et pleuray sur cette bonne mere plus que je n'avois fait des que je suis d'Eglise; mais ce fut sans amertume spirituelle, grâces a Dieu. . . .

Thus he wept freely. Again, in the same letter he referred to the death of Madame de Chantal's nine year old daughter, Charlotte, in a similar vein: Nostre pauvre petite Charlotte est bienheureuse d'estre sortie de la terre avant qu'elle l'eut bonnement touchée. Helas! il la failloit neanmoins bien un peu pleurer, car n'avons nous pas un coeur humain et un naturel sensible? Pourquoy non pleurer un peu sur nos trepassés, puisque l'Esprit de Dieu non seulement le nous permet, mais nous y semont.

On the occasion of his sister's death, moreover, he wrote to the same Saint (*op. cit.,* 13.330): Je suis tant homme que rien plus. Mon coeur s'est attrendri plusque je n'eusse jamais pensé.

In short, he shed tears upon the deaths of his dear ones, and he also bade

In the aspects of concupiscence that we have noted already, we have seen that the pleasures of concupiscence have a twofold limitation: They are transient, and they are partial, that is, they do not satisfy the whole man, but merely one specific faculty. Again, we have observed that rationalization is very often the facade behind which concupiscence hides, and that fear also has an influence in the reluctance of the individual to give up pleasures that have been found sweet.[92] The most important relationship of concupiscence, however, has not been considered so far, namely, the role of such in conflict of will, or, as it is usually called—weakness of will.

Weakness of will is one of the obstacles on the road to God. Since we shall consider it immediately in the following pages, we shall discuss also how concupiscence weakens the will. Finally, we shall point out some of the remedies mentioned by St. Augustine in his *Confessions* for the conquest of concupiscence and the enthronement of the will as the *actual* ruler of man's actions.

C. DIVISION OF WILL

In considering the problem of will in the *Confessions* one must keep in mind the Manichean background of Augustine. The Manicheans taught the convenient doctrine that in man, as in the universe at large, two fundamental principles were struggling for supremacy. One principle was good, and the other was evil; and it was the evil principle that gave rise to the bad actions of an individual. Thus this doctrine provided an escape from moral responsibility, since the individual could say that his "evil nature" had overwhelmed his better nature. This was wilful blindness.[93]

In his thirty-first year Augustine was struggling to find the truth in this matter. Now he knew at least that he had a will; and

---

others in similar circumstances to do likewise, because such sorrow is in accordance with God's will. See also Burton, *Life of St. Francis de Sales* (London: Burns, Oates, and Washbourne, 1925), 301-302, 458-459, 503-504.

[92] See *supra,* ch. 1, 6, n. 22; *supra,* ch. 3, 83-84. For a general discussion of concupiscence in all the works of St. Augustine see Mausbach, *Die Ethik des heiligen Augustinus,* 2.157-207.

[93] See *supra,* ch. 3, 63-64; 71-75. See also Bourke, *Quest of Wisdom,* 18-19.

it became clearer to him that his own will was the cause of his sins. Accepting the fact of volition, as he accepted the fact of his own existence, he knew that when he did wrong or right, it was he who did it, and no foreign substance. Yet he hesitated to draw the conclusion that man's free will was the cause of sin, because he thought it contradicted the truth of Divine Goodness.[94]

Only after he had arrived at the notion of the spirituality of God and of the privative nature of evil would he be able to see clearly that the will of man is the cause of sin. At this period, however, he regarded evil as a physical entity, and so he could not understand how an all-good God would create evil or corruption. After he had arisen from these errors, he formulated an argument to explain that man's will is the cause of sin. This argument may be stated as follows: God alone is incorruptible, inviolable and immutable. But every creature is corruptible, violable and mutable by the very limitations of its nature, and the will, as a created faculty, is mutable and violable. Therefore, it can sin, and it can be subject to forces that it does not want.

With reference to God the Saint argues further: Since God is immutable, then his will cannot slip into evil; and since He is inviolable, He cannot be subjected to force, either by another, because He is stronger than all (against the Manichean doctrine), or by Himself, since the power of God is the will of God, so that He does not use His power against His will. Hence, not the will of God, but the will of man is the cause of sin.[95]

This objective argument is reenforced by another argument of an introspective character, which is found scattered through several passages of the *Confessions*. The Saint points out that

---

[94] See *Conf.*, 5, 10, 18. See also *ibid.*, 7, 3, 5. See also Mausbach, *op. cit.*, 2.378.

[95] See *Conf.*, 7, 4, 6: Nullo enim prorsus violat corruptio Deum nostrum, nulla voluntate, nulla necessitate, nullo inproviso casu, quoniam ipse est Deus et quod sibi vult, bonum est, et ipse est idem bonum; corrumpi autem non est bonum. Nec cogeris invitus ad aliquid, quia voluntas tua non est major quam potentia tua. . . . Voluntas enim et potentia Dei Deus ipse est. Quid inprovisum tibi, qui nosti omnia? . . . Et ut quid multa dicimus, cur non sit corruptibilis substantia, quae Deus est quando si hoc esset, non esset Deus? See also Wangnereck, *Confessionum*, 222-223, n. 2.

during his Manichean darkness he was accustomed to accuse the foreign substance within him of his sins, but in truth he admits that it was completely himself. Again, as he drew nearer to the truth, he saw that he alone was responsible for his deliberate actions.[96] Finally, during the spiritual crisis in the garden immediately before his conversion, he saw how unreasonable was the Manichean doctrine that two wills, one good and one bad, fought for supremacy within man. He saw then that it was not a question of conflicting *wills,* but rather of conflicting *desires,* within the *one* soul of man. It would be ridiculous to assign a will to each variant desire of the soul of man; for there is but one soul in man, having one will, which, however, can be attracted by many different objects and so tormented by many conflicting desires.[97]

---

[96] See *Conf.*, 5, 10, 18. See also *ibid.*, 7, 3, 4-5.

[97] See *Conf.*, 8, 10, 23-24: Nam si tot sunt contrariae naturae, quot voluntates sibi resistunt, non jam duae, sed plures erunt. Si deliberet quisquam utrum ad conventiculum eorum pergat an ad theatrum, clamant isti: 'Ecce duae naturae, una bona hac ducit, altera mala illac redducit. Nam unde ista cunctatio sibimet adversantium voluntatum?' Ego autem dico ambas malas, et quae ad illos ducit et quae ad theatrum redducit. Sed non credunt nisi bonam esse qua itur ad eos. Quid? Si ergo quisquam noster deliberet et secum altercantibus duabus voluntatibus fluctuet, utrum ad theatrum pergat an ad ecclesiam nostram, nonne et isti quid respondeant fluctuabunt? Aut enim fatebuntur, quod nolunt, bona voluntate pergi in ecclesiam nostram, . . , aut duas malas naturas et duas malas mentes in uno homine confligere putabunt, et non erit verum quod solent dicere, unam bonam, alteram malam, aut convertentur ad verum, et non negabunt, *cum quisque deliberat animam unam diversis voluntatibus aestuare* (italics mine). . . . (24) Si ergo pariter delectent omnia simulque uno tempore, nonne diversae voluntates distendunt cor hominis, dum deliberatur quid potissimum arripiamus? Et omnes bonae sunt et certant secum, donec eligatur unum, quo feriatur tota voluntas una, quae in plures dividebatur. Ita etiam cum aeternitas delectat superius et temporalis boni voluptas retentat inferius, *eadem anima est non tola voluntate illud aut hoc volens* (italics mine) et ideo discerpitur gravi molestia, dum illud veritate praeponit, hoc familiaritate non ponit. See also Bourke, *op. cit.*, 64: The Manichean theory that two wills, one good and one bad, struggled within man, Augustine saw in all its unreasonableness. There were frequently more than two conflicting desires in the mind of man. To assign a will to every variant type of desire would mean a ridiculous pluralization of the faculty of choice. He saw clearly that there was but one soul in man, that it had but one will, which could be used in various ways.

This argument is directed against the Manichean heresy that there are as many contrary natures in man as there are conflicting wills. If this were so, then man would have many natures within himself; but, in reality, there is no multiplication of natures or of wills. If there is conflict within man, it occurs because at one and the same time the will may be attracted by two or more conflicting objects. Thus the will is, as it were, divided until it makes its decision and is drawn to the object of its choice.

To this question of divided will the Saint reverts again and again. Here we shall discuss some of the more important passages. It will be recalled that the effects of the Manichean heresy upon the moral life of Augustine were tremendous; but now it may be noted that even after truth was in his mind, there still remained an hiatus between the knowledge of virtue and its practice. For example, on the brink of conversion he desired not greater certitude concerning God, but more stability in the pursuit of Him.[98] He knew what he ought to do, but he hesitated in the fear that the new way of following Christ might prove too arduous for one who had been accustomed to gratify his sensual appetites. His affections needed purification now that his mind had received light: "But, as touching my temporal life, all things were still unresolved, and my heart was yet to be delivered more fully from the old leaven. The Way, the Saviour of the world, did please me well, but I could not find it in my heart to follow it through the strait gate."[99]

Although he was displeased with himself, he continued to live in carnal pleasure, considering himself as too weak to embrace the higher life of celibacy. Very aptly he compares his actions before his conversion to those of one awakening from sleep. Such a one desires to awake, since he knows that waking is better than sleeping; but he yields to drowsiness and falls asleep again. Although

---

[98] See *Conf.*, 8, 1, 1: Nec certior de te, sed stabilior in te esse cupiebam.

[99] *Loc. cit.*: De mea vero temporali vita nutabant omnia et mundandum erat cor a fermento veteri (I Cor. 5:7 ff.); et placebat via, ipse salvator, et ire per ejus angustias adhuc pigebat. See also Bourke, *Quest of Wisdom,* 66, n. 49: It must be emphasized that this conversion in the garden was a matter of the will and not of the intellect; Boyer, *Christianisme et Néo-Platonisme . . . ,* 72: C'est la vraie conversion, celle du coeur.

he is displeased with himself, yet he yields to the sleep. So also was it with Augustine, who was convinced that it was much better for him to dedicate himself to God rather than to indulge his own cupidity.[100] Thus pleasure kept him enslaved; and he could not form the resolution to do what he knew he should do. What was lacking, however, was not strength of will but PURPOSE.

This is what the Saint teaches in one of the most penetrating analyses of the will in literature. In ordinary usage when one speaks of conflict within man the term is understood to mean the flesh against the spirit. Although Augustine does speak of this struggle, he treats another division of man, which is just as fierce, namely, the battle of spirit against spirit. This latter conflict is linked with the failure to integrate one's actions under one dominant aim or purpose. For the sake of order we shall consider first the conflict between the flesh and the spirit, which the *Confessions* view in the light of St. Paul. The Saint quotes the Apostle of the Gentiles about the law of God according to the inner man in conflict with that other law in his members drawing him down to sins of the flesh. Following St. Paul, he teaches that only the grace of Christ can overcome the rebellious tendencies of the flesh.[101]

It must be noted, moreover, that the struggle between the flesh and the spirit involves another element, which we shall consider later in this section, namely, the question of habit. Speaking of the period when he had begun to battle against his habit of concupiscence, he writes:

> But the new will which I now began to have to serve thee for thyself and to enjoy thee, O God, who art our only certain joy, was not able as yet to master that other, which had been established by so long continuance. Thus did my two wills, one old and another new, one carnal

---

[100] See *Conf.*, 8, 1, 2. See also *Conf.*, 8, 5, 12.

[101] See *ibid.*, 7, 21, 27: Etsi condelectetur homo *legi Dei secundum interiorem hominem,* quid faciet de *alia lege in membris suis repugnante legi mentis* suae et *se captivum ducente in lege peccati, quae est in membris ejus?* (Rom. 7:22 ff.) . . . *Quis* eum *liberabit de corpore mortis hujus nisi gratia tua per Jesum Christum Dominum nostrum?* (Rom. 7:24 ff.) . . .

> and the other spiritual, fight one against the other, and by their discord did they drag my soul asunder.[102]

One example of this type of struggle will be sufficient to show how different it is from that described in chapters eight and nine of book eight, where the Saint portrays graphically the battle of spirit against spirit. It will be recalled that after the story of Pontitianus Augustine had entered profoundly into himself and remonstrated with himself for his delay in embracing a Christian way of life. Then he did not know the root of his procrastination, but, as he wrote the *Confessions,* he put his finger on the sore spot and diagnosed it *as a divided and therefore maimed will,* for a divided will leaves one in the state of indecision and inaction, such as he was still in.[103]

---

[102] *Ibid.,* 8, 5, 10: Voluntas autem nova, quae mihi esse coeperat, ut te gratis colere fruique te vellem, Deus, sola certa jucunditas, nondum erat idonea ad superandam priorem vetustate roboratam. Ita duae voluntates meae, una vetus, alia nova, illa carnalis, illa spiritalis, confligebant inter se atque discordando dissipabant animam meam.

[103] See *ibid.,* 8, 8, 19: Ego fremebam spiritu indignans indignatione turbulentissima, quod non irem in placitum et pactum tecum, Deus meus, in quod eundum esse omnia ossa mea clamabant et in coelum tollebant laudibus: et non illuc ibatur navibus aut quadrigis aut pedibus, quantum saltem de domo in eum locum ieram, ubi sedebamus. Nam non solum ire verum etiam pervenire illuc nihil erat aliud quam velle ire, sed *velle fortiter et integre, non semisauciam hac atque hac versare et jactare voluntatem parte adsurgente cum alia parte cadente luctantem* (italics mine).

See also Bruno Switalski, *Plotinus and the Ethics of St. Augustine,* 96-97, where the author holds that *Conf.,* 8, 8, 19, is an almost literal citation from the *Enneads of Plotinus*: In the *Enneads* we find similar expressions. To the question as to what way and what flight leads to the heavenly "fatherland" Plotinus answers that for this journey neither feet which transfer us from one land to another nor vehicles nor ships are needed, but that which is really necessary are efforts in order to acquire virtue. . . . There is no doubt that Augustine makes here an allusion to the *Enneads.* . . . And the ideas of Plotinus, treated at some length in this place, are condensed by St. Augustine into the concise phrase: "Velle ire, sed velle fortiter et integre."

With this opinion, which is based upon the comparison of the *words* of the respective texts of St. Augustine and Plotinus, Henry (*Plotin et l'Occident,* 110 ff.) is in only *partial* agreement. He points out that the general

The Saint continues to explain that willing and doing are so intimately linked that when one wills something resolutely, it is the beginning of doing. They are but two different aspects of one and the same human act. Precisely in the same area is the difficulty. The body obeys more easily the weakest nod of the soul and moves one of its limbs than the will carries out its own command. Why is this so? Why does the will have immediate power over bodily members, and not over its very self? Again, the answer is the same. What the mind commands itself to do is not done, because it does not command it *entirely*. At the same time part of its energy is being absorbed by some other object, and this prevents the execution of the command.[104]

When the will is unified, then to will the command is the same thing as to command. The fact of indecision, partly to will some-

---

movement of the thought of *Conf.*, 8, 8, 19, and *Enneads*, 1, 6, 8, is the same. Both are trying to find a spiritual pathway leading to God. But he adds: Mais comme le christianisme conquérant et presque angoissé d'Augustin diffère du rationalisme paisible et superbe de Plotin! . . . Pour l'un, il suffit de voir; pour l'autre, il faut vouloir. Entre Augustin et Plotin il y a le dogme chrétien du péché originel. *Semisauciam* est assurément un mot que Plotin n'aurait pas compris. Thus, according to Henry, St. Augustine gives to the words of Plotinus a different spirit—a Christian interpretation.

[104] See *Conf.*, 8, 8, 20: Tam multa ergo feci, ubi non hoc erat velle quod posse: et non faciebam quod et inconparabili affectu amplius mihi placebat et mox, ut vellem, possem, quia mox, *ut vellem, utique vellem* (italics mine). Ibi enim facultas ea, quae voluntas, et ipsum velle jam facere erat; et tamen non fiebat; faciliusque obtemperabat corpus tenuissimae voluntati animae, ut ad nutum membra moverentur, quam ipsa sibi anima ad voluntatem suam magnam in sola voluntate perficiendam. See also *ibid.*, 8, 9, 21: Unde hoc monstrum? . . . Imperat animus corpori, et paretur statim: imperat animus sibi, et resistitur. Imperat animus, ut moveatur manus, et tanta est facilitas ut vix a servitio discernatur imperium: et animus animus est, manus autem corpus est. Imperat animus, ut velit animus, nec alter est nec facit tamen. Unde hoc monstrum? . . . Imperat, inquam, ut velit qui non imperaret nisi vellet, et non facit quod imperat. Sed non ex toto vult: non ergo ex toto imperat. Nam in tantum imperat, in quantum vult, et in tantum non fit quod imperat, in quantum non vult, quoniam voluntas imperat, ut sit voluntas, nec alia, sed ipsa. Non itaque plena imperat; ideo non est quod imperat. Nam si plena esset, nec imperaret ut esset, quia jam esset.

thing, partly not to will it, is a disease of the mind.[105] The will is drawn in contrary directions at one and the same time. While the goal of truth pulls it upwards, the goal of inveterate carnal pleasure drags it downwards; the consequence is indecision. More accurately it may be said that one is attracted by contrary objects, but does not will either one. Thus also two partial wills are equivalent to *no* will. No matter how much an individual deliberates, he remains in a moral rut, as long as he forms no resolute purpose to amendment.

Augustine points to his own delay as an example of the effects of a divided will in the practical moral life. Since he willed not entirely, he delayed his conversion and remained in sin. One may note in this analysis of his hesitancy another common misconception exposed. He shows that weakness of will is really an illusion. The will is not weak or strong, but rather divided or unified. It is divided when it is drawn in contrary directions by contrary motives; and it is unified when it concentrates on its goal with singleness of purpose.

It is to be noted, moreover, that Augustine does not blame his "weakness of will" on any foreign intangible within himself, but assumes complete responsibility for the deliberate actions of his own person:

> Was it not I that willed, was it not I that could not will, when I was deliberating if I should serve the Lord, my

---

[105] See *loc. cit.*: Non igitur monstrum partim velle, partim nolle, sed aegritudo animi est, quia non totus assurgit veritate sublevatus, consuetudine praegravatus. Et ideo sunt duae voluntates, quia una earum tota non est et hoc adest alteri, quod deest alteri. See also Mausbach, *op. cit.*, 2.177, where he cites, *Conf.*, 8, 9, 21, as an example of the conflict *within the will itself*: Im Willen selbst herrschte Widerspruch, indem er sich gebot zu wollen und doch nicht wollte; eine Krankheit und Halbheit, indem er nicht ganz dem Zuge zur Wahrheit folgte, sondern durch schlechte Gewohnheiten sich am Boden festhalten liess. See also Rudolf Allers, *Self Improvement* (New York: Benziger, 1939), who quotes the same passage as Mausbach and notes that real willing and doing are but two sides of one and the same human act and that "weakness of will is in truth an illusion or self-deception of the mind, resulting from man's striving for two—or even more—goals at the same time; what is called weakness of will is not due so much to lack of energy as to lack of unity of the will. The trouble lies more with purpose than with will" (pp. 13-15).

> God, as I had long designed to do? Truly it was I; yet I could not fully will, or fully not will. Therefore did I strive with myself, and by myself was I dissipated, and this very dissipation of me did happen to me against my will. Yet this did not show forth the nature of a second mind, but the punishment of my own mind.[106]

Since moral acts, human acts, are essentially acts of the will, one may draw from the penetrating analysis of the will in the *Confessions* conclusions for the practical moral order. So far it has been noted that the *Confessions* discuss not only the conflict between the flesh and the spirit but also the battle between the spirit and the spirit. In this latter conflict, moreover, the will attempts to follow several conflicting goals at one and the same time. The consequence is indecision and so-called weakness of will. The remedy is concentration of the will on one goal—to the exclusion of incompatible aims. Therefore, the solution to the problem of divided will is a singleness of purpose that concentrates all the faculties of the soul—the whole person—on doing the will of God in all things in order to unite oneself with God.

The very formation and accomplishment of such a resolution is itself a gift of Divine grace, as the Saint attests: "But thou, O lord, are gracious and merciful, and thy right hand had respect unto the profoundness of my death, and from the bottom of my heart it drew forth that huge bulk of corruption. And this deliverance, what was it, but that I willed not any more that which I was wont to will, and began to will that which thou willest."[107] Hence, the will finds strength to pursue the object of its happiness as soon as it cooperates with Divine grace and forms the wholehearted and efficacious resolution to put the goal of its happiness—God—*first* in its scale of values.

[106] *Conf.*, 8, 10, 22: Ego, cum deliberabam, ut servirem Domino Deo meo, sicut diu disposueram, ego eram, qui volebam, ego qui nolebam; ego eram. Nec plene volebam, nec plene nolebam. Ideo mecum contendebam et dissipabar a me ipso, et ipsa dissipatio me invito quidem fiebat, nec tamen ostendebat naturam mentis alienae, sed poenam meae.

[107] *Ibid.*, 9, 1, 1,: Tu autem, Domine, bonus et misericors et dextera tua respiciens profunditatem mortis meae et a fundo cordis mei exhauriens abyssum corruptionis. Et hoc erat totum nolle, quod volebam, et velle, quod volebas.

"Velle fortiter et integre" is the Saint's expression for such a resolution, which God rewards by drawing the will of the person through supernatural graces. After his conversion, therefore, the will of St. Augustine was, as it were, magnetized by the Divine Beauty, so that he could exclaim that God was sweeter than all earthly pleasure.[108] God compensated him beyond measure for the renunciation of worldly pleasures—pleasures without which formerly he had feared that he could not live.

It is clear then that cooperation with Divine grace will bring singleness of aim or unity of will into the life of others afflicted with the same sort of indecision as was St. Augustine. God can cause men to be ravished by Divine Beauty and to be filled with the desire of union with Divinity. Whenever this happens the will is no longer forcibly drawn by conflicting values of earth.

D. OTHER ASPECTS OF WILL

Now it remains to consider several other aspects of will discussed in the *Confessions*. The first is the connection between the rebellion within man and original sin, to which the Saint makes several brief references. In his investigation into the cause of sin before his conversion Augustine had observed that certain motions took place in him, but *against* his will. These he regarded as punishment for sin rather than actual sins: "But whatsoever I did unwillingly, I saw that I did suffer rather than do, and I esteemed that not to be a fault but a punishment."[109] Here "unwillingly" (*invitus*) may refer to the involuntary motions of concupiscence, whose rebellion is part of the punishment of original sin. In Pauline language they are the *fomes peccati* (Rom. 7:17)

---

[108] See *loc. cit.*: Et de quo imo altoque secreto evocatum est in momento liberum arbitrium meum, quo subderem cervicem leni jugo tuo et umeros levi sarcinae tuae, Christe Jesus, . . ? Quam suave mihi subito factum est carere suavitatibus nugarum, et quas amittere metus fuerat, jam dimittere gaudium erat. See also *supra,* ch. 1, 6.

[109] *Conf.,* 7, 3, 5: Quod autem invitus facerem, pati me potius quam facere videbam et id non culpam sed poenam esse judicabam.

within us. To feel such without consenting to them is a punishment for original sin rather than an actual sin.[110]

Again, the Saint implies that division of will, "monstrum" and "aegritudo animi," as he graphically describes it, is the common penalty of the sin of Adam.[111] In his description of his infancy, moreover, he quotes Psalm Fifty to the effect that he was born in sin, and then describes the perversity of infant behavior. He recalls the inordinate motions of anger and of jealousy, and he condemns them by the name of sin in the loose sense. Although he does not impute responsibility to these infant tendencies, he does stress the truth that they are the *beginnings* of bad habits. Sagely he concludes that the "innocence" of the infant consists—not in these inordinate tendencies—but in its weakness. In short, he insists that even infants betray the effects of Adam's sin.[112]

---

[110] See Wangnereck, *Confessionum,* 220, n. 2: 'Quod autem invitus facerem.' Significat motus concupiscentiae, ejusque rebellionem esse poenam peccati originalis, quos motus nos non operamur, sed *habitans in nobis peccatum,* sive potius *fomes peccati* (Rom. 7:17), quos sentire nec consentire poena est, non culpa.

[111] See *Conf.*, 8, 9, 21: Unde hoc monstrum? . . . Et interrogem si forte mihi respondere possint latebrae poenarum hominum et tenebrosissimae contritiones filiorum Adam. See also *ibid.*, 8, 10, 22: Et ideo non jam ego operabar illam, *sed quod habitat in me peccatum* (Rom. 7:17) de supplicio liberioris peccati. quia eram filius Adam. In both these passages the Saint considers division of will as a penalty for original sin, but at the same time he insists upon the *responsibility* of the person whose will is divided. The sins of the sons of Adam are freely willed, even though not as freely committed as that of Adam. See also *Conf.,* 7, 3, 5.

[112] See *ibid.,* 1, 7, 11-12: Quis me commemorat peccatum infantiae meae? . . . Tunc ergo reprehendenda faciebam, sed quia reprehendentem intellegere non poteram, nec mos reprehendi me nec ratio sinebat. . . . An pro tempore etiam illa bona erant, flendo petere etiam quod noxie daretur, indignari acriter non subjectis hominibus liberis et majoribus hisque, a quibus genitus est, multisque praeterea prudentioribus non ad nutum voluntatis obtemperantibus feriendo nocere niti quantum potest, quia non oboeditur imperiis, quibus perniciose oboediretur? *Ita imbecillitas membrorum infantilium innocens est, non animus infantium* (italics mine). Vidi ego et expertus sum zelantem parvulum: nondum loquebatur et intuebatur pallidus amaro aspectu conlactaneum suum. . . . (12) Quod si *et in iniquitate conceptus sum et in peccatis mater mea me in utero aluit* (Ps. 50:7), . . . ubi aut quando

Another important aspect of will is habit in the sense of a regular pattern of activity that in some way depends upon the will, and that can be extirpated by the will, though sometimes with great difficulty. According to its basic meaning, the term *habit* may be used with reference to either good actions (virtue) or to evil actions (vice), but inasmuch as the *Confessions* are concerned with the habits of concupiscence and of obstinacy, we shall use the term *habit* in this section to denote a sinful pattern of activity.

In a classic passage Augustine describes his enslavement in the habit of impurity, comparing the formation of the habit to a chain, which, forged, link by link, finally enslaves the will of its maker:

> For this it was whereunto I did aspire, though I was bound as yet, albeit not with a chain of iron, but only with the iron chain of mine untoward will. Mine enemy made fast this will of mine, and thereof did he forge the chain which bound me. For through the perverseness of our affection groweth lust, and by yielding often to that lust we make a custom, and by not opposing this custom we grow subject to a kind of necessity. By these links fastened one within the other—for the which reason I have called it a chain—did bitter servitude hold me bound.[113]

---

innocens fui? See also Wangnereck, *op. cit.*, 13, n. 2, where the author explains the Saint's use of the expression "peccatum infantiae meae, etc." Although the Saint uses the term sin to condemn inordinate motions of anger or of jealousy, such do not fulfill the proper concept of sin, since they lack both reason and free will. They are no more sinful than the inordinate desires of dreamers (dormientes). Thus, nowhere else in his works does the Saint use the term *peccatum* when referring to similar actions of infants. Here it is clear that the Saint is speaking of one of the effects of original sin found in all infants. In this loose sense the infant is said to sin in his actions, and in another sense also, inasmuch as these tendencies mature into bad habits unless they are rooted up as soon as possible.

[113] *Conf.*, 8, 5, 10: Cui rei ego suspirabam ligatus non ferro alieno, sed mea ferrea voluntate. Velle meum tenebat inimicus et inde mihi catenam fecerat et constrinxerat me. Quippe voluntate perversa facta est libido, et dum servitur libidini, facta est consuetudo, et dum consuetudini non resistitur, facta est necessitas. Quibus quasi ansulis sibimet innexis—unde catenam appellavi—tenebat me obstrictum dura servitus.

One may discern four key links in this moral chain: (1) *perverse will.* This is found in the first *deliberate* act of impurity, which is primarily a rebellion of the spirit against the law of God. It is the basic deordination of the will from its *summum bonum,* God, that gives rise to the consequent rebellion of the flesh against the spirit, and such disobedience to God's law opens the way for the next stage, namely, (2) *libido or perverted lust.* The initial pleasure of lust stimulates and excites the individual to seek the same pleasure again, and with repetition comes the third stage: (3) *consuetudo,* by which the soul is drawn powerfully to the vice that it has sought frequently. Thus, an evil habit is formed from continued licence; and, as this habit becomes more deeply entrenched, the fourth stage begins, and this may be termed (4) *necessity.* Just as a chain is fashioned from the individual links, so is the will entangled by *repeated* acts of impurity until the individual believes that he *must* have the pleasure that comes from the operation of the habit. Consequently, he despairs of his ability to resist its violence and yields to its impulses, as if unavoidable.[114]

One notes also the element of Divine *punishment* in the consummate development of the vice, for the will that had abused its liberty in licentiousness becomes the slave of the very vice it had sought out.[115] If one is searching for concrete exemplification

[114] See Mausbach, *Die Ethik des heiligen Augustinus,* 2.199. See also Wangnereck, *op. cit.,* 278; B. Roland-Gosselin, *La morale de saint Augustin,* 115-117; S.T., 2-2, 142, 2: . . . aliquid dicitur esse puerile . . . secundum quandam similitudinem. . . . Peccatum enim intemperantiae est peccatum superfluae concupiscentiae. . . . Puer autem non attendit ad ordinem rationis; et similiter concupiscentiae non audit rationem, . . . ; secundo, conveniunt quantum ad eventum. Puer enim, si suae voluntati dimittatur crevit in propria voluntate. . . . Ita etiam et concupiscentiae, si ei satisfaciat major robur accipit. Unde Augustinus dicit: 'Dum servitur libidini, facta est consuetudo, et cum consuetudini non resistitur, facta est necessitas.' Thus, following St. Augustine, the Angelic Doctor shows that the habit of concupiscence has its genesis in the *childish* tendency of self-indulgence. Both the child and concupiscence grow stronger in self-will with each gratification.

[115] See *De lib. arbit.,* 3, 18, 52 (ML, 32.1296): Illa est enim peccati poena justissima, ut amittat quisque quo bene uti noluit, cum sine ulla posset difficultate, si vellet. Id est autem ut qui sciens recte non facit amittat scire quid rectum sit; et qui recte facere, cum posset, noluit, amittat posse cum velit.

of this punishment, he will find it in the many addicts of impure habits. The same truths hold with equal force in regard to the formation of the habit of drunkenness. In short, the guilt of such *habitual* sins is the culpability of forming the habit.

Since the genesis of a habit is a dynamic process of the whole person in the concrete circumstances of life, it involves more than merely volitive elements. Thus, in a brilliant analysis of the habit of lust in the early life of Augustine, Wangnereck lists, among others, the following factors: the reading of obscene poets, the bad example of vain men, the period of idleness from school during Augustine's sixteenth year, depraved companionship, and the vanity of his parents in overestimating pagan learning.[116]

Closely related to habit formation is the question of responsibility, with reference to which one may distinguish three general stages in the life of the Saint: (1) the period during which he committed sins of impurity without any struggle against them; (2) the period at Milan during which he was struggling against this vice, but still yielded to it; and (3) the period after his conversion and Baptism, which is marked by complete repudiation of the habit on the part of the will.

Concerning sins of impurity committed during the first period it may be said that he incurred the guilt of all those impure movements flowing from the habit, because he willed their causes in the development of the habit.

In regard to the second stage, the time when he was approaching the Faith, it may be stated that his guilt was not so great as during the first period. Now he had begun to battle against the vice, but rather inefficaciously, as the violence of the habit still drew the consent of his will. As he himself says, "But the new will which I now began to have to serve thee for thyself and to enjoy thee, O God . . . was not able as yet to master that other, which had been established by so long continuance."[117]

For this yielding he admits responsibility, but he feels that he is not as responsible now as he had been formerly. True, he was

---

[116] See Wangnereck, *op. cit.,* 50, n. 3.

[117] *Conf.,* 8, 5, 10: Voluntas autem nova, quae mihi esse coeperat, ut te gratis colere fruique te vellem, Deus, . . . nondum erat idonea ad superandam priorem vestustate roboratam.

responsible for the old will, because he had allowed it to gain control over him. His former will had led him into a situation which his present will did not want. Now he felt that he was more himself in his higher will, of which he approved, than in his lower will, of which he disapproved. Still, he had not yet brought unity into his formal will; he had not yet made an act of *complete repudiation* of the habit of lust. Fearful of losing the pleasure of the act, he delayed for a long time this complete renunciation of impurity;[118] hence, despite the fact that he struggled against these sins of impurity, despite the reluctance with which he gave consent to the violent movements of concupiscence, he remained guilty of all such sins.

It should be recalled, moreover, that rationalization played a role in his delay, in his divided will, and in his continuance in a vice from which he wished to be freed.[119] When at last he made the decision to give up his manner of life, and dedicate his life to God, he also repudiated the habit of lust. Thereafter, since concupiscence is a psychosomatic habit, it was not to be expected that its violent tendencies would wear off in a day. The Saint himself accepted them as Divine punishment for the sinful habit that he had formed previously, but he battled against them, and hence remained guiltless of them. As we have seen already, he still had such temptations at the time that he wrote the *Confessions*. By this time, however, they drew no consent from him, although during sleep they sometimes elicited the counterfeit of consent.[120]

Thus, while the will may repudiate the habit of lust by one spiritual act, the psychological effects and their concomitant physical effects usually remain as a fierce trial for the will. These traces of sin are so strong that they tend to draw the will after them; and if the will yields to them after repudiation, again it is seriously culpable. With the grace of God, however, the individual can resist such inveterate impulses, as Augustine succeeded in doing. These principles of responsibility in regard to habit will be

---

[118] See *ibid.*, 8, 5, 11-12. See also *ibid.*, 8, 1, 2; C. Boyer, *Christianisme et Néo-Platonisme. . .*, 134: The author points out that St. Augustine broke the chain of his bad habit little by little, but grace enabled him to make the final break.

[119] See *supra,* ch. 3, 69-74.

[120] See *supra,* ch. 3, 85-86.

given more specific application when we consider the various remedies against the habit of lust in the following chapter. There we shall correlate the positive and negative methods of helping the victim of this vice.[121]

The *Confessions,* moreover, make brief, but poignant, reference to another habit of the young Augustine, which is intellectual obstinacy. This trait is implied in Augustine's narrative of a visit paid by his mother to a certain bishop with the plea that he remonstrate with her son. The prelate replied that this would be useless, because then he was too puffed up with the novelty of Manicheanism to be capable of receiving correction.[122]

Another attitude of will discussed in the *Confessions* is the implicit denial of responsibility by the astrologers and their clients. The Saint roundly condemns the superstition of astrology, in which he had engaged as a youth. First, in book four he contrasts the Christian attitude with the astrological viewpoint. The former confessed its responsibility for sin, and its consequent need for Divine mercy, and for a firm purpose of amendment, but the latter placed the responsibility for human acts in the positions of the stars. In this way proud man projected his guilt upon the stars, but, at the same time, feeling no compunction for sin, he cut off for himself the graces of repentance and forgiveness.[123]

Later, in book seven he refutes the divinations of the astrologers with two arguments: (1) Under the same constellations, or under

[121] See *infra,* ch. 4, 150-154.

[122] See *Conf.,* 3, 12, 21.

[123] See *ibid.,* 4, 3, 4: Itaque illos planos, quos mathematicos vocant, plane consulere non desistebam. . . . Quod tamen Christiana et vera pietas consequenter repellit et damnat. Bonum est enim confiteri tibi, Domine, et dicere: *Miserere mei: cura animam meam, quoniam peccavi tibi* (Ps. 40:5), neque ad licentiam peccandi abuti indulgentia tua, sed meminisse Dominicae vocis: *Ecce sanus factus es; jam noli peccare, ne quid tibi deterius contingat* (John 5:14). Quam totam illi salubritatem interficere conantur, cum dicunt: 'De caelo tibi est inevitabilis causa peccandi' et 'Venus hoc fecit aut Saturnus aut Mars,' scilicet ut homo sine culpa sit, caro et sanguis et superba putredo, culpandus sit autem caeli et siderum creator et ordinator. See also Wangnereck, *Confessionum,* 99, n. 1: 'Quos mathematicos vocant.' Intelligit eos qui ex astris de moribus et factis hominum certa praedicere laborant, et ex situ caeli quem sidera obtinent, cum infans nascitur, ejus fortunam prosperam, etc., . . . vaticinantur.

differences in the positions of the stars too minute to be observed, Firminus and his slave were born; hence, they should have had the same lot in life. But the former, who was born in high estate, ran his course through the prosperous paths of this world, whereas the latter remained in the slavery of his birth and continued to serve his master, Firminus.

(2) According to astrology, twins have the same horoscope. Yet how different their futures have been observed to be, as, for example, in the case of Jacob and Esau. This art, therefore, is false, for either from the constellation diverse things must be predicted, and then the position of the stars is meaningless; or else a like fate is predicted for those born under the same position of the stars.

Not only are the astrologers, then, guilty of quackery, but they are also guilty of *vanity* in their divinations, for men should not seek to probe too deeply the mysteries of Divine Providence. Often God punishes such vain curiosity by allowing those things to happen to them that the astrologers had predicted; then what seems to be chance is really Divine punishment at work. Let man, therefore, take heed of his finite condition, and let him avoid the pursuit of knowledge by forbidden methods.[124] In short, then, the Saint condemns astrology both as an escape from responsibility, and as an inordinate indulgence in curiosity.

E. DEFECTIVE EDUCATION

Another impediment along the pathway of Augustine to God was a defective education. Already it has been noted how he blamed "the torrent of human custom," determining the matter of education in a tyrannical fashion, for its pernicious influence upon the morals of young students.[125] Now we shall consider what the *Confessions*

---

[124] See *Conf.*, 7, 6, 8-10.

[125] See *supra*, ch. 3, 72-73. See also Boyer, *Christianisme et Néo-Platonisme*, 190: Le laisser-aller de ses moeurs, son ignorance religieuse, la formation païenne, qu'il a reçue des grammariens et des rhéteurs—le livrent sans résistance à la critique destructrice de manichéens; Campbell and McGuire, *Confessions*, 103, n. 36, where the authors note the *repeated* criticism of the Saint against ancient Education.

say about the following aspects of education: the incentive for learning, the attitudes of parents and teachers, the correction of bad habits, and the problem of drawing the best from pagan literature.

In his description of his boyhood he criticizes his teachers for providing their students with the wrong motivation and for their failure to give good example: "Nor did those who forced me do well. . . . Those others had no deeper vision of the use to which I might put all they forced me to learn, but to sate the insatiable desire of man for wealth that is but penury and glory that is but shame."[126] Besides, these teachers did the very things for which they punished their students. Thus the Saint remarks wittily: "But the play and idleness of men are called 'business', yet when children do these things, the same men punish them."[127]

Augustine, furthermore, considered some of the compulsory subject matter to be a source of sin on account of the seductive nature of the story. Remembering how infatuated he had become with the story of Dido, he terms this sort of learning foolishness: "For such madness as this, such kind of learning, is counted more profitable and polite than that other, whereby I learned to read and write."[128] The students are enticed by the rich rewards offered to those who excel in such pagan learning. Their sole motivation is ambition.[129] Thus, later as a teacher of rhetoric and as an orator, the future Saint seeks vainly to win the plaudits of men.[130] It is

---

[126] *Conf.*, 1, 12, 19: Nec qui me urgebant bene faciebant, . . . Illi enim non intuebantur quo referrem quod me discere cogebant praeterquam ad satiandas insatiabiles cupiditates copiosae inopiae et ignominiosae gloriae. The English translation is taken from F. Sheed, *Confessions*, 11.

[127] *Ibid.*, 1, 9, 15: Sed majorum nugae negotia vocabantur; puerorum autem talia cum sint puniuntur a majoribus. See also *loc. cit.*: Aut aliud faciebat idem ipse a quo vapulabam, qui si in aliqua quaestiuncula a condoctore suo victus esset, magis bile atque invidia torqueretur quam ego, cum in certamine pilae a conlusore meo superabar?

[128] *Ibid.*, 1, 13, 21: Talis dementia honestiores et uberiores litterae putantur quam illae, quibus legere et scribere didici. See also *supra*, ch. 3, 72-73.

[129] See *Conf.*, 1, 16, 26.

[130] See *ibid.*, 6, 6, 9: Neque enim eo me praeponere illi debebam, quo doctior eram, quoniam non inde gaudebam, sed placere inde quaerebam hominibus, non ut eos *docerem*, sed tantum ut *placerem* (italics mine). See also *ibid.*, 6, 6, 10: Ego mentiendo quaerebam tyfum.

little wonder, then, that students would slip into a perverted view of morality when men were ashamed to make a mistake in grammar, and yet gloried in relating their own sinful lives in well ordered discourse.[131]

It must not be thought that St. Augustine condemns the pagan classics completely. He says that many useful things can be learned from them, but he adds that such can be learned in the study of less seductive material.[132] Thus he insinuates a working norm for those teaching the pagan classics. Let them choose passages that are representative of the period and of the author, but let them select passages that are morally unobjectionable. In the language of Augustine, let them take the gold out of Egypt.

He compares the gold taken by the Israelites from Egypt before their departure with the elements of truth found mixed with pagan errors. Following the example of Moses and St. Paul, the Saint himself had rejected the elements of falsehood in Neoplatonism, and had culled its gold, that is, its truth. Truth belongs to God, no matter where it may be buried:

> These things I found there, but I fed not thereon. For it pleased thee, O Lord, to take away the reproach of inferiority from Jacob, . . . and thou didst call the Gentiles into thine inheritance. And I myself came towards thee from among the Gentiles, and I fixed my mind upon that gold, which it was thy will that the people should carry away out of Egypt, for it was thine wheresoever it was.[133]

The Saint, however, stresses the need for discernment in reading the pagan *philosophers,* quoting St. Paul thus: *"Let no man deceive you by philosophy and vain persuasions, which are according to the*

[131] See *ibid.,* 1, 18, 28.

[132] See *ibid.,* 1, 15, 24: Didici in eis multa verba utilia; sed in rebus non vanis disci possunt, et ea via tuta est, in qua pueri ambularent.

[133] *Ibid.,* 7, 9, 15: Inveni haec ibi et non manducavi. Placuit enim tibi, Domine, auferre opprobrium diminutionis ab Jacob . . . et vocasti gentes in hereditatem tuam. Et ego ad te veneram ex gentibus et intendi in aurum, quod ab Aegypto voluisti ut auferret populus tuus, quoniam tuum erat, ubicumque erat. See also C. Boyer, *Christianisme et Néo-Platonisme dans la formation de saint Augustin,* 113, where it is shown that the Saint rejected the idolatry of Neoplatonism and accepted only its truth.

tradition of men and the principles of this world, and not according to Christ (Col. 2:8 ff.)."[134] Still, this attitude of caution did not prevent him from acknowledging his debt both to Cicero and to Plotinus. Augustine relates that his reading of the *Hortensius* of Cicero gave him a strong desire to study wisdom or philosophy.

As he relates, this book had a profound effect upon him, causing him to perceive the vanity of the pleasures that he had been pursuing and filling him with an ardent desire to return to God:

> And this book altered my affection and made me address prayers to thee, O Lord, giving me other desires and purposes than I had before, and all empty hopes did instantly grow base in mine eyes, and with incredible ardor of heart, did I aspire towards the immortality of wisdom, for now I had begun to rise that I might return to thee.[135]

Hence, just as Cicero had a salutary influence upon St. Augustine, so also other pagan authors—if chosen carefully by the teachers—may benefit students rooted in Catholic tradition.

As for the influence of the writings of Plotinus upon Augustine, it may be said that they helped him considerably in arriving at the notion of a spiritual substance. Still, their general tone was so smug and seductively attractive that they could turn unwary readers away from the solid foundations of the Faith. These writings gave the impression that salvation could be learned from them alone—so much so that the Saint declared that if he had read the Scriptures first, and then later had read the works of Plotinus, he

---

[134] *Conf.*, 3, 4, 8: *Videte ne quis vos decipiat per philosophiam et inanem seductionem secundum traditionem hominum, secundum elementa hujus mundi et non secundum Christum* (Col. 2:8 ff.).

[135] *Ibid.*, 3, 4, 7: Ille vero liber mutavit affectum meum et ad te ipsum, Domine, mutavit preces meas et vota ac desideria mea fecit alia. Viluit mihi repente omnis vana spes et inmortalitatem sapientiae concupiscebam aestu cordis incredibili et surgere coeperam, ut ad te redirem. See also *ibid.*, 3, 4, 8: Quomodo ardebam, Deus meus, . . . revolare a terrenis ad te, et nesciebam quid ageres mecum; Vega, *Obras de San Agustin,* 424, n. 20, where the author holds that the reading of the *Hortensius* was, by far, the most important influence of this period: Con toda justicia debe ser considerada como él a contecimiento mas importante y transcendental de su vida en este periode. Su influencia fué anorme y sin igual.

would have been ensnared by them, and, perhaps, would never have come to the possession of the truth,[136] for there is danger to morals in such readings. A similar peril for the Catholic college student is found in the indiscriminate perusal of secular literature, much of which possesses a peculiar seductiveness. Catholic institutions of higher learning can help the student to read with discernment by grounding him thoroughly in the understanding of sound moral principles.

Another moral aspect of education mentioned in the *Confessions* is the perversity of even young children. It is the weakness of infant limbs, and not the will, that constitutes its innocence. Inordinate tendencies to anger or to jealousy in the child should be corrected immediately, that is, as soon as they are manifest; otherwise, the pernicious habits then acquired will be transferred to more important objectives as the child matures, and then the consequences will be serious. With keen insight the Saint shows that a bad habit uncorrected remains formally the same, while the objects towards which it is directed change from the trifling playthings of childhood to the ambitions of adulthood—to gold and kingdoms and power.[137]

Probably the most important moral aspect of his early education is found in the relationship of the child, and later of the youth, to his parents. As one reads the *Confessions*, one is struck by the con-

---

[136] See *supra*, ch. 2, 42-44, nn. 141-145. See also *Conf.*, 7, 20, 26; Nam si primo sanctis tuis litteris informatus essem . . . et post in illa volumina incidissem, fortasse aut abripuissent me a solidamento pietatis, aut si in affectu, quem salubrem inbiberam, perstitissem, putarem etiam ex illis libris eum posse concipi, si eos solos quisque didicisset. Commenting on the above passage, Wangnereck (*Confessionum*, 258) holds that those who attempt to learn the love of God, contempt of the world, and the pursuit of perfection by the study of Pagan authors, like Plotinus, Plato, Seneca, etc., do great harm both to themselves and to others. They come to overestimate the value of such writings and never attain to the knowledge and practice of solid virtue, because the foundation of humility is lacking in the writings of the pagans. Indeed the virtue of humility was first taught by Christ, and among the Greek philosophers it is not known.

[137] See *supra*, ch. 3, 104-105. See also *Conf.*, 1, 19, 30: Nam haec ipsa sunt, quae a paedagogis et magistris, a nucibus et pilulis et passeribus, ad praefectos et reges, aurum, praedia, mancipia, haec ipsa omnino succedentibus majoribus aetatibus transeunt, sicuti ferulis majora supplicia succedunt.

trast between Monnica and Patricius. Imbued with a pagan attitude, Patricius did not warn his son against temptations to impurity, but, on the contrary, seemed to encourage his son to the pleasures of the flesh.[138]

Undoubtedly the ribald attitude of his father made the youth quick to despise his mother's counsels on chastity as womanish. In reprimanding himself for ignoring her advice, Augustine adds that he did not recognize the voice of God in her instructions.[139] This division of authority between his parents allowed the youth free rein during the idleness of his sixteenth year, and such license paved the way for a habit of impurity. It must be noted, however, that other elements contributed to the growth of this vice, such as the bad example of his companions, and his desire to win their approval by imitating them in their sins.[140]

Augustine censures both his parents for their overestimation of a pagan education. His father had but vain conceits for him. All that mattered was that his son become an eloquent speaker. The youth was made to feel that morals were not to be considered, since his father ignored the subject, and thus gave tacit approval to his sensual ways.[141] The Saint laments the perverted scale of values in the mind of his father, but, as we have learned already,[142] he also criticizes his mother for her attitude of compromise in allowing her desire for his education to outweigh the need of her son for continence. In a poetic figure he says that his mother had fled out of the center of Babylon, but lingered in the skirts thereof. Although she fled from the mire of sin, in which her son was, she did not depart from it completely, inasmuch as she retained vain wishes for his temporal advancement. Again, he implies that both his parents should have used due severity with him, but instead they allowed him to waste his time in sinful pleasures that blinded and enslaved him.[143]

---

[138] See *ibid.*, 2, 3, 6.

[139] See *ibid.*, 2, 3, 7.

[140] See *loc. cit.*

[141] See *ibid.*, 2, 3, 5. See also *ibid.*, 2, 2, 4.

[142] See *supra*, ch. 3, 80.

[143] See *ibid.*, 2, 3, 8. Relaxabantur etiam mihi ad ludendum habenae ultra temperamentum severitatis in dissolutionem affictionum variarum, et in omnibus erat caligo intercludens mihi, Deus meus, serenitatem veritatis

In favor of Monnica, however, it should be observed that she inculcated the doctrine of Christ into her son at a very tender age. When, as a child, he was sick, he petitioned for Baptism with great ardor, and in the years that followed he pronounced the name of Christ with a veneration that he accorded to no other name.[144] The truth that in Christ was his salvation was grounded in him by his mother, and nothing subsequently could drive this notion from his mind. During his spiritual meanderings the name of Christ was never completely forgotten; and when he began to seek the cure of his soul, he found no attraction in any teaching that lacked that sacred name. Thus, despite the fact that the *Hortensius* of Cicero won Augustine over to the pursuit of wisdom, it did not convince him of the truth of Cicero's philosophy, because it lacked the name of Christ.[145]

The lasting influence of the early teachings of Monnica upon the mind of her son shows how important it is for a mother to impress upon the receptive mind of her child the image of Christ, and the most important points in His doctrine.

F. SIN

The gravest obstacle that Augustine met in his journey towards God was sin, which is considered in the *Confessions* in a variety of

---

tuae. See also *ibid.*, 9, 8, 17, for an interesting contrast between the laxity of Augustine's parents and the strictness of Monnica's mistress, who trained her in every moderation: Hac ratione praecipiendi et auctoritate imperandi frenabat aviditatem tenerioris aetatis et ipsam puellarum sitim formabat ad honestum modum, ut eam non liberet quod non deceret.

[144] See *ibid.*, 1, 11, 17. Commenting on this section, Boyer, *Christianisme et Néo-Platonisme*, 24-25, says that Monnica ingrained the name of Christ so deeply in the mind of her child that he never subsequently forgot it: "Elle domine son évolution." Again he says (56): "Il répugne invinciblement à chercher la guérison de son âme en dehors de l'influence du Christ. . . ."

[145] See *Conf.*, 3, 4, 8: . . . hoc nomen Salvatoris mei, Fili tui, in ipso adhuc lacte matris tenerum cor meum praebiberet et alte retinebat; et quidquid sine hoc nomine fuisset, quamvis litteratum et expolitum et veridicum non me totum rapiebat. Nevertheless, as Boyer (*op. cit.*, 32 ff.) points out, the influence of *Hortensius* on the nineteen-year-old Augustine was decisive: "Cette lecture le révéla à lui-même. Dès cette époque la vérité lui apparaît comme seule digne de ces poursuites. . . . Sa conversion est commencée."

ways. For a long time he wrestled with the problem of evil, trying to reconcile the goodness of God with the existence of evil, which he considered as a material substance.[146] It was not until he read the *Enneads* of Plotinus that he found a solution to this difficulty. Basically, his difficulty lay in his materialistic conception of God and of all being. From the *Enneads* he learned that God was a spiritual being; that all things, insofar as they exist, are good; and that evil was a privation of being.[147]

From the notion of evil as a privation of being Augustine developed the notion of sin as the perversion of the will from its due order; thence, he progressed to a penetrating analysis of the diverse motivations of sin. Nor does he fail to discuss in the *Confessions* the chief forms of temptation, as well as occasions of sin. He shows clearly, moreover, the intrinsic connection between sin and its punishment.

1. *The Nature Of Sin*

In the *Confessions* St. Augustine does not give a formal definition of sin, such as he expresses in *Contra Faustum*: "Therefore sin is any deed or word or desire contrary to the eternal law."[148] The essence of sin lies in deordination from the eternal law; and in the *Confessions* this notion is implicit in the idea that sin is a perversion

---

[146] See *Conf.*, 7, 7, 11. See also *ibid.*, 7, 4, 6; *supra*, ch. 3, 63-64.

[147] See Switalski, *Plotinus and the Ethics of St. Augustine*, 69-73, where he holds that the *Enneads* of Plotinus or the "libri Platonicorum" pointed out to the Saint the solution to the problem of evil.

See also *Conf.*, 7, 12, 18: Malumque illud quod quaerebam unde esset, non est substantia, quia, si substantia esset, bonum esset. Aut enim esset incorruptibilis substantia, magnum utique bonum, aut substantia corruptibilis esset, quae nisi bona esset, corruptibilis non esset. Itaque vidi et manifestatum est mihi, quia omnia bona tu fecisti, et prorsus nullae substantiae sunt, quas tu non fecisti. Et quoniam non aequalia omnia fecisti, ideo sunt omnia, quia singula bona sunt et simul omnia valde bona, quoniam fecit Deus noster *omnia bona valde* (Gen. 1:31). Hence the Saint shows that evil is not a substance, and must be therefore the privation of substance. The same idea reoccurs: *ibid.*, 7, 13, 19.

[148] *Contra Faust.* 22, 27 (ed. Zycha, CSEL) 25.621: Ergo peccatum est factum vel dictum vel concupitum aliquid contra legem aeternam.

of the will from its highest good, its Creator, to a lower value, namely, some creature.[149]

Sin, therefore, is not a substance, nor is it what individual men may consider as good or evil in their shifting standards of thought, but it is an aversion of the will from its Creator to base things under the instigation of pride:

> And I found, and that by my own experience, how it was not strange if the same bread, which to a man of sound palate was pleasant, was a kind of punishment to him that was sick; and that the light, which to sore eyes was odious, was lovely to eyes that were sound. And that thy Justice was offensive to the wicked, . . . And still I sought what sin might be, and I found it not to be a substance, but only that it was a perversion or swerving away from thee, O God, who art the supreme substance, a deflection of the will towards lower things, *casting away its inward parts* (Ecclus. 10:10) and puffing itself up as an outlaw.[150]

There are three elements in sin: (1) *aversion* from God; (2) *conversion* to the creature; and (3) the basic motivation of

[149] See *Conf.*, 2, 5, 10: Peccatum admittitur dum inmoderata in ista inelinatione cum extrema bona sint, meliora et summa deseruntur, tu, Domine Deus noster, et veritas tua, et lex tua.

[150] *Ibid.*, 7, 16, 22: Et sensi expertus non esse mirum quod palato non sano poena est et panis, qui sano suavis est, et oculis aegris odiosa lux, quae puris amabilis. Et justitia tua displicet iniquis. . . . Et quaesivi quid esset iniquitas, et non inveni substantiam, sed a summa substantia, Te Deo, detortae in infima voluntatis perversitatem proicientis *intima sua* (Ecclus. 10:10) et tumescentis foras. (The English translation of Matthews was adapted in regard to the rendering of "iniquitas," which he translated as "this iniquity"). See also Wangnereck, *Confessionum*, 249, n. 1; Switalski, *op. cit.*, 49. Concerning "proicientis *intima sua* (Ecclus. 10:10) . . ." the Saint gives the following explanation in *De mus.*, 6, 13, 40 (ML 32.1185): Cum ergo ipsa (anima) per se nihil sit, quidquid autem illi esse est, a Deo sit; in ordine suo manens, ipsius Dei praesentia vegetatur in mente atque conscientia. Itaque hoc bonum habet intimum. Quare superbia intumescere, hoc illi est in extima progredi, et ut ita dicam, inanescere, quod est minus minusque esse. Progredi autem in extima, quid est aliud quam intima projicere; id est, longe a se facere Deum, non locorum spatio, sed mentis affectu?

pride. God is the goal of man; and creatures are meant to lead man to God. When man is turned aside from his Creator by an *immoderate* attachment to values of a lower order, he sins. He rejects the highest goods, namely, God, His truth, and His law for things that tend to deprive him of his due perfection. This rejection of higher values follows the invisible intoxication of self-will, whereby man substitutes another creature, or even himself, in place of his Creator.[151]

To exemplify this perversity of the human will in sin, moreover, Augustine refers to an apparently trifling incident, but one in which he sees "the symbol of utterly unjustifiable sin, of evil done for little more than its own sake."[152] With a gang of boys he had stolen pears from a neighbor's tree, not because of any relish for their flavor but for the sheer thrill of the escapade. Since the action, however, was of no great importance, it may be wondered why he selected this incident. The answer seems to be that he is *intent* upon the motivation of the act, considering it an example of an action done through pure malice. As he turned the incident over in his mind, he was at a loss to discover even an excuse for it. When he wrote of it, he was aware that evil was not a positive thing, but a privation of goodness, and hence incapable of being desired in itself. In this case there seemed to be nothing good to attract the will. Neither the fruit, which he threw away, nor the act was pleasurable; and so with characteristic frankness he admits that he cannot plumb the depths of his own motivation in this incident.[153]

Still, from his discussion of this incident the Saint does make it clear that the worst kind of sin is a sin of malice, or sinning merely for the sake of sin. In addition, he puts his finger on pride as the basic motive of this theft and of all sin: "For pride apes exaltation, whereas Thou alone, O God, are exalted above all things."[154] In his

---

[151] See *Conf.*, 2, 3, 6: . . . gaudens vinulentia, in qua te iste mundus oblitus est creatorem suum et creaturam tuam pro te amavit, de vino invisibili perversae atque inclinatae in ima voluntatis suae.

[152] Bourke, *Augustine's Quest of Wisdom,* 11.

[153] See *Conf.*, 2, 4, 9. See also *ibid.*, 2, 6, 12: Quid ego miser in te amavi, o furtum meum? See also *ibid.*, 2, 10, 18: Quis exaperit istam tortuosissimam et inplicatissimam nodositatem? . . .

[154] *Ibid.*, 2, 6, 13: Nam et superbia celsitudinem imitatur cum tu sis unus super omnia Deus excelsus. (The above English translation is my own.)

sin the sinner seeks to possess in an illicit way what is found in its completeness only in God; for he who turns his back upon God and lifts up his heel against Him imitates God in a perverted fashion. In a sense, then, the sinner wants to be God.[155]

Augustine asks himself what he loved in his theft. Did he want to do in a sneaking fashion, contrary to law, what he was not able to do by his might? In this way the sinner is able to mimic the power of God by doing with impunity things forbidden by the Almighty. Thus the sinner becomes a *darkened* likeness of Divine Omnipotence, and yet remains a slave, fleeing his Lord and seeking a shadow.[156]

In their very sins, then, sinners seek but a sort of likeness with God in a proud and perverted and slavish freedom. Besides viewing sin as a perverted imitation of Omnipotence the *Confessions* consider it from other angles, so that the reader is given a sort of composite descriptive definition of sin. In the following paragraphs a few of the diverse connotations of sin will be noted.

The first describes the manner in which sin separates the soul from God. Just as the soul goes to God, not by physical locomotion, but by a simple act of the will, so also one flees from God by an act of the will. It is distance in affections, not distance in space, that separates the soul from God. Distance in affections means that the soul has turned to the love of the creature in the place of the Creator. Hence the Saint calls them *darkened* affections.[157]

---

[155] See *ibid.*, 2, 6, 14: Perverse te imitantur omnes qui longe se a te faciunt et extollunt se adversum te. See also *De civ Dei,* 14, 13 (Dombart-Kalb, Leipzig-Teubner, 1929, 2.32): Perversa enim est celsitudo deserto eo, cui debet animus inhaerere, principio sibi quodam modo fieri atque esse principium. See also *Conf.,* 4, 14, 23.

[156] See *Conf.*, 2, 6, 14. See also *De Trinitate*, 11, 5 (ML 42.991): Nam et animae in ipsis peccatis suis non nisi quaedam similitudinem Dei, superba et praepostera, et, ut ita dicam, servili libertate sectantur.

[157] See *Conf.*, 1, 18, 28: Nam longe a vultu tuo in affectu tenebroso. Non enim pedibus aut spatiis locorum itur abs te aut reditur ad te, aut vero filius ille tuus equos aut currus vel naves quaesivit aut avolavit pinna visibili aut moto poplite iter egit, ut in longinqua regione vivens prodige dissiparet quod dederas proficiscenti dulcis pater, quia dederas, . . . In affectu ergo libidinoso, id enim est tenebroso atque id est longe a vultu tuo. See also S.T., 2-2, 24, 12: Unde et Augustinus dicit quod 'homo, Deo sibi praesente

Under the figure of spiritual fornication, moreover, he expresses the same idea, pointing out that the soul commits fornication whenever it turns from God, and seeks outside of Him that which is found pure and untainted only in God.[158] Once the soul wanders from God, it relapses into a life that resembles the darkness of a deep abyss, no longer possessing the God of Light; hence the state of sin is conceived as darkness.[159]

Again, sin is described as a *lie* in a passage where Augustine blames his own covetousness for wanting to possess both God and his sin; and, consequently, he lost God, who refused to be possessed by a lie, that is, God suffered no compromise with sin. He is Life, Goodness, and Truth, and sin is the privation of all these.[160]

---

illuminatur, absente autem continuo tenebratur; a quo non *locorum intervallis*, sed *voluntatis aversione disceditur*' (italics mine). Here St. Thomas shows that mortal sin, which he calls distance from God, is effected, not by change of place, but by the aversion of the will.

[158] See *Conf.*, 1, 13, 21: Non te amabam et *fornicabar abs te* (Ps. 72:27) et fornicanti sonabat undique: *'Euge, euge,'* amicitia enim mundi hujus *fornicatio est* (Ps. 39:16) abs te. See also *ibid.*, 2, 6, 14: Ita fornicatur anima, cum avertitur abs te et quaerit extra te ea quae pura et liquida non invenit, nisi cum redit ad te; J. Capello, *Confessionum,* XXXVII: Peccatum enim ab Augustino putatur quaedam dissociatio et dissipatio intima animae avertendo se ab unitate et convertendo se ad multitudinem.

[159] See *ibid.*, 13, 2, 3: Bonum autem illi est adhaerere tibi semper, ne quod adeptus est conversione aversione lumen amittat et relabatur in vitam tenebrosae abysso similem. Nam et nos qui secundum animam creatura spiritalis sumus, aversi a te nostro lumine in ea vita fuimus *aliquando tenebrae* (Eph. 5:8) et in reliquiis obscuritatis nostrae laboramus, donec simus *justitia tua* in unico tuo *sicut montes Dei:* nam, *judicia tua* fuimus sicut *multa abyssus* (Ps. 35:7). This passage may be understood also as a warning to those who have passed from the state of sin to the state of grace not to relapse again into the abyss of darkness, that is, their former manner of life. See also *ibid.*, 13, 8, 9; and 13, 21, 30.

[160] See *ibid.*, 10, 41, 66: At ego per avaritiam meam non amittere te volui, sed volui tecum possidere mendacium; sicut nemo vult ita falsum dicere, ut nesciat ipse, quid verum sit. Itaque amisi te, quia non dignaris cum mendacio possideri. Sin is considered a lie, inasmuch as it always involves the choice of an object that is not in accordance with the due and true order of things; and as a lie, it brings punishment upon the very one who commits it, shutting him off from the truth, and perverting his nature. See also *ibid.*, 3, 8, 16 and 4, 8, 13 for the same idea.

Another aspect of sin is that of choice of values, which the Saint discusses in several passages of the *Confessions*. First of all, he points out that created goods do have beauty and attractiveness, and for this reason do draw the will.[161] When men, however, form such an attachment for the various forms of natural beauty that they forsake the infinite goodness of God, then they may be said to follow a perverted scale of values.

This scale of values is found in its extreme in a pagan atmosphere, as Augustine notes; for men will observe the rules of grammar with meticulous care, while they neglect the law of God, upon the observance of which their eternal salvation depends. Again, learned pagans found it more displeasing to mispronounce the word *man* than to hate their fellowman. In the education of the lawyer, as well as in his subsequent practice, men put a high premium on deceit as a means of success. Thus men are so blind as to glory even in their blindness.[162]

In general, men commit sin either from the desire of obtaining some of those things that are called lower values or from fear of losing them. For example, the Saint observes, not even Catiline loved his own wicked deeds, but something else that motivated them.[163] Always there must be some *bonum* to cause the will to act.

If we recall, however, that Augustine could not understand completely his motives in the pear theft, it may seem that we have a difficulty. Previously he had pointed to pride as the underlying motive, and from this it may be surmised that the will of the youth was attracted by the delicious freedom of doing something forbidden without being caught and punished—a liberty rendered still sweeter by the company of likeminded youths.[164]

---

[161] See *ibid.*, 2, 5, 10. See also *ibid.*, 2, 3, 6.

[162] See *Conf.*, 1, 18, 29. See also *ibid.*, 3, 3, 6.

[163] See *ibid.*, 2, 5, 11: Cum itaque de facinore quaeritur, qua causa factum sit, credi non solet, nisi cum appetitus adipiscendi alicujus illorum bonorum, quae infima diximus esse potuisse adparuerit aut metus amittendi. . . . See also *loc. cit.*: Nec ipse igitur Catilina amavit facinora sua, sed utique aliud, cujus causa illa faciebat.

[164] See *supra*, ch. 3, 119-120, nn. 153-156. See also Wangnereck, *Confessionum*, 51: Tale bonum erat in apprehensione Augustini, libertas faciendi impune, quod non licebat, ex ipso peccantium consortio magis dulcescens.

The choice of true values entered into our discussion on friendship, where it was noted that Augustine had placed an excessive value on human friendship by loving his friend as if he were God. This inordinate affection blinded his mind, and led to more serious errors. Thus, however beautiful a human friendship may be, it will end in sorrow, unless it is referred back to God as the *summum bonum* of the human heart.[165]

Finally, after his conversion the man who had sought happiness in diverse earthly values sums up the whole question of choice: One must not search for lasting values outside of himself. It is a fact of experience that those who pretend to find their happiness by immersion in worldly activities quickly lose all inner balance. In this fashion they starve their souls, which can find no real nourishment in such things.[166]

From this discussion it is clear that sin involves not merely the will, but also the intellect. Sin involves false choice, and its repetition contributes to the formation in the mind of a set of values that is merely a shadow of real goodness.[167] Thus, the sinner may be said to choose shadow for substance.

The Saint, moreover, considers sin as self-destruction. Sin cannot harm God, but it does great injury to the soul of the sinner. By sins against nature, for example, man corrupts and perverts his own nature; and in like manner man brings injury upon himself by

---

[165] See *supra,* ch. 2, 36, nn. 119-123. See also *Conf.*, 4, 8, 13: Maxime quippe me reparabant atque recreabant aliorum amicorum solacia, cum quibus amabam quod postea amabam, et hoc erat ingens fabula et longum mendacium, cujus adulterina confricatione corrumpebatur mens nostra pruriens in auribus. See also *ibid.*, 4, 10, 15: Nam quoquoversum se verterit anima hominis ad dolores figitur alibi praeterquam in te, tametsi figitur in pulchris extra te et extra se.

[166] See *ibid.*, 9, 4, 10: Nec iam bona mea foris erant nec oculis carneis in isto sole quaerebantur. Volentes enim gaudere forinsecus facile vanescunt et effunduntur in ea, quae videntur et temporalia sunt, et imagines eorum famelica cogitatione lambiunt. See also the following passages, in which the inadequacy of temporal values to bring happiness to man is developed: *Enar. in Ps. 4,* sect. 10 (ML 36.83); *De vera rel.*, c. 21, 41 (ML 34.139); *ibid.*, c. 54, 105 (ML 34.168); and *ibid.*, c. 35, 65 (ML 34.151).

[167] See *Conf.*, 2, 6, 14: Ecce est ille servus fugiens Dominum suum et consecutus *umbram* (italics mine).

the immoderate use of creatures. In this way God allows man to be punished by his own sins.[168]

2. *Kinds And Sources Of Sin*

In the *Confessions* there are no formal divisions of sin; and, while the book describes various kinds of sin, it is far more concerned with the sources of sin, both internal and external—with their hidden dynamics, as it were, as well as with temptations and occasions of sin. Since, moreover, the divisions of sin according to St. Augustine would have to be established from a study of all his works, and would have to be expressed in his terminology—a task beyond the scope of this thesis—the writer will restrict himself to one question: In the various references to sin in the *Confessions* is Augustine describing serious violations of Divine law, i.e., mortal sin?

In reply it may be said that in most of his allusions to sin he had in mind what is called mortal sin. Mortal sin involves the selection of a creature in place of God as one's ultimate end, and the consequent death of Divine charity in the soul. Augustine describes the equivalent of this when he calls sin the perversion of the will from its highest good, the love of a creature as if he were God, the proud imitation of omnipotence, darkened affections, and spiritual fornication.[169]

Such language is too strong to characterize venial sin, which does not denote an aversion from man's true ultimate end, but merely a somewhat excessive love of the creature without the loss of the life of Divine charity within the soul. One may find examples of venial sin in the *Confessions*. When Augustine, for example, relates how he wasted time as a boy on the usual trifles that draw youngsters away from their books, he is referring to venial sins.[170]

---

[168] See *ibid.*, 3, 8, 16: Aut quae adversus te facinora cui noceri non potest? Sed hoc vindicas quod in se homines perpetrant, quia etiam cum in te peccant, inpie faciunt in animas suas et mentitur iniquitas sibi, sive corrumpendo ac pervertendo naturam suam, . . . vel inmoderate utendo concessis rebus vel in non concessa flagrando in eum *usum qui est contra naturam* (Rom. 1:26). . . . See also *supra*, ch. 2, 11.

[169] See *supra*, ch. 3, 117-123.

[170] See *Conf.*, 1, 9, 15: Et peccabamus tamen minus scribendo aut legendo aut cogitando de litteris, quam exigebatur a nobis. See also *ibid.*, 1, 13, 22.

Again, towards the end of the *Confessions* the Saint refers to the *death* of the soul of the sinner. In a beautiful antithesis he contrasts the soul that has renounced the pleasures of the world and is living for Christ with the soul that is immersed in worldly pleasures and dead to Him. The latter he calls "dead" (mortua), and the former he terms "living" (viva). Accordingly, he counsels his readers to avoid conformity with this world, the love of which leads to the death of the soul or to mortal sin. Thus the soul lives by avoiding those things from whose indulgence comes death.[171]

Furthermore, once the soul has forsaken the fountain of life, its activities are those of a *dead* soul, namely, pride, lust, and poisonous curiosity, whose tendencies render the soul the slave of this transitory world.[172] In the same passage, moreover, the Saint proposes remedies against these three fountainheads of sin, but we shall consider them in the following chapter.[173] Now we shall consider pride as the source of all sins.

After the Saint has noted the various motives that lead to sin, he concludes that they all may be reduced to the lust of the flesh, to the concupiscence of the eyes, and to the pride of life—the division of St. John, and these three, in turn, may be reduced to *pride*: "And these things are done when thou art forsaken, o thou fountain of life, . . ; and when, by a foolish and particular pride, we grow to love that which is but a part of the whole, and which really is false."[174] Another name for such pride is inordinate self-love, which causes the sinner to choose his own private good before God, who is the common good of all.[175]

---

[171] See *ibid.*, 13, 21, 29-30.

[172] See *ibid.*, 13, 21, 30.

[173] See *infra*, ch. 4 (the entire chapter), 139 ff.

[174] *Conf.*, 3, 8, 16: Et ea fiunt cum tu derelinqueris, fons vitae . . . et privata superbia diligitur in parte unum falsum. In the same section the Saint notes the triple source of sin: Haec sunt capita iniquitatis, quae pullulant principandi et spectandi et sentiendi libidine aut una aut duabus earum aut simul omnibus. The same division is found: *Ibid.*, 10, 30, 41 and 13, 21, 30. St. Thomas also follows this division: S.T., 1-2, 77, 5.

[175] *Conf.*, 3, 8, 16: . . . amplius amando proprium nostrum quam te omnium bonum. See also S.T., 1-2, 77, 4, where self-love or pride is declared to be the cause of all sin: Quod autem aliquis appetat inordinate aliquod

Since, however, the basic nature of pride as the root of all sin, has been considered already in the study of humility, and since the other two sources of sin have been explored sufficiently,[176] it will be enough to observe here that the Saint gives a clear description of pride in action in his criticism of the Platonists. There he draws a sharp distinction between the smug arrogance of the philosophers, and the humble confidence of the sinner coming back to God.[177]

From his own life, moreover, he cites an instance of one of the forms of pride, namely, *vain ambition.* Comparing himself with an intoxicated man, whom he met while he was on his way to deliver a speech, he declares that the vain desire to be acclaimed a great speaker swayed his mind more than the liquor affected the drunkard.[178] Other examples of pride could be cited, but this would but labor the obvious. Instead, it will be profitable to set down examples of other *subordinate* motives of sin that are described in the *Confessions*; and, among these, *human respect* will be depicted first.

Besides the pear tree incident, which was motivated in part by human respect and by the pleasure of complicity in a boyish prank,[179] Augustine relates how the desire to please men vitiated his early teaching career. He was filled with the desire to please

---

temporale bonum, procedit ex hoc quod inordinate amat seipsum: hoc enim est amare aliquem velle ei bonum. Unde manifestum est quod inordinatus amor sui est causa omnis peccati. See also S.T., 1-2, 77, 5.

[176] See the following references in regard to: (1) *pride: supra,* ch. 2, 43-44; 50; ch. 3, 118-119; 125-126; (2) in regard to concupiscence of the *flesh: supra,* ch. 3, 67; 77-86; and (3) in regard to concupiscence of the *eyes: supra,* ch. 2, 40; ch. 3, 88-90.

[177] See *supra,* ch. 2, 42-43. See also *Conf., 7, 21, 27*: Non habent illae paginae vultum pietatis illius, lacrimas confessionis, *sacrificium tuum, spiritum contribulatum, cor contritum et humilitatum* (Ps. 50:19); Paul Henry, *Plotin et L'Occident,* 110: Car le grand docteur de la grâce a été le premier à marquer cet écart entre l'orgueilleuse suffisance du philosophe et l'humble confiance du pécheur revenant à Dieu.

[178] See *Conf.,* 6, 6, 10. The pursuit of worldly glory keeps the soul in a state of continual uneasiness.

[179] See *ibid.,* 2, 8, 16. See also *ibid.,* 2, 9, 17: Risus erat quasi titillato corde, quod fallebamus eos, qui haec a nobis fieri non putabant et vehementer nolebant. . . . Sed cum dicitur: 'Eamus, faciamus' et pudet non esse impudentem.

men, not to instruct them. He made use of flattery and lies; and in his panegyric of the emperor he uttered many a lie, and lying, was applauded by those who knew he lied.[180]

Again, he shows how the devils tempt those who hold public office with the desire to be feared and to be loved by men, so as to forget that God is the source of all truth and goodness. In this way men come to desire human praise, not for the sake of God, but for their own sake, and, thus swelled by pride, they become the slaves of Satan.[181] Finally, Augustine cites the case of Victorinus, who delayed his conversion for a long time, because he was afraid of offending his pagan friends.[182] At last, however, Victorinus overcame his fear and entered the Church.

In fact, so well did Victorinus overcome his weakness that he made public retractation for all the false doctrines that he had taught. He felt the *duty* incumbent upon him to repair the damage done by his pagan teaching; and, even though the priests were willing to dispense him from such a difficult obligation as that of public retractation, thinking that it would be too much for him, still he chose to make a public profession of his Faith before a large assembly. In this manner Victorinus counterbalanced effectively his former pagan teachings.[183]

Four other important sources of sin mentioned in the *Confessions* are hatred, scandal, jealousy, and rash judgment. As already noted, hatred of truth has its roots in an inordinate attachment to some form of pleasure, and thus Augustine's observation that drunkards hate truth sums up this sort of hatred. Considered in its effects, hatred injures most the soul in which it releases its violent movements, producing unrest and blindness of spirit.[184]

In regard to scandal, he relates the activities of the *Eversores,* who, composed mainly of Carthaginian students, were notorious for their licentiousness in speech and action. Since this group tried to pervert other students into their manner of behavior, they were

---

[180] See *ibid.,* 6, 6, 9.

[181] See *ibid.,* 10, 36, 59.

[182] See *ibid.,* 8, 2, 4.

[183] See *ibid.,* 8, 2, 5.

[184] See *ibid.,* 1, 18, 29. For other instances of hatred see *ibid.,* 5, 12, 22 and 6, 2, 2; see also *supra,* ch. 3, 75-77 for discussion on hatred of truth.

called the *Eversores*, or "Subverters," an appellation that Augustine found very apt. Their actions resembled those of devils, who love to seduce men into the same misery as themselves, and, since these students took delight in leading others into sin, they were guilty of diabolical scandal.[185]

Out of jealousy evil servants had whispered against St. Monnica, and thus had turned her mother-in-law against her. Monnica's enduring patience and meekness faced this ordeal and won over her mother-in-law so completely that the latter disclosed the waggling tongues to her son, and insisted that he punish them with stripes. In this case, and in others, St. Monnica exemplified the virtue of counterbalancing the destructive nature of detraction. After she had listened to the bitter remarks of people at enmity with one another, she would not repeat what the other might have said, but only would add observations that would tend to reconcile the one with the other. This was the rare virtue of Monnica, for, as her son observes, most individuals, when put in a similar situation, increase the ardor of the feud by adding remarks that were never spoken by the other person, or were uttered in unthinking anger.[186]

Finally, an instance of rash judgment is found in the unusual accident that befell Augustine's friend, Alypius. Alypius had been apprehended as a thief, but his innocence had been established by the witness of an architect friend. Were it not for this intercession, Alypius would have been condemned on external appearances. From this incident the Saint draws the conclusion that God allowed this to happen to Alypius, so that he might learn thereby to avoid rash judgments when later he would judge as a bishop.[187]

From the various passages in the *Confessions* treating of *temptation* one may glean additional knowledge concerning the sources of sin. Already we have learned in this study the following facts concerning temptation: (1) It is very difficult for man to possess an adequate knowledge of himself, especially in his endeavors to examine his own reactions to the praises of men. (2) While one may accept praise, provided he refers all glory to God, still one is

---

[185] See *ibid.*, 3, 3, 6. See also *De vera rel.*, 40, 75 (ML 34.156).
[186] See *Conf.*, 9, 9, 20-21.
[187] See *ibid.*, 6, 9, 14-15.

in danger of seeking pleasure in the praises of men and of becoming thereby the devil's instrument. (3) The fear of losing the pleasure that comes from sins of the flesh retards the conversion of the sinner. (4) Carnal temptations arising from memory often remain long after the person has repudiated sins of the flesh; and (5) dreams of a carnal nature are not ordinarily imputable.[188]

Several other aspects of temptation may now be discussed. Speaking of temptations in general, the Saint quotes Job to the effect that all of life is a temptation without rest. When man becomes *full* of the love of God, then he will be wracked by temptations no longer; and Augustine adds that he has not reached this stage in the spiritual life, for he is still weighed down by long established tendencies to sin, particularly those of concupiscence.[189] Considering the fact that he wrote his *Confessions* some thirteen years after his conversion, his testimony in regard to his *continued* struggle against the tendencies of a repudiated vice should offer encouragement to others striving to overcome such carnal habits. Joyfully he describes his progress in conquering carnal temptations, and prays that he may advance to a complete victory over the flesh.[190]

As far as self-knowledge is concerned, temptations to pride and to vanity are the most difficult to eradicate. Although one can detect easily temptations to the flesh and to vain curiosity, and can measure his progress in his struggle against them, still he lacks reliable means of introspection into the motivation behind the acceptance of praise and self-complacency. Indeed it seems that the only way of discovering our attachment to praise is to note our reaction when we are deprived of it. It may be added, moreover,

---

[188] For the temptation of praise see *supra,* ch. 2, 53; and ch. 3, 126 ff.; for fear see *supra,* ch. 3, 83-84; and for carnal temptations see *supra,* ch. 3, 85-86.

[189] See *Conf.,* 10, 28, 39. See also *supra,* ch. 3, 85-86.

[190] See *Conf.,* 10, 28, 39. See also *ibid.,* 10, 30, 42: Dixi bono Domino meo *exsultans cum tremore* (Ps. 2:11) in eo quod donasti mihi, et lugens in eo, quod inconsummatus sum, sperans perfecturum te in me misericordias tuas usque ad pacem plenariam, quam tecum habebunt interiora et exteriora mea, cum *absorta fuerit mors in victoriam* (I Cor. 15:54). See also *ibid.,* 10, 5, 7.

that the experience of deprivation is a good index of other attachments also.[191]

The Saint considers the *love of praises* a most dangerous temptation, inasmuch as this tendency increases our self-esteem by soliciting the praises of men. Even when it is reproved, it continues to work in the mind, nourishing itself on the imaginary injustice of the reproof; and sometimes it assumes the attitude of *contempt-for-vain-glory,* in which self-deceit is discernible, for it glories in its very contempt of vain glory.[192]

Arising in the same subtle fashion, and from the same source, is the temptation to smugness, which causes its possessor to seek to be pleasing *merely* to himself—with utter disregard for the opinion of others. In his description of this temptation, moreover, Augustine stresses the introvert character of this tendency. One crawls, as it were, into his little shell, and therein he forms an exaggerated estimate of his self-sufficiency and excellence. This individual does not care to please even his God, whose law he adapts to fit his own ideas of goodness, nor does he acknowledge that whatever goodness he possesses comes from God. He thinks that God owes him a reward for his good deeds, which he has accomplished, not so much by God's grace, as by his own power. Even in some who acknowledge the grace of God as operative in their good works, one may discern traces of spiritual envy towards others.[193]

All these passages describing temptations to pride and to vanity suggest several practical conclusions for the moral life: (1) To counterbalance vanity, instead of examining too finely one's motives, one should purify his intentions by *continual* acts of love towards God. (2) To offset the tendency to smugness, one should

---

[191] See *ibid.,* 10, 37, 60. See also *ibid.,* 10, 32, 48: . . . quia et quod inest plerumque occultum est, nisi *experientia* (italics mine) manifestetur, et nemo securus esse debet in ista vita. . . . See also *De vera rel.,* 47, 92 (ML 34.163): Cum enim mutabilium bonorum adest copia, non eis confidit; sed cum subtrahuntur agnoscit utrum eum non ceperint, quia plerumque cum adsunt nobis, putamus quod non ea diligamus; sed cum abesse coeperint invenimus qui simus. Hoc enim sine amore nostro aderat quod sine dolore discedit.

[192] See *Conf.,* 10, 38, 63.

[193] See *ibid.,* 10, 39, 64.

repeat often *prayers of dependence* upon God's mercy to gain grace for the daily warfare against temptations.[194]

Another source of sin is the occasion of sin, to which the Saint refers in several instances. The case of Alypius is most striking. By chance one day he met several of his fellow students, who tried to persuade him to accompany them to the gladiator show. Since he detested shows of this sort, he vehemently refused; thereupon, the students bundled him off forcibly. To this friendly violence Alypius responded by the boast that despite the fact that they could carry him bodily into such a spectacle, they could not force him to gaze at the bloody battles, and consequently he would win a moral victory over them. This protest only rendered them more curious to try his will-power.

Keeping his eyes closed at first, Alypius averted his mind from the savage battle; but, upon hearing a mighty roar from the crowd, he was overcome by curiosity and decided to look, feeling superior to it, and very certain that he could despise whatever it was. As soon as he beheld the blood of the wounded warrior, he became riveted to the scene. Soon he became, as it were, intoxicated with this habit of attending gladiator shows.[195] Thus Alypius, who presumed on his own strength, fell into serious sin.

As Augustine expresses it, Alypius was bold rather than resolute. Instead of praying for Divine help when forced into this occasion of sin, he was rashly self-sufficient. Again, while he took care to guard his eyes, he failed to restrict vain curiosity, and through this weakness the gateways to sin were opened. His mistakes, then, suggest practical warnings for the person in an unavoidable occasion of sin. First of all, such a one must pray, and then he must mortify not only his external senses, but also the inordinate desire for knowledge.

This incident exemplifies also the malice of *induction,* committed by the students who forced Alypius into an occasion of serious sin.

---

[194] See *ibid.,* 10, 37, 62: Ecce in te, veritas, video non me laudibus meis propter me, sed propter proximi utilitatem moveri oportere. See *ibid.,* 10, 32, 48: Una spes, una fiducia, una firma promissio misericordia tua. See also Wangnereck, *Confessionum,* 417-418.

[195] See *Conf.,* 6, 8, 13.

The Saint mentions, moreover, the false show of continency on the part of the Manicheans as another occasion of sin, into which ingenuous Alypius fell. His untried soul was fooled easily by the attractive, but counterfeit, virtue of these heretics.[196] Finally, the reader of the *Confessions* will discover one long occasion of sin in Augustine's description of his early pagan education, with its false motivation, seductive subject matter, misleading teachers, and evil companionship.[197]

3. *Punishment For Sin*

The idea that the sinner brings punishment upon himself by the transgression of the Divine law recurs like a refrain throughout the *Confessions*. Already we have noted that sin is a form of self-injury, that hatred of truth is also spiritual blindness, and that the habit of impurity is part of the punishment of the impure.[198] Now we shall explain still further various other references made by the Saint to the manner in which God punishes the sinner.

First of all, we should note that when St. Augustine speaks of the punishment for sin, he is concerned, not with one isolated sin, but with a habit of sin. Again, in expounding the teaching of the *Confessions* on this subject, it will be necessary to use divisions for the sake of order. At the same time it has not been forgotten that in the *unity* of the sinner's person the elements of spiritual blindness, lust, and confusion are bound up with one another in a dynamically intimate way. In the vicious circle of blindness and vice, lust tends to create blindness quite as effectively as blindness contributes to the habit of lust.

In general, the Saint teaches that the sinner brings on his own punishment in the sin itself, the sin becoming, as it were, the instrument of God's justice, so that the very delights of the sinner become his torture. Thus a special kind of sin brings a special kind of punishment.[199] For example, pride produces spiritual blindness

---

[196] See *ibid.*, 6, 7, 12.

[197] See *supra*, ch. 3, 72-73; 110 ff.

[198] See *supra*, ch. 2, 37-38; ch. 3, 76.

[199] See *Conf.*, 4, 9, 14: Nam ubi non invenit legem tuam in poena sua? See also *ibid.*, 10, 4, 5: Bona mea instituta tua sunt et dona tua, mala mea delicta mea sunt et judicia tua; *ibid.*, 2, 6, 13: Opera sua malis inimica sunt. See

in the intellect, and lust generates a revolt of the lower powers against the will. Accordingly, we shall consider the punishment of pride in the intellect, the effects of lust in the volitive tendencies of man, and, finally, the general dissipation of the whole person, as the consummate development of such sins.

Augustine employs the term "poenales caecitates" to indicate that spiritual blindness is a penalty for pride.[200] Again, he stresses the truth that in the plan of God every *inordinate* affection becomes its own punishment.[201] Thus blindness and dissipation are the penalties of pride and lust. To exemplify this by concrete incidents from the life of St. Augustine will be the purpose of the following paragraphs. It must be kept in mind, however, that, while the emphasis will be on pride and its consequent blindness, the factors of lust and dissipation are integral parts of the complete dynamic pattern. First, we shall consider the dissipation of his adolescence, in the description of which he observes that he groped in a mist, which shut off from his mind the brightness of Divine truth.[202]

The mist of carnal desires prevented him from seeing the brightness of Divine truth, that is, his eyes were concentrated so much on carnal and sensual pleasures that his mind could not rise to the spiritual level.[203] During this same period, moreover, he became acquainted with the lawless students of Carthage, who inflicted injustices upon their teachers and fellow students with the mistaken notion that they were escaping punishment. The Saint notes that in their very blindness they were being punished already, since God had withdrawn from their depraved minds the light necessary to

---

also *Enar. in Ps.* 7:15 (ML 36.107): Unicuique homini supplicium fieri de peccato suo, et ejus iniquitatem in poenam converti; . . . sed (Deus) ipsa peccata sic ordinare, ut quae fuerunt delectamenta homini peccanti sint instrumenta Domini punientis.

200 See *Conf.*, 1, 18, 29: Quam tu secretus es, . . . Deus, . . . lege infatigabili spargens poenales caecitates supra inlicitas cupiditates. See also *ibid.*, 1, 4, 4: *In vetustatem perducens superbos et nesciunt* (Job 9:5); . . .

201 See *ibid.*, 1, 12, 19: Jussisti enim et sic est, ut poena sua sibi sit omnis inordinatus animus. See also Switalski, *op. cit.*, 51.

202 See *ibid.*, 2, 3, 8: In omnibus erat caligo intercludens, Deus meus, serenitatem veritatis tuae.

203 See *ibid.*, 6, 16, 26.

distinguish good from evil. They would not escape the sanctions imposed by the *eternal law* of God.[204]

The extraordinary genius and learning of the student Augustine, moreover, brought him no closer to the way of true happiness, because he lacked the virtue of humility. Thus he condemns his abuse of talents.[205] With his back, as it were, to the light he undertook the study of the Sacred Scriptures, but his pride blinded him to their true meaning. All impressed, as he was, by the eloquence and arrogance of Cicero, he was repelled by the simplicity and humility of these inspired books. Despite his sharp wit he failed at this period to penetrate their depths. By contradicting Divine truth he had raised the dust in his eyes.[206]

The same self-sufficiency caused him to fall a victim to the Manichean delusion, in which his blindness became worse. Indeed, as he himself points out, the absurdities subscribed to during this period exemplified how God was punishing him for his pride. It was a gradual darkening of his understanding that led such an intelligent man to believe that the fig tree wept when it was plucked. What St. Paul had written concerning the philosophers was fulfilled in Augustine. By his life of sin he had slipped into a *reprobate sense,* wherein he not only did evil, but also believed foolish things to be true.[207]

This reprobate sense, moreover, the Saint attributes to the learned astronomers, who have made many wonderful discoveries concerning the stars, but who lack the goodness to inquire whence they possess the intelligence to work out complicated problems. For such pride, moreover, they are punished in two ways: (1) They

---

[204] See *ibid.,* 5, 8, 14: Multa injuriosa faciunt mira hebetudine et punienda legibus, nisi consuetudo patrona sit, hoc miseriores eos ostendens, quo jam quasi liceat faciunt quod per tuam aeternam legem numquam licebit, et inpune se facere arbitrantur, cum ipsa faciendi caecitate puniantur et inconparabiliter patiantur pejora, quam faciunt. See also Vega, *Obras de San Agustin,* 423, n. 15.

[205] See *ibid.,* 4, 16, 28-31.

[206] See *ibid.,* 3, 5, 9. See also *ibid.,* 12, 16, 23.

[207] See *ibid.,* 3, 6, 10. See also *ibid.,* 3, 10, 18. See also Wangnereck, *Confessionum,* 78, 90, 136, where the author shows how pride and lust led to heresy; Mausbach, *Die Ethik des heiligen Augustinus,* 2.378; *Conf.,* 8, 10, 22 and 9, 4, 10.

have remained ignorant of the Incarnation of the Son of God; and (2) they have a perverted sense of values, inasmuch as they ascribe to themselves Divine attributes, while they attribute to God the corruptible traits of His creatures. Such is the terrible sanction for those who fail to glorify God.[208]

As it has been noted already, the Neoplatonists believed that the Word was God, but they rejected the truth of the Incarnation together with the facts of Christ's *sufferings* and *death*. As punishment for such pride, they were allowed to remain in ignorance concerning the great mysteries of Christianity. Although the Neoplatonists knew that God was the goal of human happiness, still they knew not the way of humility leading to him. In Augustine's own case, it was not until he discerned the vast difference between the confession of sin and of limitations, and the presumption of self-excellence that he cast off the proud blindness of these philosophers.[209] Just as a swollen face can impair one's vision, so had pride closed off his intellect.[210]

Finally, the Saint cites the punishment of those who through pride had sought the devils as their mediators, and had been deluded by them. Resorting to various practices of magic, they had fallen victim to the devil, who deceived them under the guise of an angel of light. It is significant, moreover, to note the motivation of such men. What made the devil so attractive to them was the fact that he had no body of flesh. This appealed to their pride.[211]

All these passages of the *Confessions* demonstrate the Divine punishment of pride. Pride and rebellion towards God also have

---

[208] See *Conf.*, 5, 3, 3-5. See also Wangnereck, *Confessionum*, 144, where he lists the vices of the learned pagans as pride, impurity, wilful ignorance, ingratitude and irreligion.

[209] See *supra*, ch. 2, 42-43; ch. 3, 125-127. See also *Conf.*, 7, 9, 13: Quia vero *in sua propria venit et sui eum non receperunt, quotquot autem receperunt eum, dedit eis potestatem filios Dei fieri credentibus in nomine ejus* (John 1:1 ff.), non ibi legi.

[210] *See Conf.*, 7, 7, 11: Et haec de vulnere meo creverant, quia *humiliasti tamquam vulneratum superbum* (Ps. 88:11), et tumore meo separabar abs te et nimis inflata facies claudebat oculos meos.

[211] See *ibid.*, 10, 42, 67. It is interesting to note how St. Thomas treats blindness of mind as a punishment for sin, pointing out that habitual sins of impurity darken the intellect. See S.T., 2-2, 15, 1-3.

another effect besides blindness. When man rebels against God, his passions rebel against his reason and will, and in punishment for his disobedience man, in turn, is disobeyed by his own powers, and the right order established by God is disturbed.[212] According to this right order, all things outside man, and all his faculties within are under the domain of his will, and his will is subject to God.

In the enslavement that results from a voluntary habit of impurity, which has been described previously,[213] one notes this perversion of right order. Instead of the passions being under the rule of the will, the reverse is true, and, more than that, the enslaved will finds it very difficult to act as a unit. It finds the pleasure of lust so attractive that it does not rise up, as it were, and tear itself from its bonds, even though it knows that it should do so, and *half* desires to free itself. Both the rebellion of the flesh against the will, as well as the civil war within the will itself, therefore, may be considered as the Divine punishment for the *voluntary* formation of a carnal vice.

Again, viewing the punishment of sin as it appears in the whole person, Augustine points out how he lost himself in the state of dissipation and confusion, so that he no longer discerned within

---

[212] See *Conf.*, 7, 7, 11: Superior enim eram istis, te vero inferior, et tu gaudium verum mihi subdito tibi, et tu mihi subjeceras quae infra me creasti. Et hoc erat rectum temperamentum et media regio salutis meae, ut manerem ad imaginem tuam et tibi serviens dominarer corpori. Sed cum superbe contra te surgerem et currerem adversus Dominum *in cervice crassa scuti mei* (Job 5:26), etiam ista infima supra me facta sunt et premebant, et nusquam erat laxamentum et respiramentum. See also *Contra advers. leg. et proph.*, 1. 14 (ML 42.613): Haec est namque poena inobedienti homini reddita in semetipso, ut ei vicissim non obediatur nec a semetipso.

[213] See *supra*, ch. 3, 79-86. It should be kept in mind, however, in considering the rebellion of the flesh a punishment for sin that here the emphasis is on actual sin, not on original sin. The punitive aspect of original sin is mentioned on page 103. On the following pages *voluntary* bad habit is shown to be *both* a Divine punishment and a state of sin. Inasmuch as one has willed the habit in its cause, he has sinned; inasmuch as he suffers from its effects, he is punished. This double point of view is expressed clearly by the Saint in another work: *Contra Ad.*, ch. 26 (CSEL 25.184): Dupliciter enim appellatur malum: unum quod homo facit; alterum quod patitur. Quod facit, peccatum est: quod patitur, poena.

himself the distinction between lust and love; and this condition he considers as the Divine retribution for his pride and lust:

> Thy wrath increased towards me, and I knew it not. I was already grown deaf by the continual noise of that chain which my sins had framed, in punishment for the pride of my soul. So I went yet further from thee, and thou sufferedst me. I was tossed up and down, and was poured out like water; I was scattered and did even seethe over in the midst of my fornications, and thou heldest thy peace.[214]

Augustine was blind even to the fact of his punishment. In this passage he specifies pride of soul as the *root* cause of the general dissipation of his soul in blindness and impurity.

Implicit in the very notion of sin itself is its punishment; for in his rejection of God the sinner deprives himself of the very source of his spiritual life, and consequently wallows in mire—as if outside his own nature.[215] At the same time habitual sin creates within the soul an intense restlessness, which remains until the soul returns to God.[216] The soul's unrest, therefore, is not merely a punishment for sin; it may be considered also as an effect of Divine mercy. This aspect of sin deserves at least passing notice.

Thus Augustine pictures the sinner as fleeing blindly from God only to stumble against Him and be injured. In this way he is justly punished, but he is also reminded that God will receive him

---

[214] *Conf.*, 2, 2, 2: Invaluerat super me ira tua et nesciebam. Obsurdueram stridore catenae mortalitatis meae, poena superbiae animae meae, et ibam longius a te, et sinebas, et jactabar et effundebar et diffluebam et ebulliebam per fornicationes meas, et tacebas. See also *ibid.*, 2, 1, 1: Dum ab uno te aversus in multa evanui. Exarsi enim aliquando satiari inferis in adolescentia et silvescere ausus sum variis et umbrosis amoribus. Campbell and McGuire (*The Confessions of St. Augustine*, 99, nn. 6-7) explain the force of the word *evanui*: In turning from God the sinner tends towards complete moral disorganization.

[215] See *supra*, ch. 3, 118, n. 150. See also *supra*, ch. 3, 123, n. 166.

[216] See *ibid.*, 6, 16, 26: Vae animae meae audaci, quae speravit, si a te recessisset, se aliquid melius habituram! Versa et reversa in tergum et in latera et in ventrem, et dura sunt omnia, et tu solus requies. See also *ibid.*, 2, 2, 4; 13, 2, 3; and 13, 17, 20.

with mercy if he repents for his sins.[217] In another passage he says that God pursued him in his sins, and scourged him with merciful rigor by sprinkling his unlawful pleasures with most bitter alloys, so that he might be persuaded to seek unmixed happiness. Again, repeating the same figure, he explains what he meant by "bitter alloys." Referring to the illicit pleasures of concubinage, he relates how it was mingled with the gall of jealousy, suspicion, fears, and quarrels.[218]

In several additional passages the Saint stresses the mercy of God, working upon the misery of the sinner, and by means of internal goads moving him back to Himself.[219] The internal misery of the sinner can be the instrument of Divine Mercy and grace.

---

[217] See *ibid.*, 5, 2, 2,

[218] See *ibid.*, 2, 2, 4. See also *ibid.*, 3, 1, 1.

[219] See *ibid.*, 6, 6, 9: Patiebar in eis cupiditatibus amarissimas difficultates te propitio tanto magis, quanto minus sinebas mihi dulcescere quod non eras tu. See also *ibid.*, 6, 10, 17: Et in omni amaritudine, quae nostros saeculares actus de *misericordia tua* (italics mine) sequebatur, intuentibus nobis finem, cur ea pateremur, occurrebant tenebrae. . . . *Ibid.*, 6, 16, 26: Ego fiebam miserior, et tu propinquior; *ibid.*, 9, 4, 7.

CHAPTER IV

Remedies

Even while Augustine describes various obstacles along the road to God, he suggests diverse ways and means of surmounting these difficulties. These positive aids are incorporated by the writer under the term *remedies.* Some of these have been discussed in Chapter II, where the teaching of the *Confessions* on the virtues of charity, humility, love of truth, and continence is summarized;[1] still others are mentioned in the consideration of such human weaknesses as division of will and vanity;[2] and, finally, several others will be outlined in this chapter. In no way, however, does this selection of remedies imply that there are no other positive aids to virtue mentioned in this work.

As always—in any discussion of concrete aids to the practice of virtue, one must keep in mind that in the dynamic interactions within the soul many factors exert their influence; and if certain factors are singled out for investigation, it is for the purpose of evaluating these in the spiritual rehabilitation of Augustine. What helped him may prove of practical value to others in their daily struggle for virtue. Accordingly, the thought of the *Confessions* on these three topics may be digested: good example, Scriptural readings, and healing grace.

A. Good Example

Two kinds of good example exercised their influence over Augustine: *group* good example, as shown by the monks of the desert; and *individual,* as reflected in Christ, St. Monnica, St. Ambrose, Simplicianus, and Victorinus.

Since the influence of the Savior upon St. Augustine was the most profound of all individuals, it is fitting that it be considered

---

[1] See *supra,* ch. 2, 32-47; 55-60.

[2] See *supra,* ch. 3, 102-103; 130-131.

first. He depicts Christ as crying out to us to follow Him by means of His words and deeds, and most especially by his ignominious death and glorious resurrection. This is regarded by Augustine as an object lesson in the practice and reward of the virtue of humility, to the practice of which the God-man also calls *us*.[3] Accordingly, the Saint exhorts *all* Christians to become lights in the firmament of the Church: "Scatter in different directions, ye holy fires, ye beautiful fires; for ye are the light of the world, nor are ye put under a bushel (Matt. 5:14). He, to whom ye did cleave, is exalted, and He hath exalted you. Spread out and become known to all nations."[4] Most particularly, however, should the ministers of Christ be the pattern of the faithful by living in such a manner as to inspire the faithful to imitate Christ.[5]

It is hardly necessary to develop the important role that the good example of St. Monnica played in the conversion of her son. Following her son in his wanderings she lavished upon him the fullness of a mother's love, while, at the same time, she rebuked him by her holy life. She remained with him as a silent but constant reproach for his flight from her Faith, and thus she helped to create within him that salutary confusion that paved the way for his conversion.[6]

Next to St. Monnica in exercising a beneficial influence upon St. Augustine comes St. Ambrose. Like St. Monnica, St. Ambrose worked his way into the heart of the wayward son in a gradual and imperceptible fashion. It was the paternal kindness and very human understanding of the bishop of Milan that first attracted the son of Monnica. Drawn by the charm of St. Ambrose, Augustine listened to his sermons, because he was curious to hear a preacher already famed for his eloquence, and despite the fact that he was interested only in the oratorical style of St. Ambrose, his mind began to drink

---

[3] See *supra*, ch. 2, 42, n. 140.

[4] *Conf.*, 13, 19, 25: Ubique discurrite, ignes sancti, ignes decori. Vos enim *estis lumen mundi* nec estis *sub modio* (Matt. 5:14). Exaltatus est, cui adhaesistis, et exaltavit vos. Discurrite et innotescite omnibus gentibus.

[5] See *ibid.*, 13, 21, 30.

[6] The following passages of the *Confessions* develop the virtues of St. Monnica: 3, 11-12, 19-21; 5, 7, 13; 5, 9, 16; and 9, 9-11, 19-28.

in *gradually* the Revealed doctrines contained in the words of this great preacher.[7]

In this slow and unconscious advance of Augustine towards the Church, the influence of St. Ambrose is beyond evaluation. His chaste and austere life, blended with his kindliness, hypnotized, as it were, the will of the youthful Augustine, and, as he listened to the exposition of Scripture from the lips of St. Ambrose, his prejudices against the Church were dissipated, and his approach to the Old Testament, in particular, was reorientated into the mold of St. Ambrose. He helped Augustine to interpret the Scriptures according to the spirit rather than merely according to the letter. In short, the bishop of Milan furnished the future Saint with the key to the understanding of the Scriptures.[8]

The virtuous life of Simplicianus was another factor in the conversion of Augustine. Hesitating on the brink of conversion, he sought out Simplicianus, who seized the opportunity to instruct him by means of a story about the conversion of the poet Victorinus. The narrative had its intended effect. Augustine was impressed by the humility and courage of Victorinus, and he burned with the desire to emulate him.[9]

---

[7] See *Conf.*, 5, 13, 23. See also *ibid.*, 5, 14, 24.

[8] See Boyer, *Christianisme et Néo-Platonisme . . .*, 52: Celui-ci sans en avoir conscience, semble-t-il, a agi profondément sur l'âme d'Augustin. Il l'a impressionnée, affrayée même, par l'exemple d'une vie singulièrement digne et chaste. Il l'a changée par sa parole. . . . Il ne l'a point retourné tout d'un coup, mais secondé par d'autres influences, il l'a amené, par degrés, à penser comme lui.

Boyer feels that it is difficult to estimate how great was the influence of St. Ambrose upon St. Augustine (see *op. cit.*, 58). See also Mausbach, *Die Ethik des heiligen Augustinus*, 1.13; Wangnereck, *Confessionum*, 171-172; Switalski, *Neoplatonism and the Ethics of St. Augustine*, 65: A significant factor in this slow and unconscious advance towards the Church and the truth was the influence of Ambrose on Augustine's will and intellect. . . . Augustine's will was wholly hypnotized by the powerful individuality of this great statesman and bishop.

[9] See *Conf.*, 8, 2, 3: Perrexi ergo ad Simplicianum. . . . Deinde, ut me exhortaretur ad humilitatem Christi sapientibus absconditam et revelatam parvulis, Victorinum ipsum recordatus est, quem, Romae cum esset, familiarissime noverat, . . . (Victorinus) non erubuerit esse puer Christi tui et infans fontis tui subjecto collo ad humilitatis jugum et edomita fronte ad

Shortly thereafter this desire was intensified still more when Pontitianus related to the restless Augustine the story of Antony and his monks in the desert, as well as the fact that St. Ambrose was in charge of a monastery outside the city of Milan. All this was *news* to Augustine, who listened avidly to the added tale of Pontitianus about the two courtiers. Upon reading the life of St. Antony, these two decided immediately to give up the vanities of their way of life and to dedicate themselves to God. The promptness of their decision shook Augustine to his very depths and drove him within himself to look at himself as he really was. The consequent comparison of himself with the two courtiers led him to a salutary self-hatred, confusion, and desire for the same sort of life.[10]

It may be noted that it was the *cumulative* force of good example from so many that penetrated gradually the heart and mind of Augustine and goaded him onwards to conversion. Immediately before his conversion, lust tempted him to remain as he was, but the acute remembrance of *so many* men and women who had embraced the practice of chastity asserted its power once again under the personification of Chastity as a beautiful lady, surrounded by a multitude of men and women of every age and condition of life.[11] When added to the powerful influence of individuals like St. Monnica, St. Ambrose, Victorinus, and others, the good example of whole groups wielded a tremendous persuasiveness over the unsettled mind of Augustine.

In his *Confessions,* moreover, the Saint stresses the effect that the conversion of the well known Victorinus had not only upon himself, but also upon the Roman populace. The good example of such an outstanding person tended to draw others after him. Among the faithful witnessing his public adjuration of paganism and his profession of the true Faith a spirit of joyous fervor spread. A common spirit of supernatural joy pervaded the entire assembly, causing each member of the group to become an in-

---

crucis opprobrium. See also *ibid.,* 8, 5, 10: Sed ubi mihi homo tuus Simplicianus de Victorino ista narravit, exarsi ad imitandum: ad hoc enim et ille narraverat; Mausbach, *op. cit.,* 1.6.

[10] See *Conf.,* 8, 6, 14-15. See *supra,* ch. 2, 19-21.

[11] See *supra,* ch. 2, 59-60.

spiration to his neighbor in the practice of virtue: "For when many men rejoice together, the joy of each man is deeper, because they mutually enkindle and enflame one another."[12]

By nourishing himself, as it were, on the common joy of the group, each member finds it easier to live the Faith, for joy is a *positive* factor in the practice of virtue. In direct contrast to that fear of human respect that intimidates the members of a crowd to participate in the sinful actions of the crowd, joy is a most powerful psychological component in the practice of virtue. Accordingly, then, in pastoral work one can strive to enkindle a similar joy for the living of Catholic ideals in the members of a particular group. Most especially can a *common enthusiasm* for virtue pervade our Catholic youth groups. This is an effective antidote to that mass fear that persuades many weak Catholics to accept certain sinful customs of the pagan world surrounding them.

It is not enough merely to warn our Catholic youth to avoid conformity with pagan customs, like that of passionate kissing among adolescents. In addition it is necessary to inculcate into Catholic youth groups a spirit of joy in the practice of purity, precisely because they are followers of Christ.

B. SCRIPTURAL READINGS

In Augustine's journey towards the Faith reading played an important role. Already it has been noted that the *Hortensius* of Cicero inspired him to search out the truth, and that the *Enneads* of Plotinus enriched his mind with correct concepts of the spirituality of God and the privative nature of evil.[13] By thus opening up the spiritual world to Augustine, the writings of Plotinus stimulated him to a deeper understanding and more ready acceptance of Catholic truth.[14] At the same time, however,

---

[12] *Conf.*, 8, 4, 9: Quando enim cum multis gaudetur, et in singulis uberius est gaudium, quia fervefaciunt se et inflammantur ex alterutro. (The above translation is my own.) See also Mausbach, *op. cit.*, 1.309.

[13] See *supra*, ch. 3, 112-113.

[14] See Switalski, *op. cit.*, 69-73: The *Enneads* solved Augustine's two fundamental difficulties, namely, the falsity of materialism and the problem of evil. And so the last two intellectual obstacles were removed. . . . The treatise of Plotinus . . . opened up to Augustine the vision of a new world.

the *Enneads* tended to create in him a smug attitude that was not at all conducive to the conversion of the will. Thus, it was only after he had read the Scriptures that he was able to form the efficacious decision to embrace the Faith.[15]

Among the books of Scripture, moreover, the writings of St. Paul exerted a most profound influence over him. From reading the Apostle of the Gentiles he learned his own misery and the necessity of dependence upon Divine grace, and thereupon he rejected the pride of the Neoplatonists. Previously, he had considered the teaching of St. Paul as contradictory to that of the Old Testament, but now these difficulties vanished, and—what is more significant—the Pauline doctrine of grace sunk into his very being: "These thoughts, by wondrous ways, did sink into my very heart, while I was reading that least of thine Apostles, and I considered thy works, and with terror was I amazed thereat."[16] Thus it was the *meditative* study of St. Paul that led Augustine to a conversion of the heart and will—to "conversion du coeur," as C. Boyer aptly terms it.[17]

Besides showing the importance of Scriptural reading in his own life, St. Augustine explains the practical moral content of the Sacred Writings, and counsels certain virtues to be utilized in the interpretation of the Revealed Word. According to him, the Scriptures teach the humble Christ. No other books are so destructive of pride as the Scriptures, and at the same time they persuade the soul to a humble service of God. In the Psalms of David, especially, one may discern a tone of simplicity and

---

[15] See *supra*, ch. 2, 43; ch. 3, 112-113.

[16] *Conf.*, 7, 21, 27: Haec mihi inviscerabantur miris modis cum minimum Apostolorum tuorum legerem, et consideraveram opera tua et expaveram. See also *supra*, ch. 2, 43; *Conf.*, 8, 12, 29: Arripui, aperui, et legi in silentio capitulum, quo primum conjecti sunt oculi mei: *Non in comisationibus et ebrietatibus, non in cubilibus et inpudicitiis, . . . sed induite Dominum Jesum Christum et carnis providentiam ne feceritis in concupiscentiis* (Rom. 13:13 ff.). Nec ultra volui legere nec opus est.

[17] See *ibid.*, 8, 6, 14. See also Boyer, *op. cit.*, 125-126: Il y a découvert, adoucie par une onction suave et par une perpétuelle exhortation à la confiance en Dieu, une leçon d'humilité. . . .

humility.[18] Again, the Saint teaches that nothing in the Sacred Books was written in vain. Even the *hidden* things are meant for our instruction; and for this reason Augustine prays that his mind may be able to understand the *deeper* meanings of such. Hence he sought a more perfect knowledge of *Christ* through all the books of the Bible.[19]

One should read the Scriptures not merely to benefit himself, but to aid others as well. Since the interpretation of these inspired writings is so difficult, one should begin his study with the prayer that God will give him light to draw profit from them and to avoid all opinionatedness and bitterness of discussion. Fraternal charity should leaven all discussions of the Revealed Word, seeing that these books were written to foster charity rather than to provide material for captious arguments.[20] It is foolish and rash, therefore, for an individual to insist that his interpretation of a particular passage of Scripture is the only correct one. Such an attitude springs from pride.

In interpreting the very difficult first chapters of Genesis, for example, some hold that Moses meant *only* what they have gathered from the text. In reality, they love not Moses' opinion, but their own, and this they love, not because it is true, but because it is theirs. Otherwise, they would love another acceptable interpretation with equal readiness, precisely because it is true. Truth does not belong to individuals in an exclusive fashion; it is meant to be *shared* by all lovers of the truth. To those who claim the truth as their exclusive possession comes the punishment of Divine Justice: They slip into most pernicious errors and sin.[21]

---

[18] See *Conf.*, 13, 15, 17. See also *ibid.*, 9, 4, 8: Quas tibi, Deus meus voces dedi, cum legerem psalmos David, cantica fidelia, sonos pietatis excludentes turgidum spiritum. . . . Et quomodo in te inflammabar ex eis et accendebar eos recitare, si possem, toto orbi terrarum adversum tyfum generis humani; *ibid.*, 4, 12, 19.

[19] See *ibid.*, 11, 2, 3. See also *ibid.*, 11, 2, 4; Mausbach, *op. cit.*, 2.367, where he points out that St. Augustine sought Christ in all the books of Scripture.

[20] See *Conf.*, 11, 2, 3. See also *ibid.*, 12, 18, 27: Quibus omnibus auditis et consideratis *nolo verbis contendere; ad nihil enim utile est nisi ad subversionem audientium* (II Tim. 2:14). . . .

[21] See *ibid.*, 12, 25, 34. See also *ibid.*, 12, 27, 37.

In stressing the fact, moreover, that Genesis has an abundance of true meanings, and that it is rash to affirm which of them Moses principally meant, Augustine expounds a practical norm to follow: Since the depth of Holy Scripture is so rich in meanings, manifold senses may and ought to be extracted from it; and hence whatever truth can be mined from its words, does, in fact, lie hidden in them.[22]

In place of bitter contentions, which tend to defeat the very purpose for which the Scriptures were written, namely, to nourish *charity*—let truth herself produce concord. Let everyone love his brother, and let all, as one body, love God, who is the source of all truth. Let not the reader of Scripture seek to force his opinion upon others; for when the inspired author wrote his book, he intended *all* those meanings that excel both for light of truth and for their *practical bearing* upon our manner of life. In a spirit of charity, then, we ought to allow and to profit by all interpretations *in accord* with the *Faith*.[23]

St. Augustine says that whenever he cannot understand a Scriptural passage, he does not assert that the passage is meaningless, but instead he leaves it to the judgment of others, whom he considers as more skilled in the interpretation of the Revealed Word than he is. In this way he exemplifies the humility with which one should read the Bible.[24] Again, in his meditative discourse on Psalm Four the Saint reveals his method of applying the Scriptures to himself, drawing from the Psalm salutary resolutions for his daily life.[25] In this way his reading of the

---

[22] See *ibid.*, 12, 25, 35. See also *ibid.*, 12, 31, 42: Nolo itaque, Deus meus, tam praeceps esse, ut hoc illum virum de te meruisse non credam. Sensit ille omnino in his verbis atque cogitavit, cum ea scriberet, quidquid hic veri potuimus invenire et quidquid nos non potuimus, aut nondum potuimus et tamen in eis inveniri potest.

[23] See *ibid.*, 12, 30, 41.

[24] See *ibid.*, 13, 24, 36: Et si ego non intellego, quid hoc eloquio significes, utantur eo melius meliores, id est intellegentiores quam ego sum, unicuique quantum sapere dedisti.

[25] See *ibid.*, 9, 4, 9-11: He shows how one of its verses was very profitable to him: Legebam *'Irascimini et nolite peccare'* (Ps. 4:5) et quomodo movebar, Deus meus, qui jam didiceram irasci mihi de praeteritis, ut de cetero

Sacred Books acquired a practical moral value. Needless to add—they possess the same value for others *if* they are read with the intense application of an Augustine.

In the study of Scripture, however, the individual must have guidance from the Church. This need is illustrated clearly in the life of St. Augustine. Before he met St. Ambrose, despite his brilliant mind, he had given to these writings purely literal interpretations with the result that he was repelled by them; but under the fatherly guidance of St. Ambrose he was able to understand the symbolic character of many events in the Old Testament, and his mind was opened to the deeper spiritual meanings of the Sacred Writings. Thus, even the most intelligent need the help of the Church for the correct interpretation of the Bible.[26] In conclusion, the Saint stresses the eminent authority of the Scriptures, comparing them to the firmament of heaven, stretched over us as a guiding light, and insisting that the words of the inspired authors are truly the voice of God.[27]

C. HEALING GRACE

More than once in the *Confessions* St. Augustine refers to Divine grace as healing his soul from the ravages of sin and restoring order and peace therein. Thus, in book two he states that it was by the grace of God alone that he was able to rise from the mire of sin, and he adds that the Divine Physician who has healed his soul has preserved many of the readers of the *Confessions*

---

non peccarem, et merito irasci, quia non alia natura gentis tenebrarum de me peccabat, sicut dicunt qui sibi non irascuntur et *thesaurizant sibi iram in die irae et revelationis justi judicii tui* (Rom. 2:5).

[26] See *supra,* ch. 2, 48-49, n. 163. See also *Conf.,* 6, 4, 6: Et tamquam regulam diligentissime conmendaret, saepe in popularibus sermonibus suis dicentem Ambrosium laetus audiebam: *Littera occidit, spiritus* autem *vivificat* (2 Cor. 3:6), cum ea quae ad litteram perversitatem docere videbantur, remoto mystico velamento spiritualiter aperiret, non dicens quod me offenderet, quamvis ea diceret, quae utrum vera essent adhuc ignorarem; *ibid.,* 6, 5, 7; Boyer, *Christianisme et Néo-Platonisme,* . . .

[27] See *Conf.,* 13, 15, 16. See also *ibid.,* 13, 29, 44. It is interesting to note that the *Confessions* are permeated by Scriptural thought. The Psalms are quoted over four hundred times, and the Epistles of St. Paul about two hundred times. (See Knöll, *Confessionum,* Leipzig: Teubner, 1898, 334-335.)

from a *moral* illness similar to that of himself. Hence let them not attribute their innocence to their own unaided powers:

> What man is there who, considering his own frailty, dares yet to attribute unto his own strength his chastity or his innocence. For then must he love thee the less, as if to him that mercy of thine had been less necessary, by which thou dost forgive their sins to them that return to thee after having fallen. He then that, being called by thee, hath followed thy voice and escaped those things which now he finds me to be remembering and confessing against myself, let him not laugh at me because I am recovered by the care of that Physician, to whom was due that he should not be sick at all.[28]

In other passages, also, the Saint describes the healing effects of Divine grace in such a way that one may use the term *healing grace* to denote that entire series of *supernatural* aids by which he overcame his spiritual blindness and carnal concupiscence, became a Christian, and continued to live in virtue despite the inveterate tendencies of bad habit. Since, however, in chapter two the necessity of grace for the practical moral life has been treated, it will suffice here to consider a few representative passages in which the function of Divine grace as a remedy for habitual sin is described.[29]

After describing how pride had swollen, as it were, his face so badly as to blind him, Augustine delineates the counterbalancing effects of Divine grace under a twofold figure. By creating a state of restlessness in his soul God activates him to seek his Creator: "And with a hidden goad thou didst urge me, that I might be

---

[28] *Conf.*, 2, 7, 15: Quis est hominum qui suam cogitans infirmitatem audet viribus suis tribuere castitatem atque innocentiam suam, ut minus amet te, quasi minus ei necessaria fuerit misericordia tua, qua donas peccata conversis ad te? Qui enim vocatus a te secutus est vocem tuam et vitavit ea, quae me de me ipso recordantem et fatentem legit, non me derideat ab eo medico aegrum sanari a quo sibi praestitum est ut non aegrotaret. See also *ibid.*, 4, 5, 11; *supra*, ch. 2, 55-61.

[29] See *supra*, ch. 2, 15-23 (grace and conscience); 25-29 (grace and the practical moral life); ch. 3, 102. See also Gilson, *Introduction à l'étude de saint Augustin*, 185.

restless until such time as the sight of my mind might discern thee for certain."[30] Such internal goads were to the soul of Augustine what healing ointment is to the eyes; for they diminished little by little the swelling of pride until spiritual eye-sight returned: "Thus did the swelling of my heart abate through thy hidden hand, which knew how to cure me, and the troubled and darksome eye of my soul was healed day by day, by the smarting eye-salve of wholesome grief."[31] Divine grace worked *gradually* through mental unrest and confusion.

In another passage the Saint compares God's grace to a fountain, to which the sinner returns burning and panting.[32] No longer does the sinner wish to lead his own life apart from God, for now he desires to become *alive* again in God: "Let me not be my own life; I have lived ill of myself, I was death unto myself, in thee do I recover life again."[33] God is more present to ourselves than we are to ourselves, and we are dependent upon Him for our continuance in existence.[34] God is the light of our heart, the

---

[30] *Conf.*, 7, 8, 12: Et stimulis internis agitabas me, ut inpatiens essem, donec mihi per interiorem aspectum certus esses. See also *ibid.*, 10, 27, 38 and 10, 36, 58.

[31] *Ibid.*, 7, 8, 12: Et residebat tumor meus ex occulta manu medicinae tuae aciesque conturbata et contenebrata mentis meae acri collyrio salubrium dolorum de die in diem sanabatur. See also Wangnereck, *Confessionum*, 234, n. 1: Collyrium proprie significat medicamentum oculorum. S.D. per translationem ita appellat internos stimulos, et aestum animi aspirantis ad veritatem, his enim Deus sensim sanavit ejus superbiam, propriis viribus aspirantem ad *notitiam* rerum divinarum, et impedientem, quominus eas recte intelligeret; J. Maritain, "St. Augustine and St. Thomas," in *A Monument to St. Augustine* (London: Sheed and Ward, 1930), 207: Furthermore, experience had taught Augustine that the sinner's wounded reason needs to be healed by *gratia sanans,* if it is actually to recover the soundness of its natural vigor, even in an order of truths accessible of themselves to the demonstration of reason.

[32] See *Conf.*, 12, 10, 10: Et nunc ecce redeo aestuans et anhelans ad fontem tuum. Nemo me prohibeat: hunc bibam et hunc vivam.

[33] *Loc. cit.*: Non ego vita mea sim; male vixi ex me, mors mihi fui; in te revivesco. See also Gilson, *op. cit.*, 140-141; *supra,* ch. 1, 1.

[34] See *Conf.*, 3, 6, 11: Tu autem eras interior intimo meo et superior summo meo. See also *ibid.*, 7, 1, 2: Ita etiam te, vita vitae meae . . . ; *ibid.*, 10, 6, 10: Deus autem tuus etiam tibi vitae vita est.

food of our soul, and the vivifying power of our spirit.[35] The idea of Divine grace as *food* is repeated again in another passage: "I am the Food of the strong, grow apace, and thou shalt feed on me; nor shalt thou convert me like common food into thy substance, but thou shalt be converted into me."[36] This was the Divine nourishment proffered to the hesitating Augustine.

Thus, in the above passage the Saint contrasts physical nourishment with spiritual. In the former the individual makes the food a part of himself by the process of biological assimilation; but in the latter the Divine food of grace makes the soul like unto God. The soul feeds, as it were, on God, and becomes like Him. Hence under a variety of figures Augustine depicts the effects of Divine grace in the soul of the sinner that he was. So firmly does he believe in the power of grace that he affirms that God could heal all the wounds of sin—all the psychological effects of bad habits still remaining in the memory and imagination—if He willed to do so.[37]

This power of grace, then, encourages the sinner to cast himself completely into the hands of God, as Augustine did just before his conversion. As already mentioned in Chapter II,[38] *fear* that he could not do without the pleasure of concupiscence held him back from the decision to give up the world; but in the vision of Lady Chastity he understood that others were able to practice chastity—not by their own strength alone, but by the grace of God. In guiding sinners who are afraid that they will fall back into their former vice, confessors can urge them to have great confidence in the grace of God. It seems that many habitual sinners give in to recurrent temptations arising from repudiated, but still rebellious, tendencies, because they feel that their will cannot hold out against them. Indeed some who are in the state of grace invite these temptations back by their very fear of a relapse. The

---

[35] See *ibid.,* 1, 13, 21: . . . Deus, lumen cordis mei et panis oris intus animae meae et virtus maritans mentem meam et sinum cogitationis meae.

[36] *Ibid.,* 7, 10, 16: Cibus sum grandium: cresce et manducabis me. Nec tu me in te mutabis sicut cibum carnis tuae, sed tu mutaberis in me. See also Wangnereck, *op. cit.,* 240, n. 1.

[37] See *supra,* ch. 3, 85-86.

[38] See *supra,* ch. 2, 59-60; ch. 3, 83-84.

remedy must be the words of Lady Chastity to Augustine: "Cast thyself upon Him and fear not, He will not withdraw Himself and let thee fall."[39]

In the study of divided will it was shown that such a conflict renders the individual helpless to rise from sin, and that an united will, or singleness of purpose, must condition any real amendment of life. The achievement of unity in the will comes only with the help of Divine grace, which must be sought after the example of both St. Augustine and St. Monnica, whose persevering prayers helped her son in the practice of virtue.[40] Augustine, for example, did not overcome the habit of concupiscence until he realized that he could conquer it only by the aid of Divine grace.[41] Like St. Paul he found in the grace of Christ an effective remedy for the violence of carnal habit: *"Unhappy man that I am, who shall deliver me from the body of this death? The grace of God, by Jesus Christ, our Lord* (Rom. 7:24-25)."[42] Thus frequently he prayed for the grace to conquer the habit of concupiscence.[43] This fact can be stressed by the confessor in guiding the victims of vices. They must pray for grace, for the least amount of grace is able to overcome the strongest impulse of concupiscence.[44]

In regard to their will, they must strive to keep it free from all those factors that held Augustine back from conversion. Among these were the rationalization of pleasure, fear, and delay in renouncing the occasions of sin, all sources of a divided will. Since, moreover, a strong will is one in which positive values and motives draw the will *away* from the pleasures of sin and center

---

[39] *Conf.*, 8, 11, 27: Proice te in eum; noli metuere, non se subtrahet, ut cadas. See also *supra*, ch. 2, 59-60.

[40] See *supra*, ch. 3, 98-103. See also *Conf.*, 5, 9, 17.

[41] See *supra*, ch. 2, 56.

[42] *Conf.*, 8, 5, 12: *Miserum ergo me quis liberaret de corpore mortis hujus nisi gratia tua per Jesum Christum Dominum Nostrum?* (Rom. 7:24-25)

[43] See *ibid.*, 10, 29, 40: Continentiam jubes: da quod jubes et jube quod vis. The same formula is repeated: *Ibid.*, 10, 31, 45 and 10, 37, 60.

[44] See S.T. 3, 62, 6, ad 3: . . . quia minima gratia potest resistere cuilibet concupiscentiae et mereri vitam aeternam. See also *ibid.*, 3, 70, 4: . . . quia minima gratia potest resistere cuilibet concupiscentiae et vitare omne peccatum mortale, quod committitur in transgressione mandatorum legis.

it on Christ as the single goal of the soul, such penitents must strive to put on the mind of Christ. The mere avoidance of the occasions of sin is inadequate; it must be reenforced by a positive spiritual renewal of the sinner.[45]

It may encourage the sinner, moreover, to realize that such a positive spiritual renovation is a *gradual* process, just as it was in Augustine's slow movement toward the Church. Working with the most varied instruments, fear of hell and compunction of conscience, mental confusion and sorrow, the warm humanity of St. Ambrose and the holy motherhood of St. Monnica, group good example, readings in Cicero, Plotinus, and most especially in the Scriptures, Divine grace prepared the soul of Augustine for that dramatic moment of decision in the garden. Since, however, the gradual character of the activity of Divine grace has been treated already,[46] it will suffice here to comment upon several incidents immediately preceding his conversion. During this period the flesh tended to hold him back, and his will remained, as it were, suspended, but with the help of grace he did not fall back into his former ways.[47]

Shortly thereafter the vision of chastity intensified the conflict within him and led him to an understanding of himself that was

---

[45] See *supra,* ch. 1, 4-5. See also *Conf.,* 13, 21, 30-32: Continete vos ab immani feritate superbiae, ab inerti voluptate luxuriae et a fallaci *nomine scientiae* (I Tim. 6:20), ut sint bestiae mansuetae et pecora edomita et innoxii serpentes. This is a figurative way of saying that one should avoid pride, lust, and inordinate curiosity. . . . In sect. 32 the Saint adds to this negative injunction a positive directive taken from St. Paul: Cum cohibitae fuerint affectiones ab amore saeculi, quibus moriebamur male vivendo, et coeperit esse anima vivens bene vivendo completumque fuerit verbum tuum, quo per apostolum tuum dixisti: *Nolite conformari huic saeculo,* consequetur illud, quod adjunxisti statim et dixisti: *Sed reformamini in novitate mentis vestrae* (Rom. 12:2 ff.). In this spiritual renewal of man love remained the activating force, as J. Capello points out (*Confessionum,* XXXVII): Voluntatis actuosum principium est amor a quo procedit bona vel mala operatio et quilibet motus animi omnesque virtutes ducuntur. Sicut amoris motus est vitae centrum affectuosae, ita amor ordinatus et rectus est centrum vitae moralis.

[46] See *supra,* ch. 2, 18-22.

[47] See *Conf.,* 8, 11, 25.

as painful to self-love as it was profitable for moral amendment.[48] This sharp perception of his own misery and consequent dependence upon the mercy of God caused him to pray for the grace of conversion: "And I cried out at large to thee, not perhaps in these very words, but to this effect, 'And thou, O Lord, how long?' . . . . For I felt myself to be still enthralled by them, and therefore did I cast forth these lamentable exclamations, 'How long, how long? . . . . Why not, even at this instant, make an end of my uncleanness?' "[49]

This prayer was heard by God. Immediately thereafter Augustine heard the mysterious voice, followed out its injunction, and made up his mind to embrace the Faith of his mother. Thereupon all his doubts gave way to a true peace of soul.[50]

From the *Confessions* the guide of souls may cull the fabrics of a reconstruction program for individuals beset with evil habits. He can point out to the penitent not merely abstract principles about the nature of virtue and of vice, but also concrete incidents in which Augustine, or someone else, overcame a vice or practiced a virtue. Again, he can show the sinner that the God of the *Confessions* is a loving Father, who works through the most mysterious channels to win back his sinful children to the ways of grace. As the soul uses the natural powers of intellect and of will, and of the other faculties as instruments of expression, so Divine grace utilizes the virtues of faith, hope, charity, humility, and continence, among others, to develop in the soul of man the supernatural life.[51]

---

[48] See *supra,* ch. 2, 60. See also *Conf.,* 8, 11, 27: Et erubescebam nimis, quia illarum nugarum murmura adhuc audiebam, et cunctabundus pendebam. Et rursus illa, quasi diceret: 'Obsurdesce adversus inmunda illa membra tua, ut mortificentur. . . .' Ista controversia in corde meo non nisi de me ipso adversus me ipsum.

[49] *Ibid.,* 8, 12, 28: Et non quidem his verbis, sed in hac sententia multa dixi tibi: *Et tu, Domine, usquequo?* . . . (Ps. 6:4) Sentiebam enim eis me teneri. Jactabam voces miserabiles: 'quamdiu, quamdiu . . . ? Quare non hac hora finis turpitudinis meae?' See also *supra,* ch. 2, 22.

[50] See *ibid.,* 8, 12, 28-29.

[51] See *supra,* ch. 2, 23 ff. (Providence and grace); 32 ff. (charity); 42 ff. (humility and love for truth); 47 ff. (faith and hope); 55 ff. (continence and other moral virtues).

The practice of these virtues, the inspiration of good example, the meditative reading of Sacred Scripture, and faithful cooperation with Divine grace by the *habit* of prayer can help both the confessor and the sinner to put on the *mind of Christ.* The individual who imitates Christ and St. Augustine by such *positive* measures weakens at the same time the hold of bad habits within his own person. While negative remedies against sin are not to be disregarded, positive measures can be stressed to a greater degree by the confessor, because they oppose to the allure of sin the greater magnetism of a life lived for God.[52]

[52] See *supra,* ch. 1, 6, n. 23. See also *Conf.,* 12, 10, 10: Et nunc ecce redeo aestuans et anhelans ad fontem tuum. Nemo me prohibeat: hunc bibam et hunc vivam. *Non ego vita mea sim: male vixi ex me, mors mihi fui: in te revivesco* (italics mine).

CHAPTER V

CONCLUSIONS

The moral teaching of the *Confessions* has a close relationship to the concrete circumstances of daily living. In regard to the desire for happiness in every man they point out the object which satisfies the desire. God is Truth in whose possession man rejoices; God is Goodness towards which the will of man gravitates; God is Infinite Beauty, ravishing all the faculties of man's soul in a way beyond feeble human understanding. While the myriad objects of sense bring disenchantment in their very possession, the unchanging Beauty of God brings a joy surpassing all the most desired pleasures of earth.

To guide man to Himself God has given him law and conscience. Man knows the basic principles of the natural law before he acquires a salutary insight into his own shortcomings. Growth in self-knowledge comes from the influence of Divine grace, for which man must pray. On the other hand, when man rejects the grace of God, his growth in self-understanding ceases, because pride and inordinate passion blind his intellect and harden his affections.

Among the virtues that lead man to his ultimate end, the *Confessions* stress three distinctly Christian ones: charity, humility and continence. Charity is a gift infused into the heart of man by the Holy Spirit. By its power man is able to love the Divine Goodness as it is reflected in creatures. Especially is this virtue necessary for the proper orientation of human friendships. As St. Augustine discovered by bitter experience, God must be in human friendships, or they will contain no true happiness. This general principle leads to several perennially practical conclusions: (1) A true friendship does not exist, unless God be the bond of union between the friends; (2) love for a friend that fails to realize his mortal limitations enslaves the soul, and exposes it to soul-shattering misery; and (3) the solution of the problem of human friendship lies in the integration of the love of man with the love of God. Far from opposing human friendship to Divine, one realizes that whatever is beautiful in his friendship is a Divine gift. Accordingly, one should exhort his friend to love God.

Not only in his relations to his neighbor, but also in his use of material creation, does man find the opportunity to exercise the virtue of charity. Corporeal wealth and beauty furnish occasion for the soul's glorification of God, provided the soul does not set her affections upon them. Too often, however, greed carries many far beyond the bounds of moderation in their use of creation's bounty; and, as a companion of greed, comes dissipation of soul. To checkmate this inordinate acquisitiveness, man should use material things only to satisfy his needs. He must not set his affections on them.

The foundation of charity is the virtue of humility, whose chief exemplar is Jesus Christ. He adapted himself to the weakness of men to teach them and to encourage them in their imitation of Him. The imitation of Christ may be called the positive side of humility, inasmuch as this virtue does not end in a sterile consideration of one's own misery, but leads to complete confidence in the Mediator, whose grace can heal all the wounds of sin. Humility is based upon the fact of man's frailty. In fact, it is synonymous with intellectual honesty, or with the sincere acknowledgment of personal shortcomings. Humility leads to truth, and truth leads to humility. In practice, this means that one is docile, willing to transform truth into action, and to accept corrections, and to seek advice for the solution of his doubts. Flowing from the virtue of humility, docility may be described as a desire to will what one understands to be God's will, even though it is not according to one's desires.

Like charity and humility, continence is a strictly supernatural virtue dependent upon the grace of God. It takes a special grace to understand by whose help one can practice this virtue, for, as long as one believes that its practice lies within the natural powers of man, he will try in vain to possess it.

Again, continence subordinates all the affections to the virtue of charity. Finite human affections must not be dissipated on too many objects or else there will be danger of losing charity itself. If, however, these human attachments are sublimated by the pervasive influence of the virtue of charity, there is no danger to the virtue of continence. Finally, the relationship of continence to Divine grace is summed up admirably in the famous dictum: "Da quod jubes, et jube quod vis." (*Conf.*, 10, 29, 40). "Lord, give us the power to do whatever you will, and order whatever you please."

In regard to the obstacles preventing one from reaching God, or slowing one's progress on the way, the first is the impediment of ignorance in the *Confessions*. From this study one learns that more than mere intellectual effort is required to come to the knowledge of the truth. The *Confessions* teach that one must reform his manner of life, and that then God will give him the light to see the truth. Whenever man neglects to use moral diligence in the pursuit of truth, the soul is sucked into the whirlpool of religious indifferentism, from which there is small chance of escape. There is no time to study and to search out the truth; there are so many worldly occupations and amusements to draw one's attention.

This intellectual and moral indifferentism seeks to justify itself by a process of reasoning known as rationalization. Far from being a purely intellectual process, it involves the will and emotional elements like concupiscence, fear and pride. Since it is frequently the disguise of concupiscence to justify a forbidden pleasure, it will be found very often in temptations to impurity. For example, delay in making a decision to give up a habit of impurity can be traced to rationalization. As the tool of pride, rationalization contributes to spiritual blindness also. Then the sin becomes incurable in the measure that the individual refuses to judge himself a sinner. A more mature form of rationalization is hatred of truth. Men hate truth, either because they love something else that is opposed to the truth, or because it exposes their faults.

It is advisable, therefore, to be on the alert for this tendency in one or in others. It has less opportunity to penetrate a mind in which personal motives are rigorously examined, and in which the various cloaks of concupiscence and of pride have been exposed. Frequent and careful examinations of conscience can help to keep one's thoughts free of rationalizing tendencies.

The next obstacle along the way to God is concupiscence. It has been noted already that concupiscence is often associated with a certain *rationalized* form of fear, seeking self-justification. The sinner fears to lose the pleasure of concupiscence. Again, this connection between fear, concupiscence, and reason should induce the sinner to take two steps: (1) Strike at fear by throwing oneself completely into the care of Divine grace. (2) Begin immediately to resist the inveterate tendencies of concupiscence. Augustine himself used these steps in his long struggle with this vice.

In St. Augustine's day, as in our own, stage dramas dealt very frequently with the illicit love theme, a subject that was an occasion of sin for theatre devotees in the fourth century as it continues to be in the twentieth. From sympathy with the sorrows of sinful lovers the young Augustine passed to the formation of seductive friendships. It is not prudery, then, to keep one's affections free from contamination. In short, one must try to draw a sharp distinction between the vicarious grief produced by the dramatization of illicit love and the feeling of true mercy. The latter leads to acts of charity towards one's neighbor; the former gives rise to nothing but inordinate pleasure and desires within the imagination of the onlookers, and sometimes it opens the way for sinful actions.

Perhaps the most important obstruction on the road to happiness is division of will, or, more precisely, the conflict of desires within the soul of man. It is contrary attractions that keep the will suspended until it makes its decision, and pursues the object of its choice. What kept Augustine indecisive for a long time was the lack of a dominant aim or purpose under which he might integrate all his actions. His indecision consisted in willing in a half-hearted fashion different objectives, so that the practical consequence was no moral amendment of his life.

This negative experience of Augustine implies the necessity of whole-hearted resolutions against sinful habits. These resolutions can be made only if the will is concentrated on one goal to the exclusion of incompatible aims. The individual who desires to practice a virtue or overcome a vice must forge that purpose with a unified will. At the same time he should remember that the very formation and accomplishment of his resolution depends upon the help of Divine grace, for which he must pray. God can cause man to be ravished by Divine beauty, and then the allurements of other objects hold no sway over the soul.

In regard to the moral chains of bad habit, it is significant that the beginning of a bad habit is found, not in the rebellion of the flesh, but in the rebellion of the spirit against God. The insurrection of the flesh against the spirit is a punishment for the more heinous revolt of the spirit against God. Therefore, the first bulwark against the habit of impurity is humble obedience to the law of God.

The fact that Augustine calls the chains of evil habit a sort of necessity implies an important psychological truth: The sinner has come to believe that he must have the pleasure that accompanies the exercise of the habit, or else he will suffer intolerable tensions, and so, despairing of his power to resist its violence, he yields to its impulses. Therefore, before the work of extirpating the habit can begin, this attitude of mind must be corrected. In some way the sinner must be convinced that he *can* resist the inveterate tendencies of bad habit.

One persuasive argument for victims of these sinful tendencies is the story of Augustine's struggle and victory over the habit of impurity. What he accomplished with the grace of God is possible also for the sinner who learns his story. Once an individual has had the courage to begin the struggle against concupiscence, he must have the wisdom to realize that the longstanding tendencies of a psychosomatic habit do not wear off in a day.

On the subject of education the *Confessions* of St. Augustine contain many acute observations among which are the following: (1) Disorderly tendencies in the child should be corrected immediately; otherwise, the pernicious habits which develop will be transferred later in life to more serious objects. When parents, therefore, neglect this duty of correction, they are at least indirectly responsible for some of the bad habits developed by their offspring; (2) divided authority in the home renders the corrections of either parent ineffectual. In the adolescence of

Augustine, for example, the warnings of St. Monnica against impurity were nullified completely by the pagan approbation of his father; (3) the education that St. Monnica gave the child Augustine is an example for all mothers. Throughout all his years of meandering in false doctrine Augustine retained her maternal teachings concerning Jesus Christ so well that no creed without the name of Christ could attract him.

In his *Confessions* St. Augustine stresses the terrible tragedy of sin. Sin involves the choice of the creature in place of the Creator. Therefore, sin is a false choice, and repeated sin forms in the mind a false set of values. The sinner seeks a counterfeit of real goodness, or shadow for substance. Likewise, sin is a perversion of the will under the motivation of pride. The sinner seeks to imitate God in a perverted fashion, trying to possess attributes that belong to God alone. This is pride, another name for which is inordinate self-love. It is pride or selfishness, then, that causes the sinner to choose his own private good before God, who is the universal good of all.

St. Augustine is concerned not merely with sin, but also with the sources of sin. He shows that concupiscence, curiosity and pride are the three chief sources of sin. This truth was already known from Scripture; his contribution, however, is found in the acuteness with which he analyzes subtle temptations to pride and vanity. He points out, for example, that it is just as much a sin to seek to be pleasing to oneself alone as it is to strive to win the praises of others. Similarly, he uncovers the pride of the smug astronomer who ignores the Giver of all knowledge. For both pride and vanity, moreover, he suggests practical antidotes. He advises the purification of personal motives by renewed acts of love towards God and by prayerful acknowledgment of one's utter dependence upon God.

The idea that the sinner brings punishment upon himself, a familiar theme of the *Confessions,* is consonant with the notion that sin is self-destruction. The blindness that is the punishment for pride, the enslavement of the will that is the direct result of habitual sins of impurity, and the complete dissipation of the whole person that follows in the wake of a life of non-observance of Divine Commandments, all reveal the personal misery implicit in a sinful life. At the same time the suffering which the sinner brings upon himself may be viewed also as an effect of Divine mercy. The bitterness alloyed with unlawful pleasure often persuades the sinner to seek true happiness in the service and love of God.

In regard to the remedies against sin St. Augustine suggests many. Chief among these are good example, the reading of Holy Scripture, and healing grace. While it is difficult to estimate the relative influence of individuals upon Augustine, it is safe to affirm that the cumulative persuasiveness of good example, from the group or from individuals, swayed him tremendously. Another aspect of group good example is the joy which it enkindles. The common spirit of joy in a group makes the practice of virtue easier for each member of the group.

In regard to the reading of Holy Scripture St. Augustine insists on a meditative study. He applied the Divine Word to himself with rigorous penetration, and amended his own life accordingly. Especially do the Scriptures teach the humble Christ, who persuades us to resist pride and to embrace the service of God.

The Saint, however, warns that in this spiritual exercise one must have guidance from the Church, because Holy Scripture is so rich with its diverse meanings, which can, and ought, to be extracted from it. In writing his book the inspired author intended all those meanings which excel both for light of truth and for their practical bearing upon our manner of life. Whatever truth one can mine from the Scripture really lies hidden within them. In a spirit of charity, then, one should be willing to allow and to profit by all interpretations that are in accordance with the Faith.

In regard to the healing power of Divine grace St. Augustine shows that it is an important element in any spiritual reconstruction program. Grace works through the most varied and mysterious channels to achieve its purposes. In its operation it usually remains imperceptible until a point in the odyssey of the soul has been reached when painful self-understanding burns out, as it were, the cancerous tissues of sin. Thereupon under the light of grace the soul understands clearly that the hand of God has been outstretched to receive it, and it clutches that hand for support. Then it begins the long arduous journey to spiritual well being with heaven at the end of the road.

The moral teaching of the *Confessions* may be recapitulated under ten headings:

1. God is the goal of man, satisfying all his aspirations in a transcendent manner.
2. The infused gift of charity is necessary for the proper orientation of human friendships. God must be the bond of union between friends.
3. The foundation of charity is the virtue of humility, whose chief exemplar is Jesus Christ. He adapted Himself to the weakness of men to encourage them to follow Him.
4. Continence is a strictly supernatural virtue, for which one must pray: "Da quod jubes et jube quod vis."
5. Rationalization is wishful thinking, refusing to face the accusations of conscience, while avoiding unpleasant obligations, and seeking the acquisition of pleasure.
6. A weak or divided will may be ascribed to the lack of dominant aim in one's personal life, while a strong or unified will rests upon the concentration of all the powers of the soul on one absorbing purpose, to the exclusion of incompatible aims.
7. The beginning of a bad habit is found, not in the rebellion of the flesh, but in the rebellion of the spirit against God. The consequence is the enslavement of the will by the flesh.
8. Motivated by pride, the sinner chooses the creature in place of the Creator—shadow for substance.
9. Each kind of sin brings its special punishment.
10. Among the remedies against sin St. Augustine stresses good example, the meditative reading of Holy Scripture, and Divine grace.

VITA

John F. Harvey, O.S.F.S., was born in Philadelphia, Pennsylvania, April 14, 1918, and received his primary education at St. Columba's School and his secondary education at Northeast Catholic High School, both in that city. Entering the novitiate of the Oblates of St. Francis de Sales at Childs, Maryland, in 1936, he made his Profession of vows in the following year. His higher studies began then at the Catholic University of America, from where he received the degree of Bachelor of Arts in 1941. On June 3, 1944, he was ordained to the Priesthood in the Cathedral of Saints Peter and Paul in Philadelphia. In January, 1945, he began teaching at the high school which he had attended, completing, at the same time, his graduate studies in Psychology at the Catholic University. He received his Master of Arts degree from there in 1946, and in the following year resumed his studies in Sacred Theology at this University. After that year of study he received the degree of Licentiate in Sacred Theology in June 1948.

INDEX